Explorations in S

British Sociological Association conference volume series

Organizing Bodies

Policy, Institutions and Work

Edited by

Linda McKie
Research Professor in Sociology
Glasgow Caledonian University

and

Nick Watson
Lecturer in Health Promotion
University of Edinburgh

Review Editors

Andrew Blaikie
Professor of Historical Sociology
University of Aberdeen

Louise Ryan
Senior Lecturer in Sociology
University of Central Lancashire

First published in Great Britain 2000 by
MACMILLAN PRESS LTD
Houndmills, Basingstoke, Hampshire RG21 6XS and London
Companies and representatives throughout the world

A catalogue record for this book is available from the British Library.

ISBN 0–333–77446–9 hardcover
ISBN 0–333–77447–7 paperback

First published in the United States of America 2000 by
ST. MARTIN'S PRESS, LLC,
Scholarly and Reference Division,
175 Fifth Avenue, New York, N.Y. 10010

ISBN 0–312–23476–7

Library of Congress Cataloging-in-Publication Data
Organizing bodies : policy, institutions and work / edited by Linda McKie and
Nick Watson.
    p.   cm.
    Includes bibliographical references and index.
    ISBN 0–312–23476–7 (cloth)
    1. Body, Human—Social aspects. I. McKie, Linda. II. Watson, Nick, 1960–

HM636 .O74 2000
306.4—dc21

                                  00–026979

This book is printed on paper suitable for recycling and made from fully managed and sustained
forest sources.

10   9   8   7   6   5   4   3   2   1
09 08 07 06 05 04 03 02 01 00

Printed and bound in Great Britain by
Antony Rowe Ltd, Chippenham, Wiltshire

Contents

Preface and Acknowledgements

This is one of four books comprising chapters originally presented as papers at the annual conference of the British Sociological Association (BSA), held at the University of Edinburgh, 6–9 April 1998. The theme of that conference was 'Making Sense of the Body: Theory, Research and Practice'. This book incorporates some of the many high-quality papers delivered on the theme of the sociology of the body in policy, institutions and work. The companion books are *Constructing Gendered Bodies*, edited by Kathryn Backett-Milburn and Linda McKie, *Exploring the Body*, edited by Sarah Cunningham-Burley and Kathryn Backett-Milburn, and *Reformulating the Body*, edited by Nick Watson and Sarah Cunningham-Burley.

The editors of these books formed the organizing committee for the 1998 BSA conference and our call for papers was rewarded with a conference embracing nearly 300 presentations and over 500 participants. The rich conference programme was organized into 21 streams and these were co-ordinated by members of BSA study groups and interested individuals. Through this process we were able to involve many sociologists, at differing stages of their careers, in the process of developing and running the conference. At the end of the conference over 180 papers were submitted for consideration by the organizing committee for inclusion in the four volumes. The editors have had an extremely difficult task in selecting papers to be revised into the format of chapters. We were greatly assisted in this task by review editors who had previously acted as co-ordinators of relevant streams at the conference.

The conference and these volumes would not have been possible without the input of many people. We would like to thank the staff of the British Sociological Association and University of Edinburgh for their support in the organization of the conference. Many members of the BSA assisted in numerous ways with the academic content of the conference and we would like to thank them for their continuing support. The editors are also grateful to their colleagues at the University of Aberdeen and University of Edinburgh. Staff at Macmillan provided much support and we would like to thank Ruth Willats for her editorial work and Karen Brazer for her advice. As ever, our families and friends helped out in practical and emotional ways; we owe them a personal debt.

We dedicate this and the other three volumes to the stream co-ordinators for the 1998 Annual BSA conference. Their enthusiastic support for our goal of running a welcoming, egalitarian and participative conference was much appreciated, and together, we hope to have achieved this.

Chapter 8, 'Social Death as Self-fulfilling Prophecy: David Sudnow's "Passing On" by Stefan Timmermans, was first published in *The Sociological Quarterly*, 1998, 39, 3 and is reprinted in this book by kind permission of the University of California Press.

Notes on the Contributors

Lisa Adkins is Research Fellow in Sociology in the Research School of Social Sciences at the Australian National University. Her research interests are in the sociologies of gender and sexuality, especially in regard to questions of economy. Publications include *Gendered Work* (Open University Press, 1995) and the co-edited volumes *Sexualizing the Social* (MacMillan, 1996) and *Sex, Sensibility and the Gendered Body* (MacMillan, 1996), as well as a number of chapters and articles. She is currently working on a book on flexible gender identities at work.

Cinnamon Bennett is a Lecturer in Sociology at Sheffield Hallam University, where she teaches gender studies and social policy. She is completing a PhD on the development of government equal opportunities policies and practice in the UK. Her particular focus is the strategy of 'mainstreaming' gender equality. She has recently contributed to a research project, completed in 1999 year under the EC 4th Community Action Programme for Equal Opportunities, which examines the criteria for success of a mainstreaming approach based on the experience of three member states.

Joanna Brewis is a lecturer in management at the University of Essex. Current research interests centre on gender, the body and sexuality in organizations. Recent publications include 'How Does it Feel? Women Managers, Embodiment and Changing Public Sector Cultures', in S. Whitehead and R. Moodley (eds.), *Transforming Managers: Gendering Change in the Public Sector* (Taylor and Francis, 1999), and 'Who Do You Think You Are? Feminism, Work, Ethics and Foucault', in M. Parker (ed.), *Ethics and Organizations* (Sage, 1998).

Harry Cowen is Principal Lecturer in social policy and Course Leader of the MSc in Applied Social Sciences at Cheltenham and Gloucester College of Higher Education. His current research interests include New Labour's social policy, communitarianism and Jewish community care. His publications include *Community Care, Ideology and Social Policy* (Prentice Hall, 1999) and *The Human Nature Debate* (Pluto Press, 1994). He is currently working on a book entitled *Critical Social and Political Thinkers in the Twentieth Century*.

Guy Daly is Head of the School of Social Sciences and Course Leader for the MA in Public Services Management at Cheltenham and Gloucester College of Higher Education. His research interests include citizenship and public accountability, user involvement and community care, and accountability in the health service. His recent publications have been on democratic accountability in the NHS and have been published in such journals as *Local Government Studie*s and *Public Money and Management*.

Tuula Gordon is Professor of Women's Studies and Social Sciences in the Department of Women's Studies, University of Tampere. She obtained her sociology degree from the London School of Economics and her doctorate from the University of London. She has also taught in the University of Helsinki. Publications include: *Democracy in One School? Progressive Education and Restructuring* (Falmer Press 1996), *Feminist Mothers* (Macmillan, 1990), *Single Women: On the Margins?* (Macmillan, 1994), *Making Spaces: Citizenship and Difference in Schools* (with Janet Holland and Elina Lahelma, Macmillan, 2000).

Craig M. Gurney is a Lecturer in Housing at the Centre for Housing Management and Development in the Department of City and Regional Planning, Cardiff University. Previously (1991–96), he was a Lecturer in Urban Sociology at Sheffield Hallam University. His research interests include the sociology of home ownership, the meaning of home, aural sociology, gender, sexuality and housing and the sociology of consumption. He is currently an external examiner at two UK universities, a management board member for a Cardiff-based Housing Association, and newsletter editor and elected committee member of the *Housing Studies Association*. He has been a member of the British Sociological Association since 1990.

Janet Holland is Professor of Social Research and Director of the Social Sciences Research Centre at South Bank University, London. Publications include: *The Male in the Head* (with Caroline Ramazanoglu, Sue Sharpe and Rachel Thomson, Tufnell Press 1996); *Sex, Sensibility and the Gendered Body* (editor with Lisa Adkins, Macmillan, 1996), and *Sexual Cultures* (editor with Jeffrey Weeks, Macmillan, 1996); *Debates and Issues in Feminist Research and Pedagogy*, and *Identity and Diversity: Gender and the Experience of Education* (both edited with Maud Blair, Multilingual Matters with The Open University 1995), and *Making Spaces: Citizenship and Difference in Schools* (with Tuula Gordon and Elina Lahelma, Macmillan, 2000).

Gordon Hughes is a Lecturer in Social Policy at the Open University. Research interests lie in politics of community and criminal justice; crime prevention and multi-agency partnerships; inspection and evaluation and the audit culture; radical communitarianism. Recent publications include *Understanding Crime Prevention: Social Control, Risk and Late Modernity* (Open University Press 1998); 'Communitarianism and Law and Order', in *Critical Social Policy*, 16 (4); *Imagining Welfare Futures* (editor, Routledge 1998); *Unsettling Welfare: Reconstruction of Social Policy* (co-editor with G. Lewis, Routledge 1998).

Debra King has recently completed her PhD and is currently teaching sociology at Flinders University, South Australia. Her research interests cover the areas of work, identity, social movements and social change, with previous research focusing on volunteer work and the work of farm women.

Elina Lahelma is Docent in Sociology of Education in the Department of Education, University of Helsinki. Currently she is a Senior Fellow at the Academy of Finland. She has written extensively on gender and education, including *Making Spaces: Citizenship and Difference in Schools* (with Tuula Gordon and Janet Holland, Macmillan, 2000).

Gail Lewis is a Lecturer in Social Policy at the Open University. Research interests lie in postcolonial social policy, intersections between 'race', gender and social policy, emergence of new welfare subjects; connections between formations of nation and discourses and practices of social policy. Recent publications include: *Welfare Settlements and Racialising Practices in Soundings* (The Public Good edition 1997), 'An Encounter with Strangers? Stuart Hall and Social Policy', in L. Grossberg et al. (eds.), *Without Guarantees* (Polity Press, 1999); *Unsettling Welfare: Reconstruction of Social Policy* (co-editor with G. Hughes, Routledge, 1998).

Celia Lury is a Lecturer in Sociology at Goldsmith's College. Her research interests include gender and cultural theory. She has just completed a book, *Global Nature, Global Culture* (with Sarah Franklin and Jackie Stacey, forthcoming) in which she considers the interrelationships between gender, nature and culture in the context of globalization. Previous publications include *Consumer Culture* (Polity 1996) and *Prosthetic Culture* (Routledge, 1998).

Linda McKie is Research Professor in Sociology at Glasgow Caledonian University. Recent publications include: 'Connecting Gender Power and the Household' (with Sophia Bowlby and Susan Gregory) in L. McKie, S. Bowlby and S. Gregory (eds.), *Gender, Power and the Household* (Macmillan, 1999) and 'Women's Public Toilets: A Serious Issue for the Body Politic' (with Julia Edwards) in *Embodied Practices. Feminist Perspectives on the Body* (Sage, 1997). Research interests include employment, caring and citizenship, disclosing domestic violence in primary health care, and lay perceptions of health and illness.

Deborah Marks is Course Director of the MA Disability Studies at the Centre for Psychotherapeutic Studies, Sheffield University. Recent publications include: *Disability: Controversial Debates and Psychosocial Perspectives* (Routledge 1999), 'Dimensions of Oppression: Theorising the Embodied Subject', in *Disability and Society* (1999) 14 (5), and 'Emancipatory Epistemology and Interdisciplinary Practice: Psychology, Psychoanalysis and Disability Studies', *Psychoanalytic Studies*, 1999, 1 (3). Her research focuses on disability theory, children's experience and group dynamics among health and educational professionals.

Sarah Neal is a Senior Lecturer in Sociology and Social Policy at Middlesex University. Her research interests centre on the issues of race, racism, gender, femininity, representations and equality policy processes. She is currently researching racism in rural England. Her recent publications include: *The Making of Equal Opportunities Policies in Universities* (Open University Press, 1998) and 'Populist Configurations of Race and Gender: the Case of Hugh Grant, Liz Hurley and Divine Brown', in A. Brah, M. Hickman and M. Mac an Ghaill (eds.), *Thinking Identities: Ethnicity, Racism and Culture* (Macmillan, 1999).

Esther Saraga is Senior Lecturer and Staff Tutor in Social Sciences at the Open University. Research interests are primarily in children, rights and social welfare. Recent publications include: *Embodying the Social: The Social Construction of Difference* (editor, Routledge 1998), and 'Children's Needs: Who Decides?', in M. Langan (ed.), *Welfare: Needs, Risks, Rights* (Routledge, 1998).

Stefan Timmermans is Assistant Professor of Sociology at Brandeis University. His research interests include medical sociology, science and technology, death and dying, the body, qualitative research methods and interpretative research methods. His publications include *Sudden Death and the Myth of CPR* (Temple University Press, 1999).

Alex Twitchen is a Senior Lecturer in the Sociology of Sport at University College Chichester. He is currently completing a research project investigating the history of safety in motor racing which reflects his interests in the sociology of sport, the body and consumption.

Nick Watson works in the Department of Nursing Studies, University of Edinburgh where he lectures in disability studies and medical sociology. Formerly he was a youth worker and health promotion officer. He is currently involved in research on disability and childhood and is co-editor (with Sarah Cunningham-Burley) of *Reframing the Body* (Macmillan, forthcoming).

Introduction

Linda McKie and Nick Watson

From being under-researched and under-theorized, the body has now become central to the sociological project. We have moved from what Freund (1988: 839) described as a 'curiously disembodied view of human beings' to one in which '[b]odies are in, in academic as well as in popular culture' (Frank 1990: 131). This interest in the body as a site of sociological analysis has in part been driven by the influence of feminism (Martin 1987; Grosz 1996), in part by the work of Michel Foucault (Foucault 1981) and developments in social theory, especially in postmodernism (Frank 1991). We all have bodies, but how we use bodies and what meaning is ascribed to a body are the products of social relations (Hurst and Woolley 1982); the body has thus provided the focus for situated historical analysis. In addition, Freund (1988: 840), amongst others, notes that there is an increasing recognition amongst sociologists that 'the social actors that populate their theories have bodies that are integral to human existence and thus a central consideration in any theory'.

Bryan Turner (1984) was one of the first theorists to bring the body into the mainstream of sociological theory, although the pioneering work of Erving Goffman (1969) should not be forgotten. Turner noted that in contrast to sociology, the 'human body has been accorded a place of importance in anthropology since the nineteenth century' (Turner 1991: 1). The work of a number of anthropologists (for example, Douglas 1970; 1973; Caplan 1987) has informed the development of a sociological theory of the body. Subsequent work by, for example, Freund (1988), Frank (1990), the edited collection by Featherstone et al. (1991), Schilling (1993), Falk (1994) and Crossley (1996) all served to ensure that the body remained in the foreground of sociological theory. The launch of *Body and Society* in 1995 signalled the establishment of the sociology of the body as an area of sociological work in its own right. Anybody doubting the upsurge of sociological interest in the body and its consequent relevance to modern-day social theory should try typing in 'body' as a key word in any social science search index.

There is, however, no single sociology of the body. In the same way that postmodernism rejects the metanarrative, so sociology of the body incorporates a plurality of theories and empirical work. It has synthesized a number of developments in sociological theory in the last 20 years (Davis 1997; Schilling 1997). In summary, these include:

- challenges to concerns that some sociology was replicating the mind/body dualism of Cartesian thought (Turner 1991; Frank 1991; Leder 1992);
- Foucault's conceptualization of power through the exploration of surveillance and control of the body and sexuality (Foucault 1981);
- feminist theorists and researchers whose examination of identity and everyday embodied experiences gave renewed impetus to debates on gender, sexuality and identity (Martin 1987; Butler 1990; Grosz 1996; Lindemann 1997);
- the critique of the medical model through sociological explanations of health and illness and social action (Goffman 1969; Fox 1993; Annandale 1998);
- the blurring of boundaries for bodies and identities, focusing on the body as a site for shifting notions of consumption (Boyne 1991; Shilling 1993; Jagger 1998); and
- the impact of social and economic changes on the body in global policies to enhance development and to tackle environmental concerns (Connell 2000).

Contributors to this book draw on a range of sociological theories and research to enhance the distinctive development of the sociology of the body. Their chapters demonstrate how the sociology of the body provides an opportunity to study the body as integral to social action and social being, and thus further the discipline of sociology.

This book is specifically concerned with the organization of the body, self and identity as evidenced in policy, politics, institutions and the workplace. The body has been strangely absent from discourses on policy and practices in institutions and the workplace. We take our body into the public domain, and the dynamic relationship between private and public embodied activities and thoughts is crucial to any exploration of social action. Yet an examination of the body in policy and practice has been slow to evolve. Thus, we contend, the contributions to this book are evidence of challenging and apposite work in the sociology of the body.

This book is divided into three parts. In Part I contributors explore the embodiment of politics and policy through a number of empirical studies; in Part II chapters examine how a number of institutions both construct and represent the body; and in Part III bodies at work and in work are considered in the theme of working bodies.

Part I: The Embodiment of Politics and Policy

The exploration of the body in politics and policy opens with a chapter by Lewis, Hughes and Saraga on the interrelationship between the body and social policy. In it they examine a number of welfare policies and practices and contend that there are tensions arising from much social policy which, on the one hand, appears to be unembodied and yet simultaneously is concerned with the effects of policies on embodied subjects. Examining documentation and policies, and in particular the treatment of children and adolescents, and dominant constructions of disability and rehabilitative welfare practices, Lewis et al. argue that policy constructs a series of representations of a diverse range of sub-ordinated bodies. Further, they contend that social policy has created its area of practice and expertise on knowledges which subordinate bodies. These tensions and resultant struggles are both epistemological and ontological, seeking to disrupt old 'knowledges' and replace them with new 'knowledges'. However, they conclude that much of the debate and construction of new knowledges is failing to reach the practice and policy communities.

Daly and Cowen examine the participation and representation of bodies in politics in their chapter on the impact of more recent conceptions of citizenship on the local polity. They contend that citizenship is historically constructed within the body politic and that social institutions may be conceived of as regulators of bodies. In contemporary notions of citizenship, citizens are regarded as users and consumers of public services. Daly and Cowen examine the challenges of, amongst others, the disability movement and feminism, to more practically oriented and conservative conceptualizations of citizenship. They present data from a study of a local authority which held a series of public meetings during a budget-setting period to discuss budgetary priorities. A similar process in implementing community care was undertaken. In the case of setting budgets, the participatory activities were said by the local authority to be evidence of a substantial shift towards participatory democracy. However, Daly and Cowen suggest that these activities blur lines of accountability and are little more than 'rubber-stamping' exercises. With community care the agenda was driven by the local authority to establish standards and assess quality rather than enhance participation. There is a rhetoric of choice and the empowered citizen that is premised on market notions of the citizen as consumer and client. This rhetoric provides a smokescreen to the realities of public accountability that local authorities must manage. Thus, the body politic in local government is dislocated from participation and also embodied notions of citizenship.

Marks examines the way in which residential institutions are designed in a manner that results in spatial and social marginalization. Marks focused on two types of residential institutions: those, for elderly people and those for people with learning difficulties. Drawing on the work of Bowlby (1988) on attachment theory, Marks argues that one element missing from theorizing on embodiment and space is the way in which certain environments are emotionally experienced. In considering the home as a secure base, there is a crucial relationship in which the spatial metaphor conveys the importance of feeling safe in a place. Making buildings accessible is not just about fitting ramps or induction loops and managing practical issues of access. Environments and institutions can disable bodies as they fail to premise policies and practice on a notion of embodied institutions.

The theme of the organization of bodies within physical space is further explored by Gurney as he considers the social space of the home. The home accommodates bodies, is a location in which a civilizing process occurs that encourages people to mask evidence of bodily substances and odours, and is a place where we can most easily be our embodied selves. In a theoretical consideration of these themes Gurney considers the storing, processing and management of corporeal dirt. He notes that it is anticipated that £736 million per annum will be spent on household cleaners and fresheners in the UK by 2001; the equivalent to the gross domestic product of a number of developing countries. He asserts that the management of corporeal dirt in the home has been an oversight in sociological work. Gurney proposes a corporeal ecology of the home whereby the body as a leaky container is managed, and moral and social constructions of self and bodies evolve. Drawing on the work of Elias (1978), Gurney concludes that the home and corporeal management in the home is crucial to 'the onward march of the civilizing process'. He challenges sociology and sociologists to undertake research on corporeal dirt and bodily taboos while noting that such topics have been avoided because of concerns about sensationalism or poor taste. Gurney closes his chapter by positing the challenge: 'is this lack of research evidence of a puritan legacy in sociology?'

Part II: Institutions Constructing and Representing Bodies

The institution of the school is the context to a consideration of embodiment and agency by Gordon et al. Data are presented from a study on citizenship, difference and marginality in schools with specific reference to gender. Observation and interview data are employed to identify and explore the practices and processes of the school. Gordon et al. argue that schooling can be understood as practice on the body. A pedagogy of the body can be traced in three intertwined layers of the school: the official (e.g. the curriculum, lessons, hierarchies); the informal (e.g. application and interpretation of rules and social interaction), and the physical school (spatiality and embodiment). The construction of gendered difference and sexuality are themes explored in the analysis of data. The authors conclude that the way that bodies are deployed in schools is gendered and there are multi-faceted layers of bodily constraint and control. Students exercise agency, selecting ways of deploying their bodies by complying with and/or transgressing both official and informal requirements in the process.

The representation and construction of bodies by the media is the subject of the chapter by Neal. Utilizing data from a content analysis of newspapers she analyses how this section of the media chose to represent Christopher Clunis and Jayne Zito. Clunis, a young man with schizophrenia, fatally stabbed Jonathan Zito. His death, and the circumstances surrounding it, dominated populist and policy debates about mental health care and treatment in the mid-1990s, in particular the changes taking place in mental health from institutional to community care. Jayne Zito, widowed after three months of marriage, became an increasingly public figure. The media represented Jayne Zito as fair, beautiful and articulate, while Christopher Clunis, a young African/ Caribbean, was described as of 'considerable height and powerful build'. Hegemonic images of gendered, feminized, racialized bodies were evident in debates and coverage. Neal cites excerpts from newspapers to identify and consider the symbols of the body and identity representations by the media. Media constructions of dichotomous bodies obscure the complexities of events and distort individuals and debates. Neal likens this aspect of the media to 'crude brush strokes' which rely on covert signposting and codes to present racialized bodies and frame polemicized populist representations.

The introduction of rigorous and far-reaching rules and regulations to promote health and safety in Grand Prix motor racing provides a second skin for the bodies of drivers. The concept of the second skin is developed by Twitchen to theorize the protection of the body against the hazards of motor racing through new rules and regulations, by acting as a supplementary skin to the body's own. In doing so Twitchen draws on the work of Douglas and Calvez (1992), who contend that the body has a double skin – that of its own and that of its community. In this chapter, the community is the institution of Grand Prix Formula One motor racing. From the early 1980s it acted to promote health and safety, resulting in a dramatic decline in accidents and fatalities. Yet, the introduction of these rules and regulations was keenly contested and posed a challenge to conceptions of masculinity and the Grand Prix driver. Thus, it took some time for initial concerns about protecting spectators to shift to an interest in protecting drivers. However, the introduction of increased standards of health and safety has enabled many individuals to sense that their body is made more comfortable and secure by the 'community' of Formula One racing. This posits an interesting challenge to individualism and promotes the notion of the body protected by communities.

Doctors and health care professionals working in emergency services manage resuscitative interventions which aim to preserve life. Timmermans observed the work of medical teams in 112 resuscitative efforts as they decided whether or not to intervene aggressively or to let the patient die with minimal medical interference. In an earlier study, Sudnow (1967) argued that the fervour of the intervention depended on the patient's perceived social worth. Certain groups of patients were more likely than others to be considered 'socially dead' and less worthy of active intervention. The idea of 'social death' (Sudnow 1967) can become a predictor for biological death. Although legislation and regulation in the United States have attempted to give protection against discrimination and social rationing in health care, Timmermans concludes that these initiatives have actually reinforced an inequality of death and dying. Emergency department staff justify and refine a moral categorization of patients by reappropriating biomedical theory and advance directives. As Timmerman notes, the social inequalities evident in attempts to resuscitate reflect broader foundations of inequality. Medical staff appear to accept and perpetuate discriminatory attitudes towards, for example, the elderly, people with disabilities or people with alcoholism.

Part III: Working Bodies

In the final part of the book the chapters explore the body at work, in work and the impact of bodies on the organization and management of workplace relations. Adkins and Lury explore the changing nature of reflexive identities in the workplace. They examine a number of techniques such as self-appraisal, performance review and forms of stress and emotion management, which, they contend, are in part constitutive of the reflexive worker, but also required acquisitions. A specific focus of their chapter is the impact of these techniques on women workers and the identity of their labour and themselves. Women's labour may be naturalized as part of their selves, and thus may not be mobilized as a resource. Adkins and Lury conclude that in contrast to men, women workers cannot claim ownership of their performance and thus may find themselves in a weaker position to undertake self-monitoring and self-appraisal. Men, they suggest, are better placed to achieve reflexive economic identities.

Gender identity and the body in the workplace are further explored by Brewis. Using data from a series of interviews she considers a number of themes including how women prepare their bodies for work, their thoughts on what their bodies signify to colleagues and clients, and how they compare their bodies and the bodies of other women to those of men. The women who participated in the research worked in a range of occupations in higher education, local government, the NHS, the Probation Service and Social Services. Brewis contends that while bodies in the workplace have a material reality, they can relate to this and the materiality of others only through the operation of prevailing discourses. For example, there is greater pressure on women to conform to particular physical appearances deemed appropriate to their workplace. The women saw their bodies as signifying to others markers of difference or otherness. Some women strove to manage that difference by, for example, seeking to present themselves as asexual, while others sought to emphasize or acknowledge difference as they considered it potentially beneficial. While the women agreed that their bodies precede and define them at work, and that female biology may pose problems in the organizational context, they also suggested that in professional, managerial and administrative work the body was relatively insignificant. These findings imply a dual status of the body as a source of human commonality and a source of difference. The women perceive their bodies as materially real (for example, their sex, weight, age, and so on), but that this materiality is accessible only through the operations of discourse and thus the body becomes a site at which, and in which, discourses (re)inscribe in a range of ways.

The Weberian concept of bureaucracies and the bureaucrat as neutral and rational is challenged by the research of Bennett on the work of women's equal opportunities officers. Bennett notes that the ideal-type bureaucrat is assumed to have a male body and to behave and experience organizational relationships from a man's perspective. This presents women or non-hegemonic males with a struggle to match their different 'lived body' experience with dominant forms of structural interactions. Women's equal opportunities officers are in a particularly complex situation from which they must seek to change hegemonic practices. Not only are their bodies different from the hegemonic male bureaucrat's, but also they are charged with changing the structural and cultural contexts that suit 'him' best. Bennett presents data from her study of Australian and British equal opportunity officers. Equal opportunity officers employ strategies of embodiment that seek to legitimate their different embodied positions through spatial, behavioural and verbal strategies. Within the nature of their bureaucrat context they must calculate strategies that range between feminist and gender-muted positions, aiming at shorter or longer agendas of change (Cockburn 1990). Bennett concludes with the reflection that progress towards a pluralistic acceptance of many different forms of embodiment is some way off and further analysis of organizational relationships is required to inform policies and practice.

The body as a powerful political tool in activist work is the subject of the chapter by King. Bodies have been used to undertake political activist work (demonstrations and direct action), but bodies have also generated activism, for example, disability and gay rights. There is a tension between considering the body as a 'thing' that can undertake activism and the body and mind as challenging hegemonic notions of human rights and equality. King reflects on the notion of energy that emerges from her empirical work of interviews with activists and an examination of her own membership in three activist organizations. King notes that activist work is not just about the work, but about performativity (Butler 1990). Energy was the term used by activists to embody themselves and their work, to illuminate and connect the corporeal to social discourses, institutions and what King terms 'universal nature'. Activists employed this wider context – of the body of the world – to harness energy for actions or explain cycles of activism.

In this book we have brought together a range of sociological work from empirical chapters presenting new data to theoretical considerations of key themes and topics. What is evident from reading the chapters is that the relationship between the body, policy, institutions and the workplace is an increasingly complex one. This relationship is often dictated by normative presentations of social class, and gendered and racialized bodies. In conclusion, the chapters presented here suggest that much remains to be researched and theorized in our quest to make sociological sense of the body.

References

Annadale, E. 1998. *The Sociology of Health and Medicine*. Cambridge: Polity.

Bowlby, J. 1988. *A Secure Base: Clinical Applications of Attachment Theory*. London: Routledge.

Boyne, R. 1991. 'The Art of the Body in the Discourse of Postmodernity', in M. Featherstone, M. Hepworth and B.S. Turner (eds.), *The Body. Social Process and Cultural Theory*. London: Sage.

Butler, J. 1990. *Gender Trouble: Feminism and the Subversion of Identity*. New York: Routledge.

Caplan, P. (ed.) 1987. *The Cultural Construction of Sexuality*. London: Tavistock.

Cockburn, C. 1990. 'Men's Power in Organisations: "Equal Opportunities" Intervenes', in J. Hearn and D. Morgan (eds.), *Men, Masculinity and Social Theory*. London: Unwin and Hyman.

Connell, R. W. 2000. 'Bodies, Intellectuals and World Society', in N. Watson and S. Cunningham-Burley (eds.), *Reframing the Body*. Basingstoke: Macmillan.

Crossley, N. 1996. *Intersubjectivity: The Fabric of Social Becoming*. London: Sage.

Davis, K. (ed.) 1997. *Embodied Practices. Feminist Perspectives on the Body*. London: Sage.

Douglas, M. 1970. *Purity and Danger: An Analysis of Concepts of Pollution and Taboo*. Harmondsworth: Penguin Books.

Douglas, M. 1973. *Natural Symbols: Explorations in Cosmology*. Harmondsworth: Penguin Books.

Douglas, M. and Calvez, M. 1990. 'The Self as a Risk Taker: A Cultural Theory of Contagion in Relation to AIDS'. *Sociological Review*, 38, 3, 445–64.

Elias, N. 1978. *The History of Manners: The Civilising Process*. Volume 1. New York: Pantheon.

Falk, P. 1994. *The Consuming Body*. London: Sage.

Featherstone, M., Hepworth, M. and Turner, B. S. 1991. *The Body. Social Process and Cultural Theory*. London: Sage.

Foucault, M. 1981. *The History of Sexuality. Volume 1: An Introduction*. Harmondsworth: Penguin Books.

Fox, N. 1993. *Postmodernism, Sociology and Health*. Buckingham: Open University Press.

Frank, A. 1990. 'Bringing Bodies Back in: A Decade Review'. *Theory, Culture and Society*, 7, 131–62.

Frank, A. 1991. 'For a Sociology of the Body: an Analytical Review', in M. Featherstone, M. Hepworth, B. S. Turner (eds.), *The Body. Social Process and Cultural Theory*. London: Sage.

Freund, P. 1988. 'Bringing Society into the Body', *Theory and Society*, 17, 839–64.

Goffman, E. 1969. *The Presentation of Self in Everyday Life*. Harmondsworth: Penguin Books.

Grosz, E. 1996. *Space, Time and Perversion. Essays on the Politics of the Body*. New York: Routledge.

Hurst, P. and Woolley, P. 1982. *Social Relations and Human Attributes*. London: Tavistock.

Jagger, E. 1989. 'Marketing the Self, Buying an Other: Dating in a Post Modern, Consumer Society', *Sociology*, 32, 4, 795–814.

Leder, D. 1992. 'A Take of Two Bodies: the Cartesian Corpse and the Lived Body', in D. Welton (ed.), *Body and Flesh: A Philosophical Reader*. Oxford: Blackwell.

Lindemann, G. 1997. 'The Body of Difference', in K. Davis (ed.), *Embodied Practices. Feminist Perspectives on the Body*. London: Sage.

Martin, E. 1987. *The Woman in the Body*. Milton Keynes: Open University Press.

Shilling, C. 1993. *The Body and Social Theory*. London: Sage.

Shilling, C. 1997. 'The Undersocialised Conception of the (Embodied) Agent in Modern Sociology', *Sociology*, 31, 4, 737–54.

Sudnow, D. 1967. *Passing On: The Social Organization of Dying*. Englewood Cliffs, NJ: Prentice-Hall.

Turner, B. S. 1984. *The Body and Society: Explorations in Social Theory*. Oxford: Blackwell.

Turner, B. S. 1991. 'Recent Developments in the Theory of the Body', *The Body. Social Process and Cultural Theory*. London: Sage.

Part I

The Embodiment of Politics and Policy

1
The Body of Social Policy: Social Policy and the Body

Gail Lewis, Gordon Hughes and Esther Saraga

Introduction

The aim of this chapter is to contribute to an emergent field of enquiry within the discipline of social policy concerning the interrelationship between the body and social policy in the sense of welfare policy and practice.[1] In this chapter we will use initial capitals 'Social Policy' to describe the academic discipline and study of social policy, and the lower case 'social policy' to describe the practices and policies of agencies of social welfare. The linguistic collapsing of the two phenomena ('study of'/practice of') itself may say much about the historial relationship between academe and policy-makers and practitioners in this field. It should also be noted that we employ a wide definiton of welfare, ranging from the archetypical social security, through education, health, to agencies operating within the criminal justice system. Our specific focus is on three main areas, each of which is interconnected. First, we want to try to think about the ways in which the body is an 'absent presence' in the discipline of social policy. In particular, we want briefly to consider the ontological and epistemological status of the body within social policy discussions of social policy practices. We argue that a tension arises in much social policy from the way in which it foregrounds an unembodied social focus and yet, simultaneously, is concerned with the effects of social policies and practices on embodied subjects. This leads to our second concern, which is to try to think through the ways in which social policy as welfare practice has both treated 'the body' as a solid, pre-social and fixed surface on which its expertise and knowledges are manifested, and, in so doing, acts socially to construct a range of embodied subjects. Finally, we move our attention to thinking about the ways in which challenges and resistances to social policy practices are often concerned to contest a series of oppressive and/or exclusionary welfare practices and to stake out a claim for the ontological and epistemological legitimacy of new constituencies, and differently embodied, welfare subjects.

Sympathetic to what might be called an emergent 'cultural turn' within the discipline of social policy, our approach is within that broad range of positions associated with social constructionism (see Saraga 1998; Lewis 1998; Langan 1998; Hughes and Lewis 1998; Hughes 1998). As a perspective within social sciences, social constructionism can alert us to the struggles over meaning and thus may be (though not necessarily) linked to a politics of articulation. By the latter we mean to indicate two things. We start with the idea of *articulation* as signalling an attempt to construct a series of connections or associations between 'bodies' as representations of 'difference', and 'bodies' as empirical subjects forming welfare constituencies. This form of association is already operative within both Social Policy as a discipline and social policy as an arena of welfare practices. The *politics* of this politics of articulation signals the contested character of these connections and the attempts to alter their form of configuration. Thus, the emergence of this perspective within the discipline of Social Policy opens up the possibility of analysing welfare subjects as *embodied* subjects constructed in and through contested discourses around social welfare. This chapter argues for a new way of 'knowing' bodies in both Social Policy and social policy and, in the process, seeks to engage critically with the work associated with medical sociology, sociology of the body and feminist theorizing of gendered embodiment. What we mean by this should become clearer as the chapter unfolds.

The chapter is organized in the following way. We begin with a brief overview of recent approaches to the body in sociological and feminist theory. This is followed by a consideration of the 'treatment' of 'the body' in the discipline of Social Policy. We then turn our attention to the links between 'the body' and social policy as a series of welfare discourses and practices. In particular we look at the ways in which welfare practices are themselves implicated within and constitutive of processes of bodily construction. Finally, we consider the ways in which challenges or contestations to welfare practices are also struggles aimed at the constitution of 'new' or differently 'known' bodies – a claim for ontological status on the basis of a series of contestatory epistemologies.

Mapping the Body: Sociological and Feminist Approaches

Approaches to the relationship between the body and society have burgeoned in recent years partly in response to the rise of feminist theory and politics; partly connected to the rise of other theoretical challenges to modernist epistemologies; partly as a result of the rise of cultures of consumption and identity politics (Davis 1997). Within this broad theoretical and empirical landscape it is possible to discern four themes or approaches.

The first of these is that of *social constructionism* (as opposed to biologism and naturalistic approaches). Despite important and distinct variations in the 'take' on social constructionism, social scientists have become increasingly attracted to the premise that the body is 'receptor, rather than a generator, of social meanings' (Shilling 1993: 70). This constructionist turn has questioned the powerful naturalizing and de-socializing logics of other discourses on the human body, not least the notion that 'anatomy is destiny'. Turner (1996: 27) captures the central proposition of this consensus as follows: 'The social constructionist approach might be summarised by the slogan – "the body has a history"' and, influenced by the poststructuralist turn, there has been a rush to find out both what that history might be and its effects for a wide range of embodied subjects. Feminism, as Bordo (1995) has noted, was profoundly influential in placing the body at the centre of theoretical and political agendas when it claimed in the late 1960s that 'the personal was political':

> What, after all, is more personal than the life of the body? And for women, associated with the body and largely confined to a life centered *on* the body (both the beautification of one's own body and the reproduction, care, and maintenance of the bodies of others), culture's grip on the body is a constant, intimate fact of everyday life.
> (Bordo 1995: 17)

A product of major shifts and reconfigurations in social, cultural, economic and political life, the 'new scholarship' on the body, with its social constructionist and deconstructive tendencies, now exists as the critical starting point of contemporary sociological enquiry into the body/society nexus. To say this, however, is not to imply that this framework constitutes the end-point or conclusion of such enquiry (Turner 1996: 29).

The second theme is that of the relationship of the body (as both physical entity and metaphor) to the *maintenance of social order* (see Douglas 1970; Turner 1984/1996). In functionalist and structuralist analyses, great play is made of the crucial role played by the body as metaphor of societal risks, pure and impure classifications and more generally as a symbol of ordered/disordered society. For example, Turner's theory of 'bodily order' proposes that societies, as functioning systems, face the central problem of what to do about bodies (rather than, say, classes). This perhaps most fully articulates the claim that the body is a major (and perhaps even the most) potent symbol of social order and that, in turn, 'disease' is the most salient metaphor of structural crisis.[2]

The third theme is associated with the work of Foucault (and other poststructuralists) on the *discursive constitution and regulation of bodies as subjects*. It is by now a common sense amongst some social scientists that rather than treat the body as a pre-social and stable entity, it is to be viewed as a site of power and control constituted through discourses and the practices to which they give rise. The substantive studies of the institutions and knowledges which have attempted to govern and regulate populations have had some impact on Social Policy, and much more centrally on sociology. Crucially, this line of enquiry has resulted in new approaches to the welfare state, as various sites for the exercise of a regulating and disciplining 'gaze' on diversely constituted populations (Leonard 1997: 43; see also Lewis 2000). It is in the work of Foucault that we have the possibility of connecting social order issues and regulation of bodies as subjects.

The fourth line of enquiry we wish to note has developed largely in response to the questions raised by, and silences associated with, the three themes outlined above. Recent theorizing on the body has noted, *inter alia*, the neglect of the phenomenology of bodily experience, a discursive reductionism allied to a minimal theorization of human agency, an ethereal (rather than corporeal) conception of our being in the world (see, for example, Frank 1991; Shilling 1993; 1997; Turner 1996; Craib 1997). Turner has described this emergent line of enquiry as being associated with the 'paradoxes of the body', which 'is at once the most solid, the most elusive, illusory, concrete, metaphorical, ever present and ever distant thing . . . a singularity and a multiplicity' (Turner 1996: 43). The phenomenology of embodiment – as lived experience – is thus now an increasing focus in analyses of the body/society nexus. As Shilling (1997: 738) has noted in his critique of debates about reflexivity and the creative potential for individual agency in late modernity, it is crucial to hold on to the idea of embodied subjects as agents 'who possess senses, sensibilities, and physical habits which are *partially* socialised but *continue to shape*, as well as be shaped, by social structures'. Similarly some feminists (for example, Young 1990), in their concern to analyse the dynamics and effects of sexual difference, have adopted phenomenological approaches as a means of making sense of the lived experience of being gendered female (Davis 1997: 9). A central concern for feminists, then, has been the ways in which the dominant conceptual structures of the body are linked to, manifest in and constitute constructions of male/female; masculinity/femininity.

Thus, in the development of theoretical and political positions aimed at deconstructing and destabilizing sexual difference, feminists have powerfully shown the material effects of representations (Nicholson 1992). They have also shown how the Cartesian mind/body split, which is central to the construction of a rational/universal subject, articulates sexual difference through its association of 'woman' and the feminine with the body (Bordo 1995). Finally, feminist work (see, for example, Braidotti 1989) has opened up debate as to the ontological status of feminist struggle.

The 'Absent Presence' of the Body in Social Policy

The irony of the relative failure of Social Policy to engage with the theorization of the body – as either socially constructed; constituted at the intersection of biology and culture; or as 'performance' (see, Butler 1989; 1993) – is that the body in diverse forms is central to the practices of social policy. Disabled bodies, 'ethnic' bodies, children's bodies, sexualized bodies, old bodies, bodies in need, bodies in danger, bodies at risk, are all at the heart of social policy. In this sense the link between social policy and the body can be said to concern the relative abilities, constraints and needs which different bodies are assumed to produce. As welfare practice, social policy is about devising ways of responding to a range of bodily derived needs. However social policy and bodies are also linked in two further ways. On the one hand, they are linked through the *uses* to which bodies are put. Thus, what people *do* with their bodies – through, for example, sexual practices, the use of legal and illegal drugs such as tobacco or heroin, or eating disorders – are all behaviours which have the potential to provoke an encounter between a range of individuals and welfare agencies. Here welfare need is not seen, in any simple or direct sense, as deriving from *natural* bodily characteristics which emerge as a function of developmental, or medical or social 'pathology'. Rather 'nature' can, and often does, creep back in through the association of particular *behaviours* with particular *types* of people: people who may be considered as having a potential genetic predisposition to certain kinds of behaviour (the 'gay' gene idea is an example). On the other hand, the body and social policy are linked through the idea that social policy practitioners work on or with issues which are not caused by the body but are *encompassed*, or 'housed', within bodies – issues relating to 'personality' or the psyche are examples. Examples used in subsequent sections of the chapter illustrate these varying connections between social policy and the body. Despite this intimate connection between social policy and the body, it is only very recently that we find some discussion of 'embodiment' in Social Policy texts (see, for example, Twigg 1997; Edwards and McKie 1997; Taylor 1998).[3]

Implicit in much mainstream work in Social Policy are two assumptions. One is that in general 'human' terms, irreducible bodily requirements establish the limits on any particularity of welfare need – after all, we all need to eat, sleep and have shelter. In this context the body is stripped of any cultural or social content and distilled to its biologically defined necessities. The body is the pre-social entity which marks the boundaries of welfare need, and welfare is the socially defined and publicly regulated or provided ensemble of services and benefits deemed necessary for the management and satisfaction of needs located in or produced by 'nature'. The limits and possibilities of welfare are constructed around the interface between two separate realms – the biological production of universal needs and the social mechanisms for their satisfaction. Questions as to the legitimate boundaries of welfare – for example, as to whether, to what extent and by what mechanisms welfare services and benefits should be distributed – are in this case political, moral or social questions which arise outside the limits imposed by biology. As a result, this assumption leaves no room for the meanings attached to bodies – for their cultural inscription. This is not quite the case for the second assumption, in which, despite humanity-wide irreducibles, the species is diversified as a result of *differences* rooted in biology – in the body – which then give rise to particular needs which manifest themselves in the specifics of 'culture' or social location. At one level this assumption works on the simple equation of the physical variability among human beings with variations in welfare requirement. Hence, for example, the assumption that old people will be physically frailer than younger people and therefore need aids in terms of mobility or strength. This formulation of the welfare effects of the assumption immediately makes clear some of the problems which arise when we start to separate physical states from their cultural inscriptions. For example, questions such as the basis of the boundaries between 'old' and 'younger' people, or at what point something becomes 'heavy', and for whom, arise. However, the assumption that inevitable biological processes or physical variations among human beings lead to particular or special welfare needs, works in more complex and overlaid ways than this. Let us illustrate the point by looking at the way a document, some 20 years old, constructs a relationship between the possibilities and provision of welfare services on the one hand, and two forms of human physical diversity on the other:

> It is much harder for older people to accept different dietary provisions, different attitudes, to learn a new language. I think that to expect an old person to settle happily into one of our old people's homes or one of our luncheon clubs is asking an awful lot if they are not reasonably assimilated....We had a suggestion come up for Urban Aid from an Indian Association for a day centre for elderly Asians and the council could not back it, specifically on the grounds that they were not supporting any type of provision for one community, only things that were being provided for the residents no matter what their ethnic origin.
>
> (CRC 1976, cited in Patel 1990: 34)

This statement is clearly full of cultural inscription. Bodies read as 'old' and as 'ethnic'[4] – and the intersection between them – determine both what is seen as legitimate for the Social Services Department to provide *and* what can reasonably be expected of 'old' people. Alongside the limits assumed to derive from age, ideas about the 'limits' imposed by 'race'/ ethnicity provide the ideological ground on which to construct a double exclusion. Thus, those constituted as both old and ethnic cannot be expected to be fully incorporated into existing local authority provision. Indeed the welfare objective of care is fulfilled by not expecting such incorporation! At the same time, ethnic specificity is not deemed a criterion sufficient to legitimate specialist provision. 'Bodies' then provide the limits of both universal and particularist needs in this scenario.

Whilst this is an example from social policy as practice, similar examples can be found within the work of writers within Social Policy as a discipline. Again a short example in relation to the construction of 'ethnic' bodies, this time 'young' ones but in connection with adoption:

> The aim of adoption must always be to provide a child without parents a suitable environment to enable the child to develop normally. The commitment must be to the child, not the parents, nor the agency. When we address ourselves to a suitable environment for the child the issue of the child's identity should be given priority above all other factors. Identity is paramount. [It is] only out of the appropriate

integration of the black child's personality that a concrete identity can be formed. If a healthy personality is to be formed, the psychic image of the child must merge with the reality of what the child actually is. That is to say, if the child is black (reality) he must first recognise and accept that he is actually black (psychic image).

(Small 1984: 139)

Again, we see that welfare needs are seen as embodied needs, but in the sense of being encompassed within the body rather than unambiguously deriving from bodily features – there is a match between particularity of need and particularity of embodied psyche.[5] In relation to fostering and adoption the extent to which this assumed correspondence should underpin the policy and practice of social services departments and other agencies operating in this field has been the subject of furious academic, official and popular debate and we do not wish to enter that debate here. What we do want to point to is the way in which ideas of the body as forming both the irreducible limit and the particular shape of welfare needs is part of a common sense which crosses social policy as practice and Social Policy as discipline. In this common sense, the body is understood as a pre-social, biological and psychic entity which is slotted into various social contexts, including those of welfare. Welfare agencies and professionals then identify and provide for needs which are either directly determined by biology or arise from forces or drives 'encompassed' in the body.

Our discussion so far has established a link between social policy and the body in at least two ways. First, social policy derives at least part of its legitimacy as a range of welfare practices from the existence of diverse and what are assumed to be naturally occurring welfare needs. The claims to, and implementation of, a specific set of welfare knowledges are manifested on the premise of the existence of a series of ontologically stable, if diverse, embodied welfare subjects. In their turn, these epistemological claims – and the practices they underwrite – act to construct categories of hierarchically ordered welfare subjects, whose very existence is understood as the product of some naturally occurring essence expressed in and by human physical diversity.

Bodies, Disciplines and Welfare Practices

Having illustrated the ways in which the body is an 'absent presence' (to invoke somewhat paradoxically this Althusserian phrase) within both social policy and Social Policy, in this section we try to show how cultural readings of bodily inscriptions can enhance analysis of social policy practices. In so doing we argue that theorizing embodiment in the contexts of social welfare may help enrich Social Policy analysis. Being 'live' to the corporeality of the subjects and objects of social policy and welfare practices will, we hope, lead to a mutually productive exchange between theorizations of 'the body' in sociology and cultural studies and Social Policy analyses of welfare practices, and the 'knowledges' which underpin them.[6]

Earlier we noted three main ways in which the body and social policy are implicated within each other. These were that different bodies are assumed to produce a series of relative welfare needs; that welfare needs derive from the uses to which bodies are put; and that bodies encompass, or 'house', welfare needs whose roots lie somewhere else (in, for example, the personality or ethnicity). Work which we have recently published (Saraga 1998) explores further these points of connection between the body and social policy. In that publication we have been concerned to consider the links between representations of a range of embodied welfare subjects and the sedimentations of these representations, and the meanings they produce and circulate, in welfare practices. On the one hand, we argue that social policy – as policy – constructs a series of representations of a diverse range of subordinated bodies. These representations in part rely on the construction of privileged, 'normal' bodies. They do this by working through a series of binary logics which act to constitute 'difference'. The binary status of these 'differences' ensures the positioning of various welfare subjects in hierarchical relations, which then structure the 'experiences' of the empirical subjects which are constituted. On the other hand, such representations of subordinated bodies are central to the ways in which social policy has historically marked out its areas of expertise and practice and constituted the very persons on whom these practices will be deployed. The embodied subjects who are inscribed within these representations then provide the corporeal surface upon which welfare practices gain epistemological legitimacy. Embodied subjects are there to be photographed, tested, hospitalized, institutionalized, categorized, analyzed and 'removed' by the relevant policy and practice experts. Bodies, then, form the 'cultural artefacts' of social policy:

> I remember too having medical photographs taken. . . . I was in the hospital and I was in the children's ward and they just put the screens round me and told me to take everything off. I couldn't understand and just did it. . . . I just knew he was taking bits, he wasn't taking me,

he was taking bits of me. It was horrid. . . . The knowledge that one's photograph is being used as an exhibit to be examined by total strangers is in itself a gross invasion of personal privacy. But, as if that were not bad enough, we are also required to perform live.

(Mason 1981, quoted in Hughes 1998: 79)

Such bodies are, therefore, living sites which facilitate the definition of a welfare 'problem/need' (or both) and also act as surfaces on which to bestow the welfare benefit/help. The body acts as a surface on which normalizing and pathologizing welfare practices are (often simultaneously) inscribed.

In the second half of this section we want to illustrate further the way in which social policy or welfare practice is a nodal point around which ideas of the body as limit, as moral issue and as the opposite of 'mind' coalesce, and we do so in relation to constructions of children's sexuality. In this context we also give more consideration to the theme of the Cartesian mind/body split and that of sexual difference.

If we include under the rubric 'welfare' that vast array of agencies and practices involved in 'public action . . . to meet fundamental human needs and to mitigate social inequalities' (Ginsburg 1996: 1) and to promote social order and social integration, then it is clear that most, if not all, of the population can be construed as welfare subjects. However, among this diverse range of people whose lives are in some way affected by the operation of welfare, children occupy a central place. Whether as the subjects of universal provisions, such as compulsory education, or as recipients of services reserved for much smaller populations of children, such as those provided by social care or criminal justice agencies, children have much of their life directly organized or regulated by the practices of welfare agencies and professionals.

In an article published in 1992, Martin explored the metaphors and imagery which predominate in biological teaching materials used in schools in the United States and Britain. She found both a highly gendered differentiation in the imagery used to depict the reproductive organs of females and males, and that femaleness or 'femininity' was equated with 'lack'. Feminist approaches to the body have shown that the association of 'women' or femininity with 'lack' is one of the dominant tropes through which sexual difference is constructed (Bordo 1995; Braidotti 1989; 1994). In this way the language and imagery of these texts reproduced this binary and its associated hierarchical valorizations. The metaphor of 'lack' in the sex education materials was possible because the dominant imagery of human reproduction was such that it was equated to a system for the production of valuable things. The extent to which such 'things' were produced provided the criteria of valorization. Once this was established as the dominant metaphor, the female monthly cycle was seen as being about the production of an egg and an environment in which fertilization can occur. Given that this double process of production is fulfilled relatively infrequently, it tended to be described in negative terms with the use of culturally laden terms such as 'debris' or 'waste' to describe menstruation (Martin 1992: 411). In contrast, the male reproductive system was depicted in terms of awe and wonderment at the continuous and voluminous process of production (of sperm) it involved. In addition to these rather telling points, Martin noted that 'passivity' and 'degeneration' were associated with the female reproductive system, in contrast to male 'activity' and renewal. These representations are related to the determination of female egg-producing capacity at birth, in opposition to the male's sperm-producing capacity being in a state of continual renewal. Female 'lack' and 'passivity' and male 'activity' and 'aggression' are, then, constructed in these textbooks through the deployment of highly gendered codes. As Martin states:

> None of these texts expresses such intense enthusiasm about any female processes, and it is surely no accident that the 'remarkable' process of making sperm involves precisely what menstruation does not in the medical view: production of something deemed valuable.
> (1992: 412)

As sex education materials used in schools, these texts form part of the repository of social policy texts. Moreover, this brief exploration through the language and imagery they deploy indicates how densely sedimented in the agencies and practices of social policy are the dominant cultural representations of sexual difference. It is this which makes Martin's work so relevant to our argument.

Located within a discursive formation, these materials illustrate the way in which anatomical differences of sexual reproduction are culturally inscribed to construct the limits of sexual difference. In this way they are one of the mechanisms used within education to inscribe boys and girls into the discursive parameters of sexual difference. It is through this that, at least in part, the bodily possibilities and experiences of young women and men are explained, constructed and valorized. Young women and men can 'know' themselves (and the differentially weighted 'wonder' of their bodies) through a set of social policy texts tied to part of the school curriculum. Moreover, embedded within the constructions of female and male reproductive capacities and sexuality is the issue of the body as a struggle over immanence and transcendence – that is, between the latent, and potentially explosive, eruption of bodily (sexual) drives, and the overcoming of these drives through the application of 'mind' and rationality – and the intersection of this binary with constructions of sexual difference. Let us elaborate this last point a little.

Within social policy as welfare practice, it is across the bodies of children and adolescents that the tension between immanence and transcendence is articulated most strongly. This takes the form, as we have already seen, of teaching children and young adults to 'know' the body and its 'drives'; to mature sufficiently, both emotionally and physically, so as to be able to control these bodily drives and express them in 'appropriate' ways and relationships; and, where necessary, to discipline and 'correct' any sexual expressions deemed 'inappropriate'. Each of these is clear from the following taken from a guide to the 1989 Children Act:

> The experience of being cared for should also include the sexual education of the young person. This may, of course, be provided by the young person's school, but if it is not, the SSD [social services department] or other caring agency responsible for the young person should provide sexual education for him. This is absolutely vital since sexuality will be one of the most potent forces affecting any young person in the transition from childhood to adulthood.
>
> Sexual education will need to cover practical issues such as contraception . . . However, it must also cover the emotional aspects of sexuality, such as the part that sexuality plays in the young person's sense of identity; the emotional implications of entering into a sexual relationship with another person; and the need to treat sexual partners with consideration and not as objects to be used. The emotional and practical implications of becoming a parent also need to be explained in some detail.
>
> (HMSO 1991: 97)

Whilst we are not concerned with the social or moral legitimacy of these aims, this official policy document is interesting for the way it constructs the relationship between the bodies (of young people) and the responsibilities of welfare agencies. Thus, the latter must assume responsibility for teaching the young person 'the facts' of sex, whilst simultaneously teaching them their 'appropriate' forms of expression.

Children as embodied subjects have generally been viewed in two dominant, essentialist but contradictory ways. As:

- innocent, vulnerable, and in need of protection from danger/abuse/labour, or as
- a social, inherently evil, and in need of firm control and socialization.

These are played out in all sorts of ways in terms of the huge variety of chronological ages at which children are seen as capable of making decisions for themselves, or as being responsible for their own actions. Children's sexuality is predominantly seen within the first view – children as 'innocent'. 'Innocence' is then understood as not 'having' adult sexuality, that is in terms of a number of 'lacks' – lack of knowledge, lack of understanding, lack of particular kinds of feelings, lack of ability to engage in certain practices and/or to handle and curtail the emotions attached to practices. It is this understanding of children's 'normal' sexuality that underwrites debates about the age of consent.[7] Crucially, pre-pubescent children's bodies are not defined as sexual, at least not in an adult sense of sexual. For example, a Law Commission Report argued the need to distinguish between an adult and a child's ability to consent to sexual activity with an adult, raising the child's intellectual competence as one of three key factors[8] (Leng 1994, cited in Barnardo's 1998: 71). Similarly, the Master of the Rolls stated in 1993:

> The reason why the law is particularly solicitous in protecting the interests of children is because they are liable to be vulnerable and impressionable, lacking the maturity to weigh the longer term against the shorter, lacking insight to know how they will react and the imagination to know how others will react in certain situations, lacking the experience to measure the probable against the possible.
> (*Re S* [1993] 2 FLR 437, cited in Barnardo's 1998: 72)

Moreover, that these ways of representing the sexuality and 'mind' of children and young people is part of journalistic and popular discourse is evident from this newspaper report of a case of alleged rape by four boys aged between ten and eleven of a nine-year-old-girl. 'Although children's sexual play can cause anxiety, intense interest is usually fleeting. This is because young children experience the world through sensations – taste, smell, touch – but when a child begins to interact and learn through the mind, these things become less important' (Cantacuzino, *The Guardian* 1998: 6).

Each of these examples provides a clear illustration of the 'Cartesian Ghost' making a presence, in which a mind/body – or immanence/transcendence – split is central. Children, like women, are on the body side of the binary – they experience the world through sensation, but are not really sexual. However, the move to adulthood is the move to 'mind'. Inscribing children's bodies through the Cartesian mind/body split opens a discursive space for the 'deviance' of having 'an adult's body and a child's mind'. A tension made possible according to one professor of paediatric endocrinology because of the increasing body mass indexes observable in children in recent years, with the result of an earlier onset of puberty (Professor Charles Brook, quoted in *The Guardian* 21 January 1998). In this sense, then, the 'innocence' of children is corrupted by a shift in the pacing of their physical development.

The idea of the 'corruptibility' of 'innocent' children opens a discursive space in which it is possible to construct boundaries between 'normal' children and their 'deviant' counterparts. Here the concept of 'evil' can be deployed and the place of the body as explanation of the differences amongst these children can be altered. Thus, it is across the bodies of child sexual abusers that the idea of the body as producer of needs or drives; as encompassing these needs or drives; and as separable from, but intimately tied to, the non-physical of the 'mind' and or emotions, coalesces in a particularly acute way. One group of professionals[9] working with juvenile sexual offenders puts it this way:

> The crux of the debate about definitional and ethical issues is whether it is the child who is being labelled or the behaviour... However, most research studies looking at the characteristics of young abusers (Becker *et al.*, 1986), and clinicians working in the field (Bremer, 1993), agree that some degree of coercion, force or persuasion coupled with unusually high levels of sexual arousal help to differentiate ordinary childhood interest in sexuality from the preoccupation with sex which can characterise even the very young abuser. In addition, the age, developmental status, physical, emotional and cognitive development of the child will all play a part in determining the extent to which the child understands the implications of his or her abusing behaviour towards other children.
>
> (Vizard et al. 1996: 259)

However, this immediately raises the question of at what point the line between childhood and adulthood is crossed. For example, is this line determined by chronological age and the physical changes which accompany this movement; or is it determined by cognitive features and capacities; or by some combination of the two? Similarly, the question is begged as to whether a distinction can be made between crossing this divide physically (in terms of bodily acts/desires) and emotionally/mentally (in terms of morality/cognition) – whether the Cartesian body/ mind dualism can be invoked quite so neatly. Despite these questions, for the welfare practitioner working within a given conceptual frame – and with difficult social and/or psychological issues to consider – normative representations of these 'problems' circulate within and between welfare agencies and act as a way through which practitioners can construct the issues and devise and legitimate the 'solutions'.

Thus, for example, there is an increasing literature on juvenile abusers who do not get prosecuted and instead are seen as welfare problems. Indeed, this is the emphasis of the 1989 Children Act. In this context, their 'welfare problems' are often understood as resulting from their own earlier abuse. This would 'fit' with a dominant discourse on the 'cycle of abuse', but it is also clear that there are ambiguities in the explanations of this type of behaviour because not all 'young abusers' have themselves been abused (see, for example, Bremer 1991; Knapp 1991). These ambiguities raise questions about the role the body may play in their 'origin'. Thus, some commentators look for explanations in the greater incidence of media representations of sexuality, which, they say, means that children are being 'sexualized' earlier – the implication here being that it is too early since there is a 'natural', age-appropriate sexual behaviour as the quote from Vizard et al., cited earlier, indicates.[10] In this case, then, the body of children is being 'acted on' in some way by the social and moral content of a repertoire of representations which circulate within and through welfare agencies and practices.

Bodies, Resistances, Subversions and Transgressions ('Making Presences Felt')

We have argued above that social policy – as policy – constructs a series of representations of a diverse range of subordinated bodies, and that these representations are central to the ways in which social policy has historically marked out its areas of expertise and practice. These practices and knowledges, however, are manifested on empirical subjects – living people who are the objects and subjects of welfare practices. This distinction between bodies as categories of representation and bodies as living, empirical subjects is a vital one to hold on to because it is at their points of intersection that the operation of power is contested. Thus, these same empirical or embodied subjects also constitute the points of contestation to social policy knowledges and practices. In this context it is important that we avoid what Williams (1996: 17), among others, has called a discursive 'determinism whereby the body as a material entity simply disappears in a post-structuralist play of signs' (see also Sheets-Johnstone 1992; Shillings, 1997). In analyses of the ways in which social policy constructs subordinated welfare subjects it is crucial that we neither lose sight of the contestations to social policy's representations and practices nor of the ways in which the body is deployed in these contestations. These subordinated bodies contest dominant representations of themselves as welfare subjects – beings subjected to different regimes of welfare practice – in specific and different ways. Perhaps the most significant areas of active contestation are associated with the struggles to resist the 'needs' which are assumed to derive from particular bodies whilst simultaneously offering counter-representations of their subordinated bodies. Such subversions of welfare practices and the policy status quo also deploy notions of the body. In this way the body – or its representation in policy and practice – constitutes the site for the contestation of professional power and other forms of privileged expertise in welfare regimes. These struggles, then, are at once *epistemological* and *ontological* struggles. On the one hand, they seek to disrupt old 'knowledges' and replace them with new 'knowledges', which are often authorized through the notion of 'experience' (see, for example, Lewis 1996). On the other hand, they are also ontological struggles since they seek to establish a form of social and philosophical 'beingness' based on a reinscription of non-normative bodies as authoritative and legitimate. Moreover, they do so by seeking to disrupt their own inscription through 'lack' and in its stead measure and valorize their subordinated bodies through positivity. They seek, then, to disrupt the binaries which act as the discursive conduits of their constitution, and, in so doing, make a claim for forms of social belonging and citizenship through the possession of non-normative bodies. In the last section of this chapter we try to illustrate these points through a brief consideration of the challenge posed to social policy as practice by the disability rights movement.

Welfare practice on disability has tended to focus on the physical or mental impairment rather than the person, and it is this 'defective' – and 'deviant' – characteristic of the body or mind which is constructed as the welfare problem. This is a quite complicated and contradictory situation. On the one hand, the impact of the disability rights movement has led (at least in part) to the emergence of a consciousness of the oppressive consequences of reducing the person to (the sum of) their impairment. On the other hand, it is still the case that in terms of the aims and targets of welfare agencies the central 'problem' is still the physical/mental 'lacks' produced by the impairment. Thus, rehabilitation rather than independence remains the prime targets for welfare agencies. In the context of resource constraints and the pressure to achieve efficiency and economy in welfare budgets even independence can be appropriated to a discourse of lack. Indeed, such is the pervasive power of this discourse that even in the 1995 Disability Discrimination Act the disadvantage disabled people face is seen in terms of the individual's impairment. In contrast to this approach, the social model of disability offers a new and contestatory framework for understanding disability. As is now widely understood, this model constructs the issue of disability not in terms of the physical, sensory, cognitive or mental impairments of the individual, but rather in terms of the disadvantages and oppression which arises from structural and normative arrangements. 'Disability' is seen as a *social process*, not an individual condition or problem. The epistemological basis of this new way of constructing, what was now termed disablement (rather than disability), is the *experience* of having their bodies defined as a site on which welfare practitioners exercised their 'expertise', as was illustrated in the quote from Mason above. This is echoed in the way in which Finkelstein draws on his own experience to analyse the process of rehabilitation:

> The aim of returning the individual to normality is the central foundation stone upon which the whole rehabilitation machine is constructed...
>
> The result, for me, was endless soul-destroying hours at Stoke Mandeville Hospital trying to approximate to able-bodied standards by 'walking' with callipers and crutches... Rehabilitation philosophy emphasises physical normality and, with this, the attainment of skills that allow the individual to approximate as closely as possible to able-bodied behaviour...
>
> (Finkelstein 1985:4–5)

Alongside this critique of dominant constructions of disability and rehabilitative welfare practices is a reordering and revalorization of the place of ability/'disability' in all human experience. Indeed, this argument strikes at the very ontological stability of the 'normal', 'able-bodied' subject. Thus Morris (1991: 38) writes:

Physical disability and illness are an important part of human experience. The non-disabled world may wish to try and ignore this and to
react to physical difference by treating us as if we are not quite
human, but we assert that our difference is both an essential part of
human experience and, given the chance, can create an important
and different way of looking at things.

Here, then, is an argument about what it means to be human. The shift
to universal human experience, rather than the particularity of the
experience of an 'abnormal' group, aims at cutting through the very
binary able-bodied/disabled and making an ontological claim for the
'wholeness' of the person by rewriting 'disabled' bodies in a way in
which their 'beingness' is no longer defined through 'lack'.

Whilst the emergence of the social model of disability has acted as a
powerful challenge to dominant inscriptions of bodies defined as disabled, this contestatory model has not been without its critics. Many of
these have come from within the movement itself and the terms of the
critique have often centred on precisely the epistemological and ontological claims contained in the social model. Thus, the feminist disabled
activist Morris (1991) has argued that the bodily figure at the heart of
much of this disabled imaginary reflected in the social model is male.
Bury (1996) has also argued that the 'social oppression' theory contained
in the social model tends to act as an ideological underpinning of the
activities of younger (mostly middle-class) people, with non-chronic,
relatively stable, though perhaps severe forms of disability. If the focus
is shifted to older people, who, Bury argues, are often affected by chronic
and disabling medical conditions, then some of the critiques of many
welfare practices – such as residential and rehabilitative care – lose some
of their potency. The challenge to medical inscriptions of the 'disabled'
body has then been subject to its own, at times internal, critique, over the
way it privileges particular experiences and particular bodies. But what
each of these shows – critique, and critique of critique – is that the body
and social policy are deeply implicated. The lesson to be learned from the
encounter of these particular bodies and the array of welfare institutions
who seek to 'service' their needs is that Social Policy and social policy
ignore the body – as site of theory and empirical subject – at its cost.

Conclusion: The 'Lived Body' and a Politics of Articulation

Our argument has been that while ideas of the body in both a normative
and differentiated sense are deeply embedded in the conceptual struc-

tures and epistemological claims of social policy as practice, Social Policy as discipline has been relatively late to respond to or engage in theorizations of the body/society nexus. Lines of enquiry into the ways in which 'the body' underwrites and is inscribed in social practices have been opened up by the convergence of two, interconnected trends: one anchored around theoretical/epistemological/ontological questions; the other, more directly political. Thus, on the one hand, questions of 'the body' have emerged from the critique and destabilization of dominant (Cartesian) conceptualizations of the body/mind split; from interrogations about the existence and character of human subjectivity; from the deconstruction of the construction of forms of difference organized around axes of human physical variation and diversity. On the other hand, questions as to the status of 'the body' have emerged from the politics of 'new social movements'. From the emergence of an array of political constituencies which sought to reveal the practical (and corporeal) implications of these dominant conceptualizations for the patterning and delivery of all forms of public goods. These 'new' constituencies also insisted on their right to be involved in the identification, design and delivery of new or altered forms of public services. However, that these constituencies pointed to the constructed character of the series of normative and differentiated bodies which stood (invisibly) at the heart of social policy practices should not, in our view, be taken to mean that the body should only be understood as discursive. Rather, it suggests the need for a theorization of the ways in which the corporeal and discursive are *mutually constitutive*. One way of beginning this is through the notion of the 'lived body', an idea developed by, among others, Merleau-Ponty (1962; 1968) and brought into the arena of contemporary debates about the body/society nexus in the work of Drew Leder (1998). The 'lived body' offers a radical alternative to the Cartesian conceptualization and articulates the corporeal and the discursive. As an 'intending' entity, the lived body 'is bound up with, and directed toward, an experienced world. It is a being in relationship ... [and] the lived body helps constitute this world-as-experienced...' (Leder, 1998: 123). Thus the 'lived body' can help provide the conceptual apparatus through which both to critique the (implicit) conceptualizations of the body which circulate within and between welfare agencies and underwrite much of their practice. Moreover, it can do this in a way which holds the insistence implicit in many of the challenges coming from diverse constituencies of welfare subjects: that is, to hold the integrity of their diverse bodies and to use them to underwrite the emergence of new forms of welfare practice and new subjectivities. It is through this critique of current discursive regimes and social practices that we see the connection to, and need for, a politics of articulation. Unless our theorizations of the connections between social policy and the body are understood as being directed towards shifting the claims of association between a series of representations and a range of differentiated embodied subjects, Social Policy's entry into contemporary debates about the body/society nexus is likely to remain academic.

Notes

1   The use of the body as a metaphor for social order has, of course, a long history, and Mary Poovey's collection of essays (1995) is a fascinating investigation of the links between this metaphor and the formation of a new social order in early nineteenth century Britain. Eileen Yeo's 'The Contest for Social Science' also explores the ways in which the body occupied a connotive role in questions of social order in nineteenth-century Britain. Particularly fascinating is her investigation of the ways in which different parts of the body became associated with specific classes after the middle of the century. For example, with 'the lower orders' frequently being described through associations with the lower parts of the body, i.e. those distant from 'mind' and connected to sexuality.

2   As Shilling (1993: 88) notes, whilst this approach has shown that 'bodies matter', their significance is determined ultimately by social structures or discourses beyond the reach of individuals. Its epistemological view of the body is as something produced by and existing in discourse. As such the approach has been charged with both a discursive and/or social overdeterminism and pessimism about change and agency.

3   At first this tended to be in the 'minority' specialist areas of disability studies, or discussions of gender and racialization in social policy (see, for example, Alcock et al. 1998). Note the exceptions on the radical margins of Social Policy such as Williams, 1996; Leonard 1997; Lavalette and Pratt 1997; and radical journals such as *Critical Social Policy* and *Disability and Society*. Even these isolated radical efforts have not generated any sustained theoretical exploration of the problem.

4   It will be immediately apparent that 'race' and ethnicity are conflated in this quote. Such conflation is, of course, a common occurrence in social science writing and serves as a clear reminder of the tendency to naturalize boundary formation, cultural inscription and social inequalities.

5   Our argument that the 'need' identified in this quote is one which is encompassed in the body rather than deriving directly from it relates to the conceptualization of 'personality' within psychology. Thus, psychologists have a dual conception of 'personality' premised on the 'I'/'me' distinction. In this dualism, the 'I' is disembodied and rational, whilst the 'me' is embodied and relational (i.e. there is a recognized social element), but precisely because 'personality' is a psychological concept its embodied materiality is somewhat evanescent. Our thanks to Ann Phoenix for alerting us to this point.

6 We would also see such a process of intellectual exchange as mutually enriching – with theorizations of 'the body' rooted in social and cultural theory benefiting from similar analyses within Social Policy.
7 There, is of course, a wide degree of inconsistency in relation to the law regarding age of consent to sexual activity. This ranges from 14 for boys engaging in vaginal intercourse, 16 for girls, to 18 for marriage without parental agreement and sexual activity between two men. See S. Edwards (1998) for a detailed discussion, albeit from a particular political perspective, of the issues.
8 The other two reasons were children's habit of obedience and adult influence on a child.
9 The authors are a group of welfare professionals from divergent fields working in the Young Abusers Project in London.
10 See also *The Guardian*, 2, 25 February 1998: 6.

References

Barnardo's 1998. *Whose Daughter Next? Children Abused through Prostitution*. Ilford: Barnardo's.

Becker, J. V., Cunningham-Rathner, J. and Kaplan, M. S. 1986. 'Adolescent Sexual Offenders, Demographics, Criminal and Sexual Histories and Recommendations for Reducing Future Offences', *Journal of Interpersonal Violence* 1: 431–45.

Bordo, S. 1995. *Unbearable Weight*. New York and London, Routledge.

Braidotti, R. 1989. 'The Politics of Ontological Struggle', In T. Brennan (ed.), *Psychoanalysis and Feminism*. London: Routledge.

Bremer, J. F. 1991. 'Intervention with the Juvenile Sex Offender. Human Systems', *The Journal of Systematic Consultation and Management* 2: 235–46.

Bremer, J. F. 1993. 'The Treatment of Children and Adolescents with Aberrant Sexual Behaviours', *Baillière's Clinical Paediatrics: International Practice and Research Child Abuse* 1: 269–82.

Bury, M. 1995. 'The Body in Question'. *Medical Sociology News* 21, no. 1: 36–48.

Bury, M. 1996. 'Disability and the Myth of the Independent Researcher: a Reply'. *Disability and Society* 11, no. 1, pp. 111–15.

Butler, J. 1989. *Gender Trouble: Feminism and the Subversion of Identity*. New York: Routledge.

Butler, J. 1993. *Bodies that Matter: On the Discursive Limits of 'Sex'*. New York: Routledge.

Community Relations Commission Report 1976. *Urban Deprivation: Racial Inequality and Social Policy*. London: CRC.

Davis, K. (ed.) 1997. *Embodied Practices, Feminist Perspectives on the Body*. London: Sage.

Douglas, M. 1970. *Purity and Danger*. Harmondsworth: Penguin Books.

Edwards, J. and McKie, L. 1997 'Women's Public Toilets: A Serious Issue for the Body Politic', in K. Davis, (ed.), *Embodied Practices: Feminist Perspectives on the Books*. London: Sage.

Edwards, S. S. M. 1998. *Abused and Exploited – Young Girls in Prostitution: A Consideration of the Legal Issues*, Ilford: Barnardos, 47–90.

Finkelstein, V. 1985. Paper delivered at World Health Organisation meeting, Netherlands, 24–28 June.

Frank, A. 1991. 'For a Sociology of the Body', M. Featherstone, M. Hepworth and B. Turner (eds), *The Body, Social Process and Cultural Theory.* London: Sage.

Giddens, A. 1992. *Self-identity and Late Modernity.* Oxford: Polity.

Ginsburg, N. 1996. 'The Future of the Welfare State'. Inaugural Lecture: University of North London.

Goffman, E 1969. *The Presentation of Self in Everyday Life.* Harmondsworth: Penguin Books.

HMSO 1991. 'The Children Act: Guidance and Regulations', *Family Placements* 3 London.

The Guardian 1998. 21 January.

The Guardian 1998. 25 February.

Hughes, G. 1998. 'A Suitable Case for Treatment? Constructions of Disability', in E. Saraga (ed). *Embodying the social constructions of Difference.* London: Open University in association with Routledge.

Hughes, G. (ed.) 1998. *Imagining Welfare Futures.* London: Open University in association with Routledge.

Hughes, G. and Lewis, G. (eds.) 1998. *Unsettling Welfare: The Reconstruction of Social Policy.* London: Open University in association with Routledge.

Knopp, F. H. 1991. *The Youthful Sex Offender: The Rationale and Goals of Early Intervention and Treatment.* Syracuse, NY: Safer Society Press.

Langan, M. (ed.) 1998. *Welfare: Needs, Rights and Risks.* London: Open University in association with Routledge.

Lavalette, M. and Pratt, A. 1997. *Social Policy: A Conceptual and Theoretical Introduction.* London: Sage.

Leder, D. 1998 [1992]. 'A Take of Two Bodies: the Cartesian Corpse and the Lived Body', in D. Welton (ed.) *Body and Flesh: A Philosophical Reader.* Oxford: Blackwell.

Leng, R. 1994. 'Consent and Offences against the Person: Law Commission Consultation Paper'. *Crim. L.R.* 134: 480–8.

Leonard, P. 1997. *Postmodern Welfare.* London: Sage.

Lewis, G. (ed.) 1998. *Forming Nation, Framing Welfare.* D218 Book 2: London: Open University in association with Routledge.

Lewis, G. 1996. 'Situated Voices: "Black Women's Experience" and Social Work', *Feminist Review* 53 summer: 24–56.

Lewis, G. 2000. *'Race', Gender, Social Welfare: Encounters in a Postcolonial Society,* Oxford: Polity Press.

Martin, E. 1992 'Body Narratives, Body Boundaries', in L., Grossberg, C. Nelson and P. A. Treichler (eds) *Cultural Studies.* New York and London: Routledge.

Mason, 1981. 'On the Children's Ward', *Embodying the Social: Constructions of Difference* D218 Book 1: London Open University in association with Routledge.

Merleau-Ponty, M. 1962. *Phenomenology of Perception.* London: Routledge and Kegan Paul.

Merleau-Ponty, M. 1968. *The Visible and the Invisible.* Evanston, Ill.: Northwestern University Press.

Morris, J. 1991. *Pride against Prejudice.* London: The Women's Press.

Patel, N. 1990. *A 'Race' Against Time? Social Services Provision to Black Elders.* London: Runnymede Trust.

Poovey, M. 1995. *Making a Social Body: British Cultural Formation 1830–1864*. Chicago, Illinois, and London: University of Chicago Press.

Saraga, E. (ed.) 1998. *Embodying the Social: Constructions of Difference*. London: Open University in association with Routledge.

Sheets-Johnstone, M. 1992. 'Corporeal Archetypes and Power: Preliminary Clarifications and Considerations of Sex'. *Hypatia* 7: 39–76.

Shilling, C. 1993. *The Body and Social Theory* London: Sage.

Shilling, C. 1997. 'The Under-socialised Conception of the Embodied Agent in Modern Sociology', *Sociology* 31: 4, 737–54.

Taylor, D. 1998. 'Social Identity and Social Policy: Engagements with Postmodern Theory', *Journal of Social Policy* 27: 329–50.

Turner, B. 1996. *The Body and Society*, second edition. London: Sage.

Turner, B. 1997. 'What is the Sociology of the Body?', *Body and Society* 3, no. 1: 103–7.

Twigg, J. 1997. 'Demonstrating the "Social Bath"', *Journal of Social Policy* 26: 211–32.

Vizard, F., Wynick, S., Hawkes, C., Woods, J. and Jenkins, J. 1996. 'Juvenile Sexual Offenders: Assessment Issues'. *British Journal of Psychiatry* 168: 259–62.

Williams, F. 1996. 'Post-modernism, Feminism and the Question of Difference', in N. Parton (ed.), *Social Theory, Social Change and Social Work*. London: Routledge.

Yeo, E. J. 1996. *The Contest for Social Science: Relations and Representations of Gender and Class*. London: Rivers Oram Press.

Young, I. M. 1990. *Throwing Like a Girl and Other Essays in Feminist Philosophy and Social Theory*. Bloomington and Indianapolis: Indiana University Press.

2

Redefining the Local Citizen

Guy Daly and Harry Cowen

Introduction: Body Politic and Citizenship

Proposals to reform the nature of local democracy, implying a reduction in the emphasis on representative forms of participation, question the very essence of the body politic and the meaning of citizenship (Blair 1998; Department of Environment, Transport and Regions 1998; Hecke and Ward 1998). However, the argument of this chapter is that with the restructuring of the local polity, we are witnessing a further retreat to narrow individualistic conceptions of citizenship and concomitant constrictions of public, that is, political accountability (Daly 1997). Accordingly, the chapter casts doubt on the belief that a 'consumerist' model of participation, whether under the New Right or New Labour, reflects an enhancement of citizenship, although it may appear to do so. In this respect, current policies and debates regarding citizenship may be understood in a longer historical context: citizenship is historically constructed within the body politic.

The social body politic, it is contended, mediates the social relationships of human beings, the body which regulates the movements of the individual (MacKenzie 1979; Masters 1989). Social institutions, thus, may be seen as regulators: hence, the concept of the public body (Hobbes [1651] 1968; Schatzki and Natter 1996; Turner 1996). The social institutions and constitutions, being part of the social order, regulate and order individual identities. But humans are conscious agents too. While 'human' is both biologically and morally constructed, the teleological element of life is not simply a product of biology, but is concerned with the social and philosophical. Living as a moral being is an ineliminable part of one's humanity, and moral equality requires equality in the body politic (Clarke 1994). Nor are moral precepts *individual* constructions; rather they are defined and refined in a social context. Indeed, sociality and social purpose are essential facets of our 'human nature' (Cowen 1994). We would argue that a viable model of citizenship must position the human agent within their political and communal habitat, rather than treat the human actor as an atomistic, self-centred autonomous individual.

The classical perspective views the relationships between the 'institutional' and the 'individual' as symbiotic (or 'communitas'). Basically, it is a communitarianism which interprets the citizen's decision-making capacities as inseparable from the communal process. Yet this perspective has not survived uncontested. Our understanding of citizenship is itself historically and politically shaped (Oliver and Heater 1994), particularly affected by the rise of capitalism and the enhanced significance of the atomistic individual as distinct from the communal citizen and the body politic. One must question to what extent the rearticulation of formal communitarian precepts represents policies which challenge the idea of the redefined consumerist citizen in the arena of social care and local service delivery.

In the course of this chapter, we unpack the theoretical and empirical dimensions of the argument, by discussing the historical genesis of the relationships between the body politic and the citizen, the more recent forms of citizenship, and corresponding changes in the forms of public accountability,with the recomposition of public bodies. We then evaluate particular changes in the form of local decision-making bodies, especially relating these to a particular local authority's policies, the implications for contemporary citizenship, the delivery of community care in this local authority and how this reconstructs the meaning of citizenship and citizen.

The Body Politic and Citizenship Constructed: An Historical Analysis

Citizenship: The Two Traditions

The notion of citizenship as actively belonging to and participating in a body politic originated in ancient Greece. The concept of the citizen received its fullest expression in the Athens of classical Greece (Oliver and Heater 1994; Clarke 1994: 4–6).

Aristotle's *Politics* represents the classic statement of the idea of the body politic as regulator of the community and the citizen's activities. In classical Rome, the enjoyment of Roman citizenship and the cultivation of virtue was a civic republicanism, but the new definition formally incorporated the distinction of status into citizenship, that is, a second-class category was recognized as a legal, but not political, citizenship.

The period of medievalism was dominated by the precepts of the Church and universal order in which humans inhabited a fixed, preordained space. But in the eighteenth century civic republicanism reemerged with a stress on the *duties* incumbent on the citizen in their activities within the republic. Civic virtue is expounded in Rousseau's *Social Contract* (1772 1: vii): 'Those who are associated in [the body politic] take collectively the name of a *people*, and call themselves *citizens*, in so far as they share in the sovereign power.'

On the other hand, from the seventeenth century onwards and the rise of capitalism, the liberal tradition stressed the autonomous individual and their individual citizen rights. Political and civil freedom is emphasized rather than the symbiotic communal body. The rise of industrial capitalism (Turner 1985), with its affirmation of self-help and entrepreneurialism, could not but run counter to the concept of citizenship as communalism, as in the classical tradition.

Hobbes' *Leviathan* (1651) best expresses a political system under which social relationships are reduced to relationships of exchange between individuals, so that the only solution for binding the individual to the state is a contract based on fear. Hobbes grounds the very nature of political power in the body's physiological movements – the body politic literally regulates the dynamism of the individual organism to minimize conflict (Plant 1991) and maximize general stability and security. Indeed, *Leviathan* has been characterized as the rationalized history of a healthy body politic (Wilkins 1973). Hobbes' political body is the human body extended; the body politic is thus 'the artificial body which provides the framework within which the real bodies of men can find security and peace' (Turner 1996: 105).

Locke's later liberalist espousal, *Two Treatises of Government* (1690) conceptualised the state as the result of a contract arrived at between government and citizens that would meet their respective interests – a legal bond where the citizens were property holders, and the government protected the property to ensure freedom. Locke's bourgeois citizen legally *contracts* with the state for freedoms in civic society. Later, citizen relationships were circumscribed by the power of nineteenth-century market forces (Adam Smith's *Wealth of Nations* 1766) in a society where the citizen is a liberal individualist, but cannot be a citizen in the communitarian sense.

The Twentieth Century, Social Citizenship and Welfare

In the twentieth century, it may be argued, the arrival of the welfare state, founded on collectivist political principles, heralded a revisiting of the communitarian reassertion of the citizen as an integral part of the social organism. For T. H. Marshall (1950), whose work on the citizenship debate was seminal during the late years of the twentieth century (Barbalet 1988; Turner 1993; van Steenbergen 1994; Bulmer and Rees 1996), the *social* rights invested in citizens under welfare capitalism reflected an evolution of citizenship rights from the civil or legal rights of the seventeenth century through the political rights of the eighteenth and early nineteenth centuries (an evolution not without struggle), but culminating in the social rights of the late nineteenth century and first part of the twentieth century (Marshall 1950). However, the means for participation in the political body (the public arena) were made available for the practice of citizenship, e.g. through local involvement or participation in local government and representations on various public welfarist institutions). Leftist critiques (Giddens 1982; D. Taylor 1989), however are less convinced that equality of citizenship is possible in an economically unequal and basically unchallenged capitalist society.

The New Right and Markets

Such ambivalence towards citizenship's instrinsic relationship weakened over the final decades of the twentieth century with the rise of a New Right ideology which: (i) reasserted the seventeenth century's fundamental atomistic concept of the citizen as individual, protected by civic and legal rights; (ii) reasserted the hegemony of private market values over those of the public arena; (iii) dismantled the pillars of the public polity (the body politic) within which the welfare state's citizens were politically participating – for example, local government bodies, health authorities, educational institutions; (iv) substituted quasi-market and managerialist relationships, which redefined the citizen not as an intrinsic member of a body politic but as consumer and customer, exerting one's choice and preferences in relation to services offered (Andrews 1991; Culpitt 1992; Saunders 1993; Haworth 1994; Clarke and Newman 1997).

Communitarianism

Despite the dominance exerted by New Right philosophy since the mid-1970s in redefining the citizen as individual, the civic republican, communitarian tradition has persisted. The tradition reasserts human beings' essential communal nature and the inviolability of social duties and responsibilities, notably in the critiques of individual citizen rights by North America-based philosophers (Walzer 1983; MacIntyre 1985; C. Taylor 1989). For instance, Sandel (1982) holds participation as the defining element in developing the citizen's sense of identity and belonging to a specific community or republic. Charles Taylor (1989) emphasizes commitment within the community.

The more practically oriented and conservative new communitarianism of Etzioni (1993) appealing to New Labour, although it fails to take account of socio-economic inequalities, social class and gender (Lister 1997), has re-entered the political agenda. Witness the contemporary political social movements. Their pressures on the public body politic have hinged on redefining the public institution in terms of biological definitions of their location as non-citizen in the body politic. To quote Schatzki and Natter (1996: 11):

> Since, on the one hand, subjects are constituted through the molding of bodies, corporeality is an important focus for feminists, gay activists, and others who politicize identity formation by locating it within and relating it to the public realm. At the same time, since the body politic is maintained through the sociocultural investment of bodies, the management of corporeality becomes an important focus for the decision-making and executive bodies that attend to general arrangements.

The politics of the disability movement incorporates the sense of body by celebrating and valuing the disability, challenging the idea of the able-bodied, and indeed confronting the mythic split between the disabled and the able-bodied (Hughes 1998: 82). The movement defies the body politic to broaden its definition by offering citizenship and equal rights collectively to disabled individuals. This movement within the body politic hinges on the body as identity. If one comprehends disability as socially created, then political action is capable of shifting its meaning (Hughes 1998: 83). The social model, politically grounded, dethrones the medical model.

The 'Grey Power' movement offers a further example of organizing around (against) a traditional definition of identity whereby the group in question is imprisoned (and defined by) their body/ies, as distinct from their goals, aspirations, sense of self and emotions. Laws, rules and regulations serve to marginalize older people from participation in the institutions of the body politic (regulatory body). Old people are defined by biological age, i.e. age equals body, and hence merit less value for the body politic. 'Declining bodily powers' (the body clock) have been used to exclude elderly people from participatory citizenship.

The women's movement too characterizes the political challenge to an imposed bodily/biological definition of their identity as individuals, and to the institutional form of the body politic which is public (domain of the intellect) and participatory for men: a political citizenship which confines women to the private (domain of the emotions and caring for the body). One of the prominent features of the women's movement organizationally has been the need for child care, so as not to exclude women from participation and to remove the 'private' barrier to public discourse (Lister 1997: 40–1). This public/private schism (Elshtain: 1993) may be construed as the political expression of the Cartesian mind/body split. Sevenhuijsen (1997: 15) has argued for a construction of citizenship which locates within itself 'the ethics of care', so that care is not relegated to the private domain. Instead, 'the concept of citizenship will be enriched and thus better able to cope with diversity and plurality, and care will be "de-romanticised"', enabling us to consider its values as political virtues'.

Historically, symbolic tactics in the political arena of both the feminist movement and the disability movement include demonstrators chaining themselves to the railings of Parliament and disabled people rolling their bodies in red paint on the pavement outside the Westminster Parliament gates.

Again, just as the woman is precluded from the body politic by dint of the public/private split (mirroring the mind/body dichotomy), minority ethnic groups are left stranded, marginalized citizens beyond the reaches of the white body politic. Bodily features serve to exclude black people from legal, social and political citizenship. But the history of the ethnic marginalization and subordination – the representation 'of their subordinated bodies' – is also contested by black peoples (Lewis et al. 1998). Turner (1996) observes that under colonialism, '[t]here existed a complex relationship between the notion of subordinate and free peoples on the one hand and the subordination of the body to the mind on the other, a paradox or tension which lay behind the Enlightenment as a whole.' The Cartesian mind/body duality facilitating the hierarchical class structure of western societies reflects the superiority of the mind over body – the rule of the administrator in the body politic over the worker equated with body. Given the black population's predominance in the menial ranks of the occupational hierarchy, the equation becomes instantaneously transposed into the rule of white over black – the mind of the white colonial administrator over the body of the black labourer (Hodge et al. 1975).

Contemporary Forms of Citizenship and Accountability

The reconstituting of public bodies has in turn meant a transformation in the nature of public accountability. At both national and local levels, the old state and its local decision-making bodies have been refashioned into an enabling state (Brooke 1989) with its provider agencies. Public bodies, such as health authorities, and local authorities are increasingly regarded as enablers and no longer as essentially direct service providers. Instead, these bodies purchase on behalf of citizens. Citizens are then redefined as users and customers with consumer and market rights. Increased emphasis is simultaneously placed on public bodies and providers of pubic services (which may be private sector bodies) to involve their users and customers and to be responsive to them.

The emphasis on the maximal state delivering social welfare to *passive* citizens has altered. Instead citizens are *active*: they can now make choices as users and customers. Accordingly, public services have been encouraged to alter their approach (at least theoretically) from being supplier-dominant to being user- and customer-oriented. Citizens are now assured their rights as customers with consumer rights to public services.

Gyford et al. (1989) have characterized this shift of focus as a change in the nature of democracy. The traditional representative model of democracy has been tugged in three different directions, creating three alternative versions of democracy: *delegate, participatory* and *market* democracy. We shall refer to the market and participatory versions of democracy in considering how the reorientation of public bodies (as strategic enablers) and the redefining of local citizens (as users and consumers) has impacted upon public acountability. What has this reorientation of public bodies and redefining of citizenship meant to the 'shape' of public accountability?

Public Accountability

Under the contemporary reconstruction of citizenship, citizens are regarded simply as users and consumers of public services. Public accountability is to be achieved through the public services being responsive to these consumer citizens. However, this reconstruction of accountability in terms of accountability to users and consumer citizens poses a number of problems.

Definitions of accountability typically identify two aspects (Oliver 1991; Day 1993; Stewart 1995). First is the requirement for those in positions of responsibility to explain or 'give an account' of their behaviour. Second is the expectation that the public can apply sanctions or 'hold to account' their public servants – if necessary by punishing them or imposing sanctions on them, or (ultimately) by removing from public office those being held to account. A third aspect, unique to *public* accountability, is 'the public domain' (Ranson and Stewart 1994). The new forms of public accountability concentrate on market accountability, but also reduce the duty of explanation or availability of sanction. In equating accountability with market accountability, they ignore the specific location of accountability in the public domain. But three main criticisms of the change in emphasis to market accountability are in order: the absence of 'sanctions', the difficulty in identifying who is the customer, and the disjuncture between 'responsiveness' to the consumer and accountability in the public realm.

First, the consumer has no facility of sanction other than to complain. They cannot usually, or readily, 'exit' (Hirschman 1970), either in terms of being able to choose another supplier or of removing those responsible for the current provision. A second concern is the confusion in identification of the customer of public services. In fact, one encounters a plurality of customers and users with a plurality of needs and demands. Third, public sector professionals and managers and, ultimately, public representatives have to prioritize provision. In the public arena, as distinct from the marketplace, one is endeavouring to reconcile the irreconcilable: whose needs should be met, who counts as a priority, who is to be ignored? This cannot be achieved simply by listening and responding to those who are the most vociferous or articulate. Whilst being responsive is a necessary attribute in the accountability of public services, in that it allows for better informed decision-making, it does not replace the requirement for the decision-makers to be held to account.

Redefined Local Decision–making Bodies and the Local Citizen

Local authorities and other agencies of the 'local state' have been busily reconstructing themselves and their relationship with the 'local citizen' since the mid-1980s when 'citizenship' seemed to emerge as the 'big idea' (Young 1985). This section will assess how local authorities and other local agencies have tackled reconstructing themselves and what this has meant in terms of citizenship and citizens. In doing so, reference will be made to one local authority in particular. The local state, that is to say not just local government but also local health services, local quangos and other public services operating at a local level, has been subject to dramatic change over the last 20 years (Cochrane 1993; Stewart and Stoker 1995). It is within this context that agencies of the local state, specifically local government but also local health authorities and other local public bodies, have attempted to redefine themselves and their relationships with the 'local citizen'. They have increasingly construed themselves as 'enabling' (Brooke 1989) and strategic authorities responsible for purchasing services for their citizens and for representing them through providing a 'governance' role (Stewart 1997). To this end, local authorities, along with other areas of the local state, have used a number of 'techniques' – citizen juries and panels, user forums, local referenda, specific service charters, liaison boards, forms of decentralization and devolution, to 'get closer' to their customers and citizens. Health authorities, NHS Trusts, GP Fund-holders and non-fundholding practices have adopted similar approaches, as part of *Local Voices* and *Priority Setting* and *Patient Participation* initiatives (Daly 1996).

The Local Authority Experience

The particular local body under scrutiny has utilized a number of these approaches in its attempts to redefine itself and its local citizens. In general terms the local authority has adopted a range of strategies in its goal to redefine itself and its relationship with local citizens, and although its approach may not be as radical as that of some authorities (for example, Walsall, Lewisham or Kirklees), it has gained a reputation for creating a 'community governance' tendency. Amongst the discrete initiatives, the authority has devolved and decentralized specific aspects of provision. It has decentralized the management of its own housing stock and its benefits advice service into neighbourhood offices, and instituted sub-committees in each electoral ward. In addition, it has attempted to generate greater participation, not least in involving local citizens in the decisions over budget priorities. The local authority has held a series of public meetings during the budget-setting period to discuss the budgetary priorities with local citizens so that local decision-makers (councillors) may be better informed of the priorities of local citizens when setting the authority budget. It has embarked on a 'Local Involvement, Local Action' initiative (reported in *Labour Party: Agenda*, February 1998) including a Housing Action Trust and a City Challenge initiative (Prior 1996).

Such innovations are claimed as a substantial shift towards participatory democracy, whereby citizens are given a genuine voice over budgetary and therefore council service priorities. However, we would contend that they may be seen as little more than a rubber-stamping exercise which legitimizes the decisions of the local authority. They are certainly capable of producing confusion over the lines of accountability. Our contention is that this particular authority has not fully decided whether it wishes to pursue the goal of *participatory* democracy to any great extent, or whether it wishes to remain wedded to the traditional *representative* democratic form. If it aimed to be truly participatory, it would give real power to its local communities, devolve budgets and decision-making down to local communities, ensure that these were representative, and utilize citizen juries and forums to a much greater extent. Alternatively, if it does not wish to follow the *participatory* route, it should recognize its approaches for what they are: merely forums which act as a supplement to the representative structures to provide information and test out local public opinion.

Local Decision-making Bodies, Community Care and the Local Citizen

Below, we explore the impact of the emphasis on citizenship and user-centredness on local decision-making bodies in terms of community care provision. We will evaluate in particular the extent to which the growing discourse around citizenship and user involvement coincides with how local bodies have implemented community care policies 'on the ground'.

What have these changes meant to local citizens and to local decision-making bodies? Both SSDs and health authorities have espoused the rhetoric of citizenship, of user involvement and of customer choices and responsiveness (Daly 1996). However, these efforts have generally not met with great satisfaction from users and citizens. A plethora of research studies suggests that users and citizens do not really feel empowered by the changes in the way that community care has been delivered (Ellis 1993; Hoyes et al. 1993; Ross 1994; Wilson 1995; Humphreys 1996; Lewis and Glennerster 1996; Barnes 1997; Cowen 1999). Furthermore, a number of judicial reviews and court case verdicts imply that users and citizens are unhappy with the changed arrangements for social care provision (e.g. cases involving Gloucestershire County Council, Sefton, Devon) or the health services (e.g. the case of 'Child B').

Rather than local citizens being more empowered by the changes in community care and health policy, the opposite would seem to prevail.

User studies (Hoyes et al. 1993; Carpenter and Sbaraini 1997) point to a lack of choice and the progressive diminution of limited choice. Rationing – dependent on both need and 'means' – and the use of charges feature regularly (Edwards and Kenny 1997). An expectation lingers that 'the family' will provide (informal) care and that women specifically will take on this responsibility (Dalley 1996). Moreover, involvement of users and citizens is treated at best as minimal and more often as tokenistic (Croft and Beresford 1992).

A Local Approach to Implementing Community Care

In the authority that we have been investigating, the Social Services Department (SSD) takes lead responsibility for managing 'Community Care', and the SSD has undertaken various initiatives to facilitate citizen and user involvement, including: service improvement groups (SIGs), a search team, carers' panels/forums, a group of lay assessors, as well as its own Community Care Charter in addition to the government's own Charter. These are additional to the requirement for the authority to produce an annual Community Care Plan (Barnes 1997)

Clearly, then, the local authority has implemented a variety of programmes to facilitate greater user and carer involvement in the provision of community care. However, they are geared particularly towards setting standards and measuring quality rather than producing any more substantial direct involvement. For the most part, users and carers have not been empowered in the sense of possessing greater choice in meeting their own needs. They are assessed and provided with an appropriate care package. Except for the Direct Payments initiative, they are not provided with a voucher or cheque in order to make their personal purchasing choice, such as domestic or shopping assistance (which the SSD will perceive as non-essential needs). This hardly amounts to user choice or empowerment.

In the meantime, the SSD, in concert with other authorities, has had to adjust its definition of need regarding entitlement to community care assistance. The SSD is currently using its third set of need criteria by dint of having to restrict provision increasingly to needier individuals. And with respect to participation versus representation, users are not empowered to determine collectively the needs criteria. Whilst they may be consulted, this does not mean that they are in control (or should be?). Such decisions remain within the province of officers and politicians. Meanwhile, users must meet stricter criteria in order to receive community care. Increasingly stringent criteria are applied to their financial means. In other words, their ability to pay is taken into account when a care package is assembled.

Users and carers have not become more empowered through greater choice *vis-à-vis* actual provision. To summarize, local citizens seem to have experienced a deterioration rather than an enhancement in their status. Their (social) rights to caring facilities are very much conditional on need and ability to provide for oneself. Indeed, as a former Chair of Social Services Committee suggested in an interview, the local authority and its Social Services Committee felt obliged to ration eligibility to services that may satisfy perceived needs. At the same time, citizens' political rights to have their say and to choose have not been enhanced. They may have actually contracted with the emphasis on consumer rights.

Conclusion

Historically, as we have observed, two traditions have prevailed in the definition of citizenship and its relationship to the body politic: that of civic republicanism or the communitarian tradition, and the tradition of individualism. In recent decades, the New Right's adulation of individual enterprise has driven the formal policy agenda, although the collective opposition of many socially marginalized groups is an impressive demonstration of communitarian tenacity. We are now witnessing in Britain a further redefining of the body politic and the local citizen. In summarizing the changes in the focus of local decision-making bodies – especially those concerned with the provision of community care – and their impacts on contemporary citizenship, there lies a seeming chasm between the rhetoric and the reality. On the one hand, is the rhetoric of choice and empowered citizens; on the other, the reality of a fragmented local body politic and the atomization of citizenship. Local authorities, in pursuing the aim of promoting active citizenship, have involved themselves in such initiatives as organizational decentralization, user forums, panels and service improvement groups. But citizens are exerting no real control over needs critieria, e.g. the criteria used to assess entitlement to community care provision. Public expenditure imperatives eventually nullify the effectiveness of citizen involvement, suggesting the paradox of greater participation and choice obtaining as long as one is adjudged to be in need in the first place. This redefinition may well have been presented as an advance in the evolution of citizenship. Nevertheless, as we have demonstrated in this study of local authority policies, it is problematic for two reasons. First, the attempts to enthuse citizenship through the market, whereby citizens are redefined as customers and consumers, are insuffcent. As we know, market responsiveness inherently accedes to the strongest voices at the expense of those of the more vulnerable groups. Therefore, instead of creating communitas (where citizens experience at the very least a sense of sociality in decision-making), what effectively transpires is a fragmented, dislocated body politic. Second, programmes to invigorate citizenship through extended participatory mechanisms are also problematic. Accountability in the public domain is about reconciling the irreconcilable. Therefore, representative democratic structures remain necessary, but must be *informed* by participatory democracy. However, such participatory democratic mechanisms must be inclusive and not act as a substitute for representative democracy (Sevenhuijsen 1997).

To conclude, the chapter has traced a set of transformations in the body politic of contemporary capitalism that runs counter, it is argued, to the classical communal forms. The re-emergence of the discourse of citizenship echoes that of the classical period. However, whilst the classical citizen was part of the body politic and defined by their relationship to it, the current discourse expresses a citizenship within a fragmented and atomistic society. As articulated earlier, citizenship suggests an organic equality between citizens, such that the individual citizen's moral decisions are intertwined with their political and communal environment. However, the contemporary individualized models of citizenship misguidedly construe the body politic as dislocated from its constituent parts. Hence, participatory citizens remain unequal, resembling those 'Hobbesian' atoms irrevocably colliding inside a fragmented body politic.

References

Andrews, G. (ed.) 1991. *Citizenship*. London: Lawrence & Wishart.
Aristotle. 1946. *The Politics of Aristotle*. trans. E. Barker. Oxford: Oxford University Press.
Barbalet, J. M. 1988. *Citizenship*. Buckingham: Open University Press.
Barnes, M. 1997. *Care, Communities and Citizens*. Harlow: Longman.
Blair, T. 1998. *Leading the Way: A New Vision for Local Government*. London: Institute for Public Policy Research.
Brooke, R. 1989. *Managing the Enabling Authority*. London: Longman.
Bulmer, M. and Rees, A. M. (eds.) 1996. *Citizenship Today: The Contemporary Relevance of T. H. Marshall*. London: UCL Press.
Carpenter, J. and Sbaraini, S. 1997. *Choice, Information and Dignity*. Bristol: Policy Press.
Clarke, J. and Newman, J. 1997. *The Managerial State*. London: Sage.
Clarke, P. 1994. *Citizenship*. London: Pluto Press.

Cochrane, A. 1993. *Whatever Happened to Local Government?*. Milton Keynes: Open University Press.

Cowen, H. 1994. *The Human Nature Debate: Social Theory, Social Policy and the Caring Professions*. London: Pluto Press.

Cowen, H. 1999. *Community Care, Ideology and Social Policy*. Hemel Hempstead: Prentice Hall Europe.

Croft, S. and Beresford, P. 1992. 'The Politics of Participation'. *Critical Social Policy* 35: 20–44.

Culpitt, I. 1992. *Welfare and Citizenship: Beyond the Crisis of the Welfare State?*. London: Sage.

Dalley, G. 1996. *Ideologies of Caring – Rethinking Community and Collectivism*. 2nd edition. Basingstoke: Macmillan.

Daly, G. 1996. 'Public Accountability in Today's Health Service', in H. Davis (ed.), *Quangos and Local Government: A Changing World*. London: Frank Cass.

Daly, G. 1997. 'Participatory Citizenship and Public Accountability: Whatever Happened to Social and Political Rights?' Paper presented at the conference: 'Citizenship for the 21st Century?'. University of Central Lancashire, 29 October.

Day, P. 1993. 'Accountability', in N. Thomas, N. Deakin and J. Doling (eds.) 1993. *Learning from Innovation: Housing and Social Care in the 1990s*. Birmingham: Birmingham Academic Press.

Department of Environment, Transport and Regions. 1998. *Modernising Local Government: Local Government and Community Leadership*. London: HMSO.

Edwards, P. and Kenny, D. 1997. *Community Care Trends 1997 Report: The Impact of Funding on Local Authorities*. London: Local Government Management Board.

Ellis, K. 1993. *Squaring the Circle: User and Carer Participation in Needs Assessment*. Bristol: Policy Press.

Elshtain, B. 1993. *Public Man: Private Woman: Women in Social and Political Thought*. 2nd edition. Princeton, NJ: Princeton University Press.

Etzioni, A. 1993. *Spirit of Community*. London: HarperCollins.

Giddens, A. 1982. 'Class Division, Class Conflict and Citizenship Rights', in A. Giddens, *Profiles and Critiques in Social Theory*. London: Macmillan.

Gyford, J., Leach, S. and Game, C. 1989. *The Changing Politics of Local Government*. London: Unwin Hyman.

Haworth, A. 1994. *Anti-Libertarianism: Markets, Philosophy and Myth*. London: Routledge.

Hecke, D. and Ward, L. 1998. 'Blair Gives Ultimatum to Councils'. *The Guardian*. 4 March.

Hirschman, A. O. 1970. *Exit, Voice and Loyalty*. Cambridge, Mass.: Harvard University Press.

Hobbes, T. 1651. *Leviathan*, ed. C. B. Macpherson. Harmondsworth: Penguin Books, 1968.

Hodge, J. L., Struckman, D. K. and Trost, L. D. 1975. *Cultural Bases of Racism and Group Oppression: An Examination of Traditional 'Western' Concepts, Values and Institutional Structures which Support Racism, Sexism and Elitism.*. Berkeley, Calif.: Two Riders Press.

Hoyes, L., Jeffers, S., Lart, R., Means, R. and Taylor, M. 1993. *User Empowerment and the Reform of Community Care: An Interim Assessment*. Bristol: School for Advanced Urban Studies.

Hughes, G. 1998. 'A Suitable Case for Treatment? Constructions of Disability', in E. Saraga (ed.), *Embodying the Social Construction of Difference*. London: Open University/Routledge.

Humphreys, B. 1996. *Critical Perspectives on Empowerment*. Birmingham: Venture Press.

Labour Party 1998. 'Renewing Democracy in Practice', *Agenda: The Magazine of the Association of Labour Councillors*. February, 24: 11.

Lewis, G., Hughes, G. and Saraga, E. 1998. *The Body of Social Policy: Policy and the Body*. Paper presented to the British Sociological Annual Conference, Edinburgh, April.

Lewis, J. and Glennerster, H. 1996. *Implementing the New Community Care*. Buckingham: Open University Press.

Lister, R. 1997. *Citizenship: Feminist Perspectives*. London: Macmillan.

Locke, J. 1690. Two Treatises of Government. Ed. P. Laslett. Cambridge: Cambridge University Press, 1967.

Macintyre, A. 1985. *After Virtue*. London: Duckworth.

Mackenzie, W. J. 1979. *Biological Ideas in Politics*. Manchester: Manchester University Press.

Marshall, T. H. (1950) 'Citizenship and Social Class', reprinted in T. H. Marshall and T. Bottomore. 1992. *Citizenship and Social Class* . London: Pluto Press.

Masters, R. D. 1989. *The Nature of Politics*. New Haven, Conn.: Yale University Press.

Oliver, D. 1991. *Government in the United Kingdom: The Search for Accountability, Effectiveness and Citizenship*. Milton Keynes: Open University Press.

Oliver, D. and Heater, D. 1994. *The Foundations of Citizenship*. Hemel Hempstead: Harvester Wheatsheaf.

Plant, R. 1991. *Modern Political Thought*. Oxford: Blackwell.

Prior, D. 1996. 'Working the Network: Local Authority Strategies in the Reticulated Local State', in H. Davis (ed.), *Quangos and Local Government: A Changing World*. London: Frank Cass.

Ranson, S. and Stewart, J. 1994. *Management for the Public Domain.*. Basingstoke: Macmillan.

Ross, K. 1994. 'Customer Caring?'. *Local Government Studies*. 20. 2: 186–92.

Rousseau, J-J. 1772. *Social Contract*: Essays by Locke, Hume and Rousseau. Oxford: Oxford University Press, 1968.

Sandel, M. 1982. *Liberalism and the Limits of Justice*. Cambridge: Cambridge University Press.

Saunders, P. 1993. 'Citizenship in a Liberal Society', in B. S. Turner (ed.), *Citizenship and Social Theory*. London: Sage.

Schatzki, T. R and Natter, N. 1996. 'Sociocultural Bodies, Bodies Sociopolitical' in T. R. Schatzki and N. Natter (eds.), *The Social and Political Body*. Aldershot: The Guilford Press.

Sevenhuijsen, S. 1998. *Citizenship and the Ethics of Care: Feminist Considerations on Justice, Morality and Politics*. London: Routledge.

Smith, A. 1776. Wealth of Nations. Oxford: Oxford University Press, 1976.

Stewart, J. 1995. 'Responding to the Defenders of Appointed Bodies', in H. Davis (ed.), *Quangos and Local Government: Issues and Responses*. Birmingham: INLO-GOV, University of Birmingham.

Stewart, J. 1997. 'The Need for Community Governance', in Local Government Information Unit, *A Framework for the Future: An Agenda for Councils in a Changing World*. London: LGIU.

Stewart, J. and Stoker, G. 1995. 'Introduction', in J. Stewart and G. Stoker (eds.) *Local Government in the 1990s*. Basingstoke: Macmillan.

Taylor, C. 1989. *Sources of the Self*. Cambridge: Cambridge University Press.

Taylor, D. 1989. 'Citizenship and Social Power'. *Critical Social Policy* 26: 19–31.

Turner, B. S. 1985. *Citizenship and Capitalism*. London: Unwin Hyman.

Turner, B. S. (ed.) 1993. *Citizenship and Social Theory*. London: Sage.

Turner, B. S. 1996. *The Body and Society*. 2nd edition. London: Sage.

Van Steenbergen, B. (ed.) 1994. *The Condition of Citizenship*. London: Sage.

Walzer, M. 1983. *Spheres of Justice*. Oxford: Martin Robertson.

Wilkins, J. W. N. 1973. *Hobbes' System of Ideas*. London: Hutchinson.

Wilson, G. (ed.) 1995. *Community Care: Asking the User*. London: Chapman and Hall.

Young, H. 1985. 'Citizens! The Cure-all Rallying Cry', *Guardian*. 22 November.

3
A Secure Base? Attachment Theory and Disabling Design

Deborah Marks

Introduction

Since the work of Goffman (1961) there has been a large body of work exposing the oppressive nature of residential institutions, such as mental hospitals (Ryan and Thomas 1980) and residential schools (Rieser and Mason 1990). This work locates the origins of problems with such institutions less in the abusive behaviour of individual members of staff than in the practices and structures within the institution and the wider social system that segregates certain people to the margins.

  This chapter follows in the tradition of critiquing 'special' institutions. However, rather than exploring interactions within institutions (Goffman 1961) or wider economic or social factors which generate the existence of institutions (Finkelstein 1980; Oliver 1990), I identify some oppressive aspects of *environmental design* and speculate on the way they are likely to be experienced by residents. Using Mary Ainsworth's (1982) concept of 'the secure base', I examine the way physical environments in some institutions erode the boundary between public and private realms. In doing this, they not only violate privacy, but also undermine social interaction. This is because social engagement is predicated on having a space in which to withdraw from the public gaze.

  I focus on two kinds of residential institution; for elderly people and people with learning difficulties and challenging behaviour.[1] I argue that whilst the design features I discuss might be justified on practical grounds (for example, on the grounds of safety and security), such defences do not stand up to critical scrutiny. In the latter half of

the chapter I identify some of the problems with the design of adaptations to make 'mainstream' buildings accessible to disabled people.
I argue that the legacy of segregation continues in the way in which
'mainstream' buildings are 'adapted' for disabled users. 'Disability'
design features tend to be concerned primarily with 'practical considerations' and are often aesthetically out of tune with the wider environmental context.

Spatial Marginalization

Since Foucault (1995; 1977), there has been a growing interest in social
theory in the organization of space. Much of this work is interdisciplinary in nature. For example, Lefebvre's (1991; 1996) analysis of
the production of space seeks to bridge disciplinary gaps between the
realms of theory and practice, between the psychological and the social
and between 'the living organism' and its 'extensions, from the space
that it reaches and produces'. This chapter attempts to make similar
disciplinary links by using psychoanalytic concepts to make sense of
the meaning of certain design features and social organisation.

Lefebvre sees the organization of space as shaping both thought and
action. Space can be 'a means of control, and hence of domination and
power' (1991: 26). Similarly, Kitchen (1988: 344) points out that space is
'not just a passive container of life, but [is] also . . . dynamic and ambiguous, claimed and contested'. Whilst scholars within the growing new
discipline of Disability Studies have tended to focus on the political,
economic (Finkelstein 1980; Oliver 1990) and cultural (Shakespeare
1994a; 1994b) oppression of disabled people, there is growing apprecia-
tion of the importance of examining the social construction and hierarchical organization of space (Imrie 1996) and the marginalization of
embodied 'impaired' subjects (Patterson and Hughes 1997). Latent rules
about a person's spatial 'place' tells us a great deal about what Pukulsky
(1996: 77) refers to as 'cultural citizenship', that is, the degree to which
they are respected, valued and included in communities, in ways that
allow for the 'active cultivation of these identities and their symbolic
correlates'.

Much of the work that has been done examining built environments
within Disability Studies focuses on ways in which the public sphere is
made hazardous for disabled people. Pavements littered with obstacles
make journeys difficult for people with visual impairments (Imrie 1996).
Disabled people frequently risk anxiety, confusion and humiliation
when venturing into new territory (see Keith 1996; Hockenberrry

1997; Hull 1997; for vivid narrative accounts). Few public buildings or transportation systems are fully accessible to disabled people (Imrie and Kumar 1998). The wide range of access needs within a community are not held in mind by local authorities, planners and designers, who continue to conceive of disability as a medical rather than an environmental issue (Imrie 1997). By contrast, those institutions designed *specifically* for disabled residents are made ultra-protective, with a high level of supervisory 'care' for residents. Whilst a premium is placed on the health care needs of residents, far less attention is given to the sense of well-being engendered by a readable, safe environment.

Institutional Care

Segregated institutions are both a product of and serve to reproduce the socially constructed dependency of disabled people (Finkelstein 1980; Barnes 1990). As Miller and Gwynne (1972) argue in their analysis of some of the Cheshire Homes for physically disabled people, residents experienced 'social death' as a prelude to physical death. They had little involvement in, or capacity to contribute to, the wider community. Miller and Gwynne's 'solution' to the distress generated by such arrangements was to improve the organization of the homes in order to make life more bearable for its residents and help staff cope with their stressful work. Such an approach has become notorious among social model theorists, many of whom were residents of such institutions; (Hunt 1981; Finkelstein 1998), for failing to recognize that the structure of segregated care is inherently oppressive (Barnes 1990). Ultimately, Miller and Gwynne's approach is a functionalist one; it is concerned with helping institutions operate more effectively, but fails to look critically at the values of these institutions or beyond what exists to how things might be different. Residential care deprived disabled people of a number of rights, including sexual (Shakespeare et al. 1996), parental (Booth and Booth 1998) and consumer rights (Barnes 1997), and often involves traumatic separations of residents from their families and communities (Humphries and Gorden 1992).

Most disability theorists have argued that the economic conditions that brought about segregation (industrial capitalism and large-scale factory production) have ended. With the development of new technologies, services and the knowledge of how to build environments that are accessible to all people (rather than just to young, fit, able-bodied people), there is no justifiable reason to continue excluding disabled people (Oliver 1996).

Over the last 30 years most of the large residential institutions for disabled people have closed.[2] There has, however, been an opposing trend in the growth in the number of secure units for young offenders (many of whom have learning difficulties) and residential homes for elderly people. In addition, the move of many disabled and mentally ill people into the 'community' has merely replaced segregated residential institutions for 'institutionalisation in the community' (Morris 1993). For example, 'special needs housing' usually means small clusters of accessible homes set within mainstream housing estates where disabled people are cut off from their families, their friends and the able-bodied community as a whole' (Barnes 1991: 150). Often, 'special' facilities in the community are difficult to use, and are marked in ways that stigmatize and segregate the user.

For this reason, it is useful to return to examine some of the organizational and design features within segregated institutions in order to see how the values of the institution are imported back into the community, within 'special' design practices. This chapter focuses specifically on the organization of space and the prioritization of concerns about the *functional* needs of disabled people. It identifies the failure to address the requirements which all people, disabled as well as non-disabled, have, for buildings to be 'readable', comfortable and secure. What I mean by these three factors will become clear as the discussion progresses.

Attachment Theory

One element which is missing from most social theorizing on the organization of space and embodiment is attention to the way certain environments are *emotionally experienced* (see Marks 1999a; 1999b for further discussion of this point). Generally, such a dimension of analysis tends to be left to relatively untheorized narrative and biographical accounts. Yet the question of how particular designs affect a person's sense of self, foster a sense of inclusion or are experienced as an attack on identity, represents an important dimension of disablism (Mason 1992).

For this reason, I draw on attachment theory (Bowlby 1988) in order to reflect on ways in which environments can be enabling or oppressive. Of all psychoanalytic and developmental psychological models and approaches, attachment theory is perhaps most suited to thinking about design environments, since it is essentially a spatial theory. Attachment theory is built on the premise that the needs for a key attachment figure in one's early life is a fundamental and universal human need (Karen 1998). As Bowlby (quoted in Holmes 1993) puts it, 'all of us, from the cradle to the grave, are happiest when life is organised as a series of excursions, long or short, from the secure base provided by our attachment figures.' These attachments are mediated by the senses of touch, vision and hearing (Holmes 1993). Attachment theory, alongside the 'independent tradition' of British psychoanalysis (Gomez 1998; Raynor 1991), is concerned to understand the effects of the environment on emotional experience and human development. Such work represents an attempt within psychoanalysis to move beyond reductive and individualist Freudian and Kleinian work which prioritized physiological drives and unconscious fantasies (Holmes 1998). By contrast, attachment theory takes seriously not just dyadic relations (for example, between mother and child), but also larger institutional, social and contextual factors that shape experience (Robertson and Robertson 1989). As such, it is the school of psychoanalytic theory which is perhaps most compatible with sociological theorizing.

The Home as a Secure Base

Ainsworth (1982) first used the phrase the 'secure base' to describe the sense of safety offered by attachment figures for infants, who used this security as a springboard for exploration of the external world. Ideally, the attachment figure will adapt to the needs of the infant, and provide what Winnicott has termed a 'facilitating environment'; that is, one that is 'attuned' to the needs of the infant (Hurry 1999). In this way, an infant does not need to attend greatly to the external world; she can just get on with the tasks of exploring, enjoying and interacting with her external world. Holmes (1993: 70) offers a very helpful description of attachment as exerting 'an invisible pull on the child, just as heavenly bodies are connected by gravitational forces. But unlike gravity attachment makes its presence known by a negative inverse square law: the further an attached person is from there secure base, the greater the pull of attachment.' Thus, when in touch with our 'secure base' we enter 'a relaxed state in which one can begin to "get on with things", pursue one's projects, to explore' (Holmes 1993: 67).

Whilst Ainsworth used the concept of a secure *base* to refer to a key *relationship*, the spatial metaphor conveys the importance of feeling safe in a *place*. The metaphor works so well because many of us invest our homes with the qualities of a secure base. A home provides a familiar context, where it is possible to 'be', to feel safe and not to have to worry about external demands or unfamiliar environments. The availability of such a base is something that most people take for granted. Thus, whilst we are alert to the external world when exploring a new neighbourhood or going into an unfamiliar institution, we can enter a state of trusting familiarity when we return to our home base (Holmes 1993).[3] Home is an environment in which we can both socialize with others but also have a relatively high degree of control over what might be called self-nurturing activities; that is, over the preparation of food, washing and dressing and engaging in intimate activities such as going to the toilet or having sex.

The relevance of the psychoanalytic concept of the 'secure base' is that it helps us to identify the nature of certain privations within residential settings, which make it difficult for residents to feel safe and to use their home as a secure point of departure to take risks in the wider social world. Where an environment is not designed with consideration of the user in mind, it demands additional energies, which might otherwise be used more productively. The architect John Van Rooyan has made just such a connection in applying Winnicott's concept of a 'facilitating environment' to the design of built environments. He writes (Van Rooyan 1997: 5):

> The built environment can be containing, comforting and holding, or hostile, obstructive and difficult . . . I often notice how little people register about the spaces they are in and why they feel comfortable or otherwise. In a way, this lack of awareness places the individual in a child-like reliance of the spaces to contain them, much as an infant relies on its mother's holding environment.

Van Rooyan (1997: 5) adds that whilst physically disabled people have begun to challenge successfully 'unnecessary barriers and negative impingement's on their lives . . .' we need to examine the person/environment set-up as it affects people with learning disabilities, because those members of society find it most difficult to adapt to unfamiliar demands and are most dependent on a 'holding environment'. If we look at two quite different forms of residential homes – those for elderly people and a home for people with learning difficulties and challenging behaviour – we find that both often lack the qualities required of a secure base, which provides a restful space which adapts to the needs of its user.

'Homes' for the Elderly

A study by Willcocks et al. (1998) of 100 residential homes for the elderly found that only half of all residents had a room of their own and only eight of the homes had lockable bedrooms. Residents in only two homes were permitted to lock their rooms from the inside. The implications of such limited capacity of residents to defend their privacy and security is an undermining of 'the sense of ownership which residents may wish to attach to their rooms; without such control this private space becomes common territory' (Willcocks et al. 1998: 82). Given this lack of private space, it is unsurprising that residents in most of the homes tried to create personal privacy within public spaces. One example of this is the lining up of chairs around walls or in rows, rather than grouped around coffee tables or in positions which fostered communication between residents. As the authors (Willcocks et al. 1998: 83) comment,

> this arrangement allows residents to avoid prolonged social interaction and to withdraw to relative anonymity... The 'backs to the wall' strategy may be construed as a retreat position, and the somewhat uninterested focusing upon the television as a further strategy for avoiding eye contact with other residents.

In addition to ritual avoidance of spontaneous social engagement, residents were prevented from having free access to a number of rooms where key domestic activities take place. These included:

> kitchens, laundries, boiler rooms, garages... staff living-in accommodation, night duty rooms and staff common rooms... such exclusions will distance residents from tasks which concern basic activities such as providing and preparing food, washing clothing, and arranging for heating... It is only in recent years that homes have given residents facilities for making tea or coffee when they wish, an amenity which is still not universal.
>
> (Willcocks et al. 1998: 85)

Practical justifications for denying elderly residents keys to their own rooms or access to areas in which basic nurturing activities such as food preparation takes place are often put forward. These frequently take the form of concerns about 'safety' or 'practicality' such as 'keys had been lost' (Willcocks et al. 1998: 89). However, allowing residents keys does not preclude staff having master keys to be used in emergencies. As with the cliché of telling wheelchair users they represent a 'fire hazard', such defences appear to be post hoc rationalizations.

This inversion of conventional distinctions between social space that is privatized and private space that is exposed is also reflected in the experiences of residents in a secure unit for people with challenging behaviour and learning difficulties.

A 'Home' For Young People with Challenging Behaviour

This section is based on an analysis of a secure unit for the assessment and treatment of people with learning disabilities and challenging behaviour (Marks et al. 1998). The original proposal documents, written prior to setting up the unit, suggested that it should have 'a domestic rather than institutional character, a robust construction, a therapeutic suit and spacious and secure grounds' (Marks et al. 1998: 13). The site eventually chosen for the unit displayed none of these characteristics. The unit was housed in a prefabricated building located in the grounds of a large nineteenth-century teaching hospital. The building had originally been used as a children's unit. It had low ceilings. Its walls were thin (in fact, they were so flimsy that on one occasion, a resident had smashed through a wall) and bare. It had no secure perimeter fence around the garden, which meant residents were rarely allowed to go outside unless accompanied by a member of staff. Although the size and purpose of this unit differed markedly from the homes for elderly people described by Willcocks et al. (1998), we see similar practices relating to residents' privacy, and their exclusion from a number of domestic activities.

Most of the residents in the unit had lived there since the unit had opened, approximately 18 months earlier. The unit consisted of three flats, each containing a bathroom, a living room and three bedrooms, radiating out from a large room at the centre of the unit. This room was empty of any furniture and lined with noticeboards, used (and this point seems particularly significant) for *staff* information. Whilst this central room was certainly big enough to provide a forum for collective activities and meetings, it actually functioned as a corridor. Each living room contained a TV and two sofas.

The doors to each flat automatically locked residents in, although staff and visitors could walk in from the outside, without knowing the combination code. Given the unit was a secure facility and 'patients' were deemed to be dangerous, such locking might be justifiable.[4] However, the experience of doors locking 'the wrong way' to allow free movement in but not out represented an inversion of normal boundaries marking a secure base. Residents could not restrict free movement of 'visitors' into their 'flats'. Moreover, there were no doorbells or devices to alert residents of someone entering their 'flat'.

In terms of bathroom facilities, the design of the lavatories resembled those found at motorway service stations, and other large public institutions, with large gaps above and below the doors.[5] It was interesting to note that there were no full-length mirrors in the unit, so residents did not have the opportunity to develop an accurate image of themselves and their bodies.

None of the bedroom doors was lockable. Staff wishing to enter a resident's room would generally give a cursory knock before walking in. As a researcher examining the unit, I was surprised that staff felt in a position to invite me to 'look at X's bedroom'. The powerlessness of residents to resist such incursions was demonstrated by the relatively unsuccessful request written on one bedroom door: 'Knock and Wait for an Answer'.

As with the home for elderly people, the communal rooms were not a space in which spontaneous interaction took place between residents. Generally, they received very limited use and were rarely occupied by more than one resident at a time. Communication in both the homes for elderly people and people with learning difficulties took place primarily between staff and residents. Staff tended to explain this in terms of lack of interest among residents in communicating with each other, or even conflict between residents. However, to the extent that this was true, the origin of such difficulties seemed to lie in the lack of institutional structures that would foster horizontal communication.

Community Accommodations

Most people would not find the descriptions of life in the residential 'homes' for elderly people or the unit for people with learning difficulties particularly appealing. The failure to establish collective social spaces where communication with others could take place was paralleled by the failure to provide a private space into which residents could withdraw. Indeed, these two failures might be seen as two sides of the same coin. Where there is no safe private sphere to retreat into, the prospect of permanent engagement with others can threaten to overwhelm and engulf the individual.

It is interesting to note that the privations suffered by people living in residential institutions also occur, albeit in a modified form in the facilities offered to disabled people within public institutions. At my own place of work, an accessible toilet was installed without a mirror. Yet mirrors are routinely supplied in all non-accessible staff and student toilets in the university. The door of this toilet was initially hinged so that it swung inwards. This meant that anyone going past would be able to see a wheelchair user back into the room fully before a series of complex manoeuvres would need to be undertaken in order to close the door. There continues to be no make-up shelf or coat hook in this toilet.[6] These failings might be seen as small oversights that say more about the poor quality of the building department of the university. However, I wish to argue that they should be seen as slips; that is, as accurate expressions of the unacknowledged (latent) assumptions which designers and planners have about disabled people. The focus in design for disabled people tends to be on catering for particular *functional* needs. The importance of privacy and recognition of aesthetic requirement (such as the desire to see oneself in a mirror or apply make-up) are not seen as relevant. This is because often disabled people are not recognized as being autonomous, desiring cultural citizens.

Conclusion

This chapter has argued that making buildings accessible requires not just fitting ramps, induction loops and other 'accommodations' for disabled people. Rather, it means thinking about and respecting the diverse needs of users, including the need for privacy, as a prerequisite for the possibility of socializing. The importance of thinking beyond the question of practical access is a point made by Napolitano (1996: 34) in relation to work on design aesthetics and thinking about the dignity of users. She writes of elegant Victorian buildings, that they reflect and engender 'a sense of pride in citizenship, a sense of belonging to something larger than self and family'. When adaptations are made without consideration of the extent to which they are in tune with the environment, they reinforce associations of disability as something that cannot be harmoniously included into the 'able' world. Napolitano (1996: 34–5) expresses this well:

> I wasn't at all happy with the idea that getting my share of what goes on in those buildings should inevitably produce an aesthetic blot on the cityscape. If my participation could only be made possibly by some ugly contraption, what did that say about me? What would it do to my sense of pride in citizenship? Being able to use the environment is about more than being able to 'get about'. At a deeper level it is about a sense of belonging. Until the environment supports

mobility impaired people's participation with dignity and pride intact, this sense will continue to evade them.

Similarly, when disabled people are required to gain access to buildings through real entrances of buildings, or with the assistance of others, this reinforces their position as a group of outsiders. Like children at nursery school, people living in total institutions are infantilized and controlled by those 'responsible' for them. Focus tends to be placed on their 'basic' functional needs rather than their adult need for privacy, involvement in domestic activities and or decision-making, and communication with other.

The problems identified in this chapter would be partially addressed by thoroughgoing adoption of the principles of universal design (Weissman 1992). This would involve buildings which recognize the wide range of potential users and working in a way which is thoughtful both regarding the access requirements and concerns about aesthetics, privacy, sociability and comfort. Such a change would clearly need to be based on consultation with as wide as possible range of disabled people. Thus, there would be far less need for a separate and secure 'supportive' space for those people who are disabled by an environment that places not only physical but aesthetic and psychological barriers on the inclusion of all people within a society.

Notes

1   These two groups have tended to receive less attention within the disability literature and also have a far lower profile within the disabled people's movement. See Campbell and Oliver (1996).
2   I am including within the definition 'disabled' all those people who are currently eligible for benefits, services or come under the auspices of the Disability Discrimination Act and other such legislation.
3   Of course, the level of anxiety when exploring unfamiliar circumstances is much greater for disabled people who are faced with constant battles with hostile environments.
4   A Levels of 'incidents' (when residents presented a 'challenge') varied enormously according to the managerial regime, suggesting that the difficulties in the unit depended less on the intrinsic 'challenge' presented by a particular resident, than on the context into which they were placed.
5   Toilets in institutions for people with learning difficulties are often designed more for the convenience of care assistance than with the dignity of the user in mind. As Thomas has noted on his arrival for work at a hospital ward for the 'mentally handicapped', 'I was shown the shower-room and toilets – cold floors, high ceilings, glaring lights, a row of lavatories with no doors...' (1987: 32). Similarly, one reason that so many young people with learning

difficulties wear track suit trousers is that it is much easier to assist a person wearing them in dressing and undressing.
6 I would like to acknowledge Anna Ravetz and other students at Sheffield MA course, regarding the failings of this and so many other 'accessible' loos.

References

Ainsworth, M. 1982. 'Attachment: Retrospect and Prospect', in C. M. Parkes and J. Stevenson-Hinde (eds.), *The Place of Attachment in Human Behaviour*. London: Tavistock.

Barnes, C. 1990. *Cabbage Syndrome: The Social Construction of Dependency*. London: Falmer Press.

Barnes, C. 1991. *Disabled People in Britain and Discrimination: A Case for Anti-Discrimination Legislation*. London: Hurst & Company/BCODP.

Barnes, M. 1997. *Care, Communities and Citizens*. London: Longman.

Booth, T. and Booth, W. 1998. *Growing up with Parents Who Have Learning Difficulties*. London: Routledge.

Bowlby, J. 1988. *A Secure Base: Clinical Applications of Attachment Theory*. London: Routledge.

Campbell, J. and Oliver, M. 1996. *Disability Politics: Understanding Our Past, Changing Our Future*. London: Routledge.

Davis, L. 1995. *Enforcing Normalcy: Disability, Deafness and the Body*. London: Verso.

Finkelstein, V. 1980. *Attitudes and Disabled People: Issues for Discussion*. New York: World Rehabilitation Fund.

Foucault, M. 1977. *Discipline and Punish: The Birth of the Prison*, Alan Sheridan (trans). New York: Pantheon.

Foucault, M. 1995. *Madness and Civilization: A History of Insanity in the Age of Reason*. Richard Howard (trans). London: Routledge.

French, S. 1994. 'Disability, Impairment or Something in Between', in J. Swain, V. Finkelstein, S. French and M. Oliver, *Disabling Barriers – Enabling Environment*. London: The Open University and Sage.

Goffman, E. G. 1961. *Asylums*. New York: Doubleday, Anchor Books.

Hockenberry, J. 1996. *Declarations of Independence: War Zones and Wheelchairs*. London: Viking.

Holmes, J. 1993. *John Bowlby and Attachment Theory*. London: Routledge.

Holmes, J. 1998. 'The Changing Aims of Psychoanalytic Psychotherapy: An Integrative Perspective'. *The International Journal of Psycho-Analysis*, 79 (2), April.

Hull, J. 1997. *On Sight and Insight: A Journey into the World of Blindness*. Oxford: One World.

Humphries, S. and Gordon, P. 1992. *Out of Sight: The Experiences of Disability 1900–1950*. Plymouth, C4/Northcote House.

Hunt, P. 1981. 'Settling Accounts with the Parasite People', *Disability Challenge*, 1, London: UPIAS.

Hurry, A. 1998. (ed.), *Psychoanalysis and Developmental Therapy*. London: Karnac.

Imrie, R. 1996. *Disability and the City: International Perspectives*. London: Paul Chapman Publishing.

Imrie, R. and Kumar, M. 1998. 'Focusing on Disability and Access in the Built Environment', *Disability and Society*, 13 (3): 357–74.

Karen, R. 1998. *Becoming Attached: First Relationships and How They Shape Our Capacity to Love*. Oxford: Oxford University Press.

Keith, L. (ed.) 1994. *Mustn't Grumble: Writings by Disabled Women*. London: The Women's Press.

Kitchen, R. 1998. 'Out of Place, "Knowing One's Place": Space, Power and the Exclusion of Disabled People'. *Disability and Society*, 13 (3): 343–56.

Lefebvre, H. 1991. *The Production of Space*, D. Nicholson–Smith (trans). Oxford: Blackwell.

Marks, D., Kendall, T. and Dudley, M. 1998. *Training Needs Assessment for the Assessment and Treatment Unit*, Sheffield: Community Health Sheffield.

Marks, D. 1999. *Disability: Controversial Debates and Psycho-Social Perspectives*, London: Routledge.

Marks, D. 1999. 'Dimensions of Oppression: Theorising the Embodied Subject', in Disability and Society, Special Issue: '*Theory and Experience*', 14 (5): 614–28.

Mason, M. 1992. 'Internalised Oppression', in R. Rieser and M. Mason (eds.), *Disability Equality in the Classroom: A Human Rights Issue*. London: Disability Equality in Education.

Morris, J. 1993. *Independent Lives: Community Care and Disabled People*. London: Macmillan.

Napolitano, S. 1996. 'Mobility Impairment', in G. Hales (ed.) *Beyond Disability: Towards and Enabling Society*. London: Sage, in association with The Open University Press.

Oliver, M. 1990. *The Politics of Disablement*. London: Macmillan.

Oliver, M. 1996. *Understanding Disability: From Theory to Practice*, London: Macmillan.

Patterson, K. and Hughes, B. 1997. 'The Social Model of Disability and the Disappearing Body: Towards a Sociology of Impairment'. *Disability and Society* 12 (3): 325–40.

Pukulski, J. 1996. 'Cultural Citizenship', *Cultural Studies*, 1 (1): 73–86.

Raynor, E. 1991. *The Independent Mind in British Psychoanalysis*. London: Free Association Books.

Rieser, R. and Mason, M. (eds.) 1992. *Disability Equality in the Classroom: A Human Rights Issue*. London: Disability Equality in Education.

Robertson, J. and Robertson, J. 1989. *Separation and the Very Young*. London: Free Association Books.

Ryan, J. with Thomas, F. 1987. *The Politics of Mental Handicap*. London: Free Association Books.

Shakespeare, T., Gillespie-Sells, K. and Davies, D. 1996. *The Sexual Politics of Disability*. London: Cassell.

Van Rooyan, J. 1997. 'The Baby and the Bathwater', *The Squiggle Foundation Newsletter*. London: The Squiggle Foundation, October.

Weisman, L. 1992. *Discrimination By Design*. Evanston, Illinois: University of Illinois Press.

Willcocks, D., Peace, S. and Kellaher, L. 1998. 'The Physical World', in M. Allott and M. Robb (eds.), *Understanding Health and Social Care: An Introductory Reader*. London: Sage, in association with the Open University Press.

4
Accommodating Bodies: The Organization of Corporeal Dirt in the Embodied Home

Craig M. Gurney

Introduction

This theoretical chapter considers the organization of bodies within the physical space of the dwelling and the social space of the 'home'. It suggests that there are important, but hitherto unexplained, relationships between home, the presentation and impression management of the body and attitudes towards corporeal dirt. The unifying thread of the chapter is that home (in various unique ways) accommodates bodies. The word 'accommodating' is used here to denote compromise and reconciliation as well as a synonym for dwelling or residing. This is to draw attention to the fact that we train, manage, regulate, discipline and present our bodies at home in ways which we cannot elsewhere. Following on from that, it is argued that home can be conceptualized in relation to a civilizing process that masks evidence of bodily substances and odours.

By accommodating bodies the home allows the storing, processing and management of corporeal dirt. It is also a social and physical space in which we can most easily be our (embodied) selves. It provides a locale in which we may drop the Goffmanesque mask that attaches a socially constructed decorum to 'dirty' elimination activities such as defecation, urination, menstruation, flatulence, vomiting and expectorating. Our bodies are leaky and odoriferous containers. Consequently, our homes become containers that are both polluted and olid. Thinking about home as a container and processor of corporeal dirt in this way provides a context within which to read some quite remarkable statistics.

In 2001, £524 million will be spent in the UK on household cleaners[1] (Mintel 1997a) and a further £212 million will be spent on household fresheners[2] (Mintel 1997b). For purposes of comprehension it is note-worthy that the combined sum is greater than the gross domestic product of a number of developing countries including, for instance, Lesotho, Chad, Sierra Leonne and Guyana (Euromonitor 1999). Given the self-evident economic and social significances attached to the processing of corporeal dirt in contemporary British society, the neglected relationship between the home and the body in the sociological literature appears to constitute a stark oversight.

This contribution to the literature is influenced by an apparent 'rediscovery' of the work of Goffman (1959), Douglas (1966) and Elias (1978) in a putative *embodied turn* in sociology (Turner 1992; Scott and Morgan 1993; Shilling 1993; Synott 1993) and geography (Rodaway 1994; Bell and Valentine 1995; Sibley 1995; Duncan 1996). These classic sociological texts have been widely discussed elsewhere so this chapter assumes the reader has at least a working knowledge of their import. No primary empirical data are presented here, but the results of a study which uses the theoretical framework suggested are discussed elsewhere (Gurney 1998; 2000).

The main body of the chapter is organized around five themes. It begins with two short sections discussing the disembodied housing imagination and the embodied home. It then goes on to demonstrate how Elias's (1978) concept of the 'civilizing process' has a number of important implications for the accommodation of bodies in the contemporary home. Next, the chapter conceptualizes the body as a leaky container. This idea is used to suggest a corporeal ecology of home in which some spaces are imitative of the corporeal dirt extruded there. The chapter then goes on to demonstrate the relationship between odour and the moral construction of self in order to make sense of home as an olidic (foul-smelling) locale. Finally, the chapter concludes by outlining some possibilities for further research on the home as a processor of dirt and the relationship between bodies and dwellings.

The Disembodied Housing Imagination

Housing continues to languish in the doldrums of the sociological imagination with much recent housing research insulated from some of the most significant developments in recent sociology. The failure to view housing through the lens of an embodied turn in sociology is one such example of this. The so-called 'absent presence of the body' (Shilling 1993) has not been recognized in a(ny) sociology of housing.[3] So whilst there is a well-defined literature on health and housing and disability and housing, the body has never seriously been accorded a central role as the *subject* of housing research (Allen 1997). Despite decades of policy-driven research on the most appropriate ways to provide warm, dry, sanitary, ergonomically designed dwellings, which provide privacy whilst minimizing overcrowding for people with a variety of housing needs, the accumulated stock of knowledge which loosely constitutes the subject area of *housing studies* has overlooked the fact that home is a place where bodies are accommodated.

Thinking about home as a sensuous space within which bodies are smelly and smelling, noisy and hearing, touching and tasting seems an obvious thing to do when one considers the type of things we do where we live. Moreover, the failure to recognize the accommodated body as a subject of study in its own right appears an even greater oversight when one considers the amount of time we spend at home. Stretton (1976: 183) once remarked that 'more than half of all waking time is spent at home or near it'. We might add to this that we are not often naked, but when we are we are most often at home. In addition, we plainly prefer to defecate and urinate at home rather than in public lavatories where strangers have been before or where they might overhear us or burst in (Kira 1974). Seen in this way, home can be understood as a place where bodies are both vulnerable and safe. At the heart of this paradox is the need routinely to cleanse the body of dirt and eliminate waste or residue (Sibley 1995: 78). Despite the centrality of home in the organization of bodies, our understanding of home as a specifically embodied space remains underdeveloped. In fact, we know much more about the organization of the corpse in cemeteries and crematoria (Jupp and Howarth 1997; Rugg 1998) and the organization of bodies in the street and shopping mall than we do about the organization of bodies in the spaces of the home where they are most often to be found (Longhurst 1995; Duncan 1996). In short, the complex relationships between the body and the home remain as fascinating as they are under researched.[4]

The Embodied Home: Being Yourself/Being and Self

Home is one of those delicious concepts that only becomes visible in its full sociological complexity when one pauses to think about it. Thinking about *your home*, images of love or hate, of safety or danger, or of freedom or restraint will – depending on your biography – spring to mind. Typically, these images will be articulated through stylized descriptions of home as a place where you can – or would, at least, like to be able to – *be yourself*. Such descriptions are frequently found in the

burgeoning trans-disciplinary literature on the meaning and significance of the home (Appleyard 1979; Duncan 1981; Altman and Werner
1985; Rybczynski 1986; Sixsmith 1986; Saunders and Williams 1988;
Allan and Crow 1989; Crow and Allan 1989; Gurney 1990; 1997; Newton and Putnam 1990; Despres 1991; Somerville 1992, 1997; Darke
1994, 1996; Benjamin with Stea 1995; Cooper Marcus 1995; Bowlby et
al. 1997; Dupius and Thorns 1998). But what does *being yourself* really
mean in this context, and why is this important in a book about bodies?

Being yourself in your home might mean, for example, having the
freedom to represent or practise your sexuality without fear of ridicule,
rejection or threat of violence (Egerton 1990; Smailes 1994; Johnston
and Valentine 1995). It might mean the opportunity to be fully or partly
undressed in some or all rooms without fear of reproach from, or
embarrassment to, other householders. It might mean being able to
flout conventional etiquette by belching or by breaking the 'fart taboo'
which usually restricts flatulence outside the home (Largey and Watson
1972: 1023). It might mean relaxing by not putting on make-up, not
shaving, not washing, not combing your hair. It might mean being able
to ingest forbidden foods and drink, or consume certain illegal substances. For some, it is undoubtedly interpreted as the opportunity to
exercise violence, control or surveillance over *other people's bodies* (Pizzey
1978; Malos and Hague 1997). The following extract from fieldwork
data, collected as part of a study on the meaning of home,[5] provides a
vivid illustration of the consanguinity of patriarchy and the surveillance
of the body to demonstrate this point:

> He made sure that every month he burnt their private parts on the
> fire [pause] That's how it was, to make sure that every month...
> [detecting incredulity] No, no, it's true, their *Dr Whites'* [trade mark
> name for a sanitary towel] and all that, he made sure that he burnt
> them on the fire to make sure that none of the daughters was expect-
> ing again. That's how he was.... Every month he used to say to them
> 'Got something to put on the fire?'
>
> (quoted in Gurney 1996: 301)

A number of observers (Madigan et al. 1990; Barrett and McIntosh
1991; Watson 1991) have questioned the dominant view of the home as
a 'benign social space' in research on domestic environments (Sibley
1995: 93). The extract above provides evidence of a very literal (rule
by the father) form of patriarchal repression and lends support to
Sibley's (1995: 77–8) perspective on the home as a site of conflict over

bodily residue. Most importantly, it demonstrates that having the freedom to *be yourself* can have deleterious consequences for the (embodied) selves of others. Nevertheless, the theoretical connections between the body, the home and the freedom to be yourself are not well established.

Whilst the relationship between home and the body appears crucial in making sense of ideas of privacy, the majority of work in this area remains distinctly disembodied (Lawrence 1984; Allan 1989; Munro and Madigan 1993). Thus, ideas of *being yourself* at home are most frequently understood in the existing literature in relation to ideas of private space or relaxation. The foregoing discussion has highlighted, however, that being yourself is also a profoundly embodied notion. This in turn raises a range of questions about privacy. For example, is privacy about mine-ness or alone-ness? Is privacy about power or about resistance? Is the individual privacy between insiders of a different order to the privacy of insiders from outsiders? Can privacy be understood in relation to the senses? To what extent is privacy related to the management of the body? Some clues to answering these questions can be found in Erving Goffman's work.

The organizing principle of *The presentation of self in everyday life* (Goffman 1959) is the metaphor of a theatrical performance. This metaphor provides a framework which allows Goffman to draw on the staging and management of a play to explain the reasons why individual or group behaviour is dependent upon the nature of their audience. Ideas of 'performance', 'impression management', 'front region', 'back region' and going 'off-stage' or 'out of play' being the techniques used to avoid various social 'gaffs' or faux pas (Goffman 1959: 203–30). Elsewhere (Gurney 2000) it has been suggested that, even when we live alone, we (still) enact various kinds of Goffmanesque performances to an 'internalized audience' (Duncan 1962: 303–4). This argument is significant because it suggests that we might only really be able to be ourselves when, in Goffman's terms, we go off-stage. He explains this by using defecation as an example:

> In our society defecation involves an individual in an activity which is defined as inconsistent with the cleanliness and purity standards expressed in many of our performances. Such activity also causes the individual to disarrange his [sic] clothing and to 'go out of play', that is, to drop from his face the expressive mask that he employs in face-to-face interaction. At the same time it becomes difficult for him to reassemble his personal front should the need to enter into interac-

tion suddenly occur. Perhaps that is a reason why toilet doors in our society have locks on them.

(Goffman 1959: 123)

Goffman's observations on defecation provide an insight into an activity which, paradoxically, renders us simultaneously safe (because we are off-stage) and vulnerable (because we just might be disturbed and, thus, have to adopt a *front* or *back* persona). The nature of this vulnerability is tied up with the question of the relationship between being ourselves, the maintenance of a performance and taboo attitudes surrounding corporeal dirt. This vulnerability is so deep-seated for many people that even when people live alone or when they know that no one else is at home they still use the lock on the toilet door to which Goffman alludes (Gurney 1998). The remainder of the chapter will explore in some detail some of the taboos surrounding off-stage activities in the embodied home. An understanding of the power of the civilizing process and the internalized audience seems crucial in making sense of this safe yet vulnerable paradox, and is explored below.

The Civilizing Process and the Accommodated Body

Norbert Elias's (1978) *The Civilizing Process* occupies a crucial role in the new sociology of the body.[6] His work draws on historical case-study material of sixteenth-century court society to outline the emergence of taboos and highlight the importance of regulating the body. Drawing on a number of contemporary guides to manners and civility, Elias demonstrates how the civilizing process can be understood as a relative, on-going accomplishment which socializes the body and forces each successive generation to renegotiate their embodied existence. The following examples are typical of the kind of bodily instructions to which Elias refers:

> Do not be afraid of vomiting if you must, for it is not vomiting, but holding the vomit in your throat that is foul...It is impolite to greet someone who is urinating of defecating....The sound of farting, especially of those who stand on elevated ground, is horrible. One should make sacrifices with the buttocks pressed firmly together.
>
> (quoted in Elias 1978: 58–9; 129–30).

Elias argues that civilization can be understood as a 'specific transformation of human behaviour' from primitive barbarism to the self-conscious manners, sensibilities and etiquette of the present (1978: 1–5). The emergence of new notions of civility, etiquette and indelicacy from the sixteenth century onwards began to privatize the body. An important outcome of this was that people increasingly sought to distance themselves from their own (and others') bodily functions.

Of course, ideas of uncivilized behaviour and standards of moral repugnance are constantly changing. Barbara Cartland's advice from the early 1970s appears anachronistic (if it wasn't so when it was published):

> The self-discipline of good behaviour should never be dropped within the home, least of all by the husband and the wife.... Cleanliness is one of the essentials of marriage but it is excruciatingly bad manners to leave the bathroom and the basin in a dirty wet mess for the next occupier.
>
> (Cartland 1972: 16–19)

Elias suggests that 'our behaviour, will arouse in our descendants feelings of embarrassment similar to those we sometimes feel concerning the behaviour of our ancestors' (Elias 1978: 59). Thus, Largey and Watson (1972) illustrate how late twentieth-century attitudes to the restraint of flatus in public places are more or less taken for granted, but their discussion about 'letting go' might, for future generations, seem as indelicate as some of the sixteenth-century advice on civility marshalled by Elias does now:

> [T]he rule of etiquette that restricts flatus...is so widely agreed upon that formal etiquette books do not even discuss it, and certainly anyone who 'lets go a fart' in public is usually considered somewhat crass and undisciplined...One also might note that the stigmatization of an individual for so 'letting go' often involves an attempt by the 'crass one' to convince others that it was someone else.
>
> (Largey and Watson 1972: 1023–4)

The civilizing process is constantly moving forward to redefine what is acceptable behaviour and what is bad manners. It has a number of important implications for understanding the organization of bodies in homes. Two are discussed here.

The first concerns the internalization of body management norms. Shilling argues that self-imposed regulation is now so widespread that civilized behaviour becomes taken for granted whilst at home:

Codes of behaviour become adopted at partly a subconscious level to the point that they are followed *irrespective of the presence of others . . .* people usually dress in the mornings even if they are spending the day at home with no intention of seeing anyone.

(Shilling 1993: 158; emphasis added)

Home, as we have already seen, allows us to be our (embodied) selves, but this 'partly subconscious' desire to maintain a performance even when the audience has gone must force a reassessment of how we understand privacy. Part of this reassessment should include a consideration of privacy and the senses. The next extract, for instance, illustrates the importance of aural, visual and olfactory privacy when carrying out elimination activities:

The very strong need to be visually private [in the bathroom] is matched by the desire not to be heard, or for one's whereabouts not to be sensed in any other way and this has implications for the location of the room, its entrance, its size, location, window glazing and for its acoustical treatment.

(Lee 1976: 67–8)

The taboos which surround elimination activities are an established part of the civilizing process which has moved them back stage then off stage. This movement constitutes the second link between the civilizing process and the accommodation of bodies.

The management of elimination activities has become an increasingly individualized experience. The work of Wright (1960), Kira (1974) and Best (1979) provide evidence of a link between the civilizing process and dwelling design with respect to trends in the siting of the toilet and the bathroom in Britain since the mid-nineteenth century. These facilities shifted from collective outside privies (earth or dry closets, wet middens, pail closets or water closets) and communal exterior baths to household privies with cisterns, local baths and household bath-nights. Postwar (1945) housing design in Great Britain saw the continuation of this trend with the embarrassment of being seen entering or leaving an outside lavatory by one's neighbours (Kuper 1953) removed by the integration of the toilet into the dwelling structure. More recently, the process has continued with increasing provision for a second (downstairs) toilet (or more euphemistically, cloakroom), en-suite bathing and elimination facilities, and the introduction of the bidet and the jacuzzi as higher-status positional goods. Most recently, there has been a move towards separate en-suite facilities in luxury master bedrooms.

Such spatial reorganization of polluting activities is far from a universal experience of British housing consumption, however. Anecdotal evidence suggests that, in the 1990s, older home owners in Huddersfield refused grants for the installation of indoor lavatories because they regarded indoor elimination as unhygienic.[7] This does seem to suggest that by bringing faeces, urine or menses indoors, the civilizing process has created an entirely new set of problems for the accommodation of leaky and odoriferous bodies. Elias's thesis would suggest that, over time, expectations about the efficacy of corporeal pollution management in the home would increase. The late twentieth-century obsession with anti-bacterial cleanliness seems to provide some justification for this. Here, home is socially constructed as at risk from a rising tide of somatic dirt and germs (panics concerning Salmonella and *E. coli* providing the most well known examples of this).[8] Attitudes towards a home which was not only clean but *hygienic* appear to have been manipulated (and continue to be manipulated) to stimulate demand for new product development in 'women's magazines' and elsewhere. Furnival reminds us that during the 1960s and 1970s, 'TV commercials emphasised higher hygiene standards for anything from teeth to kitchen surfaces' (Furnival 1998: 20). Further evidence for the onward march of the civilizing process can be detected in trends on cleaning regimen advice. In 1981, the following advice was offered on disinfecting toilet cistern flush handles: 'clean *once a week* with a bleach solution' (Good Housekeeping Institute 1981: 116; emphasis added). A little over a decade later the advice on cleaning regimens had escalated: 'Clean *every day* to keep the germs at bay. Wipe the rim of the bowl and the seat with a solution of washing-up liquid' (Wilkinson 1994: 281; emphasis added). Such advice on hygiene is often accompanied by the conflation of the clean home with the healthy family. Contemporary attitudes to infants' fecal matter is insightful in this respect. Recent product innovation includes the introduction of the scented disposable nappy (diaper), scented nappy sacks, scented baby-wipes, scented potty liners, specially formulated nursery air fresheners and delicately fragranced infant body sprays. We may not be able to stem the flow of infant faeces but we can, at least, make them smell sweeter.

The image of the clean child is a pervasive marketing icon in the lucrative home cleansing industry. Children and infants are portrayed as being particularly vulnerable to dirt and in constant need of civilization (although there is convincing evidence to suggest that it is their lack of contact with germs which is compromising their immune system).

> The children are portrayed as 'naturally' wild but it is clear that *Persil* [trade mark name for a washing powder] is a civilizing influence, a necessary commodity in the suburban home, contributing to the creation of a purified environment... The family home is the setting for a struggle against dirt and natural wildness.
>
> (Sibley 1995: 64)

Sibley points to an important link here between cleanliness and socialization. There is extensive evidence to suggest that parental attitudes towards dirt are used to control children's bodies. The child as dirty, stubborn, in need of breaking in, training or taming was popularized in Wesleyan preaching. Early Victorian child care experts such as Pye Henry Chavasse were quite clear that 'a dirty child was a mother's disgrace' and that it was possible to potty train from the age of three months. More recently, Dr Spock's advice convinced mothers that 'a dry child was a good child' (Jackson 1993: 136–48). Children are socialized from an early stage about the dangers of dirt, with the result that cleanliness becomes unavoidably associated with (hetero-)sexual purity with sometimes profound psychological consequences for later life (Jackson 1993: 82–4).

The civilized home of the early twenty-first century seems to have its origins in a late twentieth-century moral panic about germs under the rim and wipe-clean surfaces. Current attitudes towards the bodies which continue to pollute them with taboo substances and odours have a different history. A moral panic about an unruly mass of unwashed proletarians is clearly identifiable in the discourses of the public health reformers and social philanthropists of the late nineteenth-century. The history of state intervention in housing policy in Great Britain begins with a crusade against dirt. For Victorian reformers such as Octavia Hill, Robert Owen and Ebeneezer Howard, the association between corporeal dirt and moral dirt was often implicit. The capacity for bodies to produce dirt, in fact, became an important strategy for excluding some groups whilst benefiting others:

> The aspiring middle classes wanted to get away from the *dirt* – moral as well as physical – of the labouring poor which is why, for the bourgeoisie 'cleanliness was next to godliness'. The preoccupation

with dirt and its elimination at this time *preceded* any knowledge about germs.

(Walter 1982: 63; emphasis in original)

We should not delude ourselves about the exclusionary power of the civilizing process. Sibley's (1995) work on the importance of dirt and boundaries in sustaining homophobia and racism is crucial to understanding the socio-spatial organization of bodies in the twenty-first century. The long journey from barbarism to civility is far from complete. New standards of body regulation and management using techniques from eugenics or genetic engineering and the spatial purification of urban areas through panoptic technologies and gated communities might lead our descendants to regard our present lifestyle in much the same way as we currently regard Engels' accounts of mid-Victorian middens oozing cess into the overcrowded cellar homes of illiterate Irish immigrants in nineteenth-century Liverpool (Lawless and Brown 1986: 22–7). The repulsion associated with the leaky body is explored in more detail in the following section.

The Moist Home? A Corporeal Ecology of Leaky Bodies

Bodies can be understood as essentially unfinished social products which are inherently prone to disorder and in careful need of management, training and presentation. Extending this argument we can point towards the home as the place where the regulation of leaky bodies routinely and most frequently takes place. This presents certain staging difficulties given the discussions on performance and the civilizing process above. In particular the feelings of repulsion associated with menstrual blood, faeces, urine, semen, sputum, mucus and vomit must be resolved since they are most frequently discharged in the home.

This section of the chapter outlines a complex corporeal ecology of home by drawing upon Mary Douglas's (1966) work on the anthropology of the body and socially constructed attitudes towards dirt. It argues that this ecology imbues some spaces with associations imitative of leaky bodies and that this has hitherto unexplicated consequences for bodies being 'in place' or 'out of place' in the dwelling. Douglas reminds us that 'dirt is essentially disorder' (1966: 2). Thus we can suggest that moist somatic excretions are regarded as dangerous and repulsive because they come from the margins of the body and are seeped out through vulnerable orifices. Douglas (1966: 121) suggests that *all* margins are regarded as a dangerous threat to order and that is it mistake 'to treat bodily margins in isolation from all other margins'. Kira outlines what this means in relation to the home:

> Attitudes surrounding the elimination processes – urination, defecation, flatulence, spitting and so on – tend by and large to be negative in outlook. . . . Urine and feces [sic], in particular, are generally regarded by contemporary Western societies as filth of the worst sort, so much so that the individual not only wants to dispose of them as quickly as possible but also wishes in many instances to be completely disassociated from the act of producing them.
>
> (Kira 1974: 93)

This argument suggests that the bathroom/toilet has a crucial and symbolic role to play in the management of bodies. It is, in Douglas's terms a marginal and dangerous place because it is representative of our embodiment and our pollution. Given this, it is surprising how little attention has been devoted to this room in the housing and design literature (Wright 1960; Kira 1974).

Of course, since attitudes towards dirt are socially constructed we should not be surprised to find cultural variations in what constitutes polluting and non-polluting activities. These may have profound consequences for the design of dwellings and the experience of home. Lawrence, (1987: 104–6), for example, illustrates contrasting attitudes to laundry activities in Great Britain and Australia. In the latter the washing of clothes by hand or in a washing machine is clearly a polluting activity and thus *never* undertaken in a room where food is prepared. This, of course, contrasts markedly with the British experience of house design where washing machines are routinely located in kitchens. It is significant to note, however, that a degree of cultural convergence is occurring in the trend towards providing utility rooms (ostensibly for washing machines) in 1990s new-build houses.

The foregoing discussion has suggested that impression management, performance and privacy are interrelated and that parts of dwellings imitative of moist corporeal dirt are regarded as dirty spaces. It is important to remember that, as part of this corporeal ecology, these spaces might also hide secret objects with dirty corporeal associations and that these are consequently assiduously hidden from view. Back region rooms such as the bedroom may come under such scrutiny from guests or visitors as to invalidate all attempts at impression management (indeed, this corporeal ecology might prove crucial in making sense of etiquette in research on hospitality). This may necessitate some thought in the storage of contraception, and those devices and clothing euphemistically referred to as *marital aids*. Comfort (1993: 51) recognizes this and provides some reassuring advice, arguing that 'a well-designed bedroom can be a sexual gymnasium without it being embarrassing to let elderly relatives leave their coats there'. Beyond this, careful consideration may have to be given to the placing of items traditionally stored (and/or used) in the bathroom/toilet. Thus, sanitary protection, soiled underwear, oral contraceptives, certain types of intimate medication (such as haemorrhoid ointment, suppositories, vaginal deodorants or lubricants), denture fixative cream, cotton buds and even lavatory paper and toilet brushes are hidden away in cabinets, or camouflaged behind crocheted dollies or cheery animal-shaped dispensers, whilst items associated with cleansing the body such as towels, soap or toothpaste are more frequently left on open display. *The House Style Book* – another contemporary source on twentieth-century etiquette – advises that 'the sort of detritus that accumulates in bathrooms always looks unpleasant lying about in wastepaper baskets' (Sujdic 1984: 221). Implicit in this advice is further evidence for an ecology of leaky bodies based on negative ideas about bodies being (or becoming) dirty and more positive ideas about bodies being (or becoming) clean. Other secret objects suggestive of the leaky body can be located elsewhere in this ecology. They might include evidence of masturbation (pornography, erotic fiction), of eating disorders (forbidden food and laxatives), of addiction (non-prescription drugs and out-of-place socially acceptable drugs) or of sick or unregulated bodies (vomit, urine, faeces or blood stains on mattresses, carpets, fabrics or upholstery).

The taboo substances which attract the most revulsion are undoubtedly those which inundate the human senses. Although the sight of fecal matter or vomit is, in itself, universally regarded as unpleasant, it is their conjunction with a distinctive smell, or (on elimination) sound and texture which makes them so repulsive. We may avert our eyes but we may still smell, hear or feel dirt. Whilst a consideration of corporeal noise has been made elsewhere (Gurney 1998), the following section explores the neglected significance of odour for the accommodation of bodies.

The Olidic Home? The Impression Management of the Odoriferous Body

> Odour is a significant component of our moral construction of reality and our construction of moral reality…what smells good *is* good. Conversely, what smells bad *is* bad.
>
> (Synott 1993: 190)

> In everyday terms, one's house has a characteristic smell readily perceived by visitors but apparent to the occupant only after having been away from home for some time.
>
> (Porteous 1985: 358)

> Originally meant for kitchens and toilets, air fresheners are now used in all rooms of the house and have become more sophisticated, designed to create a perfumed atmosphere and increase olfactory comfort inside the home.
>
> (Euromonitor 1998: 4)

These quotations all demonstrate the importance of odour for an under-standing of the relationship between the body and home. They tell us three things. First, odour is closely tied up with identity, the construction of the self and of morality. Second, as a result of habituation we become immune to the smell of the familiar. Third, when taken together, observations one and two provide an explanation for the emergence of notions such as 'olfactory comfort' which sustain an odour management to assuage fears about social gaffs surrounding dirty bodies.

Given the importance attached to masking the visual evidence of corporeal dirt discussed in the previous section perhaps we should not be surprised at the emergence of an odour management in the home. What is surprising, however, is how little has been written about the sociological significance of smell. This section briefly reviews the literature on this topic before arguing that the body was an implicit subject in much of the institutional racism and housing allocation research of the mid-1980s in which issues of cooking smells often seemed to be used as euphemisms for body odours. It concludes by assessing the role of the civilizing process in the creation of an odourless and perfumed home and considers the role of the household fresheners and fragrances market in creating a twenty-first century moral panic around the olidic home.

Largey and Watson's (1972) article has already been cited in this chapter and is one of only a very few sources on the sociology of odours. In concluding their position paper they suggest a list of questions for further research which stretches over 25 lines. Their list ends with the following summary question;

> In short, how do interactants become conscious of how to feel about or define a given odor perceived to emanate from a given other in a given social setting at a given time?
>
> (Largey and Watson 1972: 1033)

Although there have been anthropological (Corbin 1986) and geographical (Porteous 1985) accounts of smell, the sociological questions raised by Largey and Watson have been largely neglected. However, it seems that the relationship between body and smell is crucial to the management and regulation of the embodied home. Following on from this, it appears inevitable that the management of odours becomes an important part of the construction of the self. Synott is quite clear on this. He suggests that the association of odour with bestial sexual behaviour has created a deodorizing imperative. It is clear that this imperative will be felt much more keenly at home than elsewhere:

> Indeed *ordinary* human odours are to be eliminated, in the body, the bathroom, the bedroom, the kitchen and at work; deodorants, air fresheners, extractor fans, open windows...all combine for this one purpose.
>
> (Synott 1993: 185; emphasis added)

Largey and Watson suggest that odours carry a widely understood social meaning and that this can be used to mobilize prejudice against people who emanate a specific odour. There is clearly a powerful socialization process at work here. Engen (1982) for example, points out that few smell preferences are innate, but that children have a much higher tolerance to bodily odours. Synott (1993) and Porteous (1985) both argue that smell can invoke memory and vice-versa. Most significant of all, however, is the widespread association of certain odours with distinctive social classes or 'racial' groups.

The role of odour in distinguishing groups of people is well established (Corbin 1986), being used to justify 'racial' segregation and class prejudice by imputing a negative moral identity to the olfactory traces of culturally specific diets. There is, in fact, quite recent evidence to demonstrate the use of odour in discrimination against minority ethnic groups. During the mid-1980s a number of studies into local authority housing allocation policies were carried out (Commission for Racial Equality 1984, Phillips 1986, Henderson and Karn 1987). These studies all suggested that institutional racism was widespread and was sustained by discretionary moral judgements about housekeeping, dirt and cleanliness. Smells, and in particular cooking smells, often seemed to be a material consideration in allocating suitable properties to applicants. The following extract provides an example:

> The housing of one Asian family on this estate has prompted much discontent from other families who are affected by the more exotic aroma which tends to add spice to the atmosphere in the internal corridor access . . . Many tenants find this situation unacceptable and their objections are certainly not racist but merely traditional.
>
> (internal memorandum quoted in Phillips 1986: 28–9)

Phillips points out that the negative reactions to cooking smells from white tenants were accorded a greater significance than the specific housing needs of one Bengali family. Phillips' research found that Bengali families were socially and morally constructed as both smelly and dirty by housing staff. These disturbing findings shed new light on ideas of impression management and illustrate that the body has an implicit presence in (widely cited) housing research. Although a study of the role of odour in sustaining racism lies beyond the scope of this chapter, these observations do highlight the theoretical possibilities of a more embodied housing imagination. Familiar debates about 'deserving' versus 'undeserving' poor which can be traced back to the embodied attitudes of the Victorian philanthropists discussed earlier in this chapter still play an important role in the mobilization of discretion amongst housing managers.

The paradox of the safe but vulnerable home is well developed in relation to odour. Perspiration, fecal matter, flatulence, urine and vomit all have a distinctive odour which are most frequently emanated within the home. Similarly the distinctive odours of malfunctioning chemical toilets, blocked drains and urine-sodden carpets cannot easily be disassociated from an embodied home. In short, by accommodating bodies the home can very quickly become an olid (foul-smelling) container. Moreover, as a result of habituation and the immense individual variation in response to odour, the management of these embodied smells is a particularly difficult task. Whilst we can detect an unkempt physical appearance in a mirror, it is less easy to make such judgements about how we smell or about how spaces in our homes smell. After establishing a clear relationship between odour, the self and morality, the management of bodily odours seems crucial if any front region performance is to be sustained.

The fear of corporeal odour inside and outside the home became an important part of the civilizing process during the latter half of the twentieth century. The usage of deodorants, for example, grew from 81 per cent of all women and 68 per cent of all men in the UK in 1980 to 91 per cent and 85 per cent respectively in 1996 (Mintel 1996). Recent years have also seen a growing effort to create a demand for products which not only clean but deodorize, fragrance and freshen the home. The phenomenal growth in the size of the UK air freshener market alluded to in the introduction and contextualized in Table 4.1 demonstrates the consumer response to this. Even allowing for inflation, this is a phenomenal growth. Mintel suggest that it is a function of an increasing number of households, a shift towards more expensive, slow-release products and a growing interest in perfuming the home. This final trend offers a number of fascinating possibilities for further research.

Writing at the turn of the twenty-first century, it seems as though the civilizing process currently attaches a particular etiquette to the odour management of the home. The growing sophistication of home fragrancing, the increasing interest in enhancing a specific mood or ambience through scent and the conflation of *feng shui*, aromatherapy and impression management (Gregory and Gurney 1999) all point towards the final removal of any odoriferous traces of corporeal dirt in the home. But of course, as Elias reminds us, our descendants will probably regard such trends as futile, primitive and indelicate attempts to mask the odours of our leaky, odoriferous bodies.

Table 4.1   Actual and forecast retail sale of household fresheners, 1992–2001

Year	£m (current prices)
1992 (actual)	95
1994 (actual)	125
1996 (actual)	159
1998 (forecast)	185
2001 (forecast)	212

Source: Mintel (1997).

The Civilising Processor? Some Concluding Remarks on Accommodating Bodies and Thoughts for Further Research

This theoretical chapter has contributed to sociological debates about the organization of bodies through a focus on the social and physical space of the home. By making the body the subject of this thesis, the chapter makes a contribution to the sociology of housing. The organizing principle of the chapter was that the home is a place within which the accommodation of bodies is accomplished. The onward march of the 'civilizing process' proved crucial in sustaining this argument and was identifiable in changing attitudes towards the containment, dilution, damming up and masking of bodily fluids and odours. A number of opportunities for further research might be suggested by this chapter. The outcome of these will be contingent on the way in which the home is conceptualized. Building on the ideas discussed in this chapter there seem to be at least four ways in which this might be done. Thus, home might be conceptualized as a sensorium; as a processor of dirt; as a container of secrets; or as a site where the civilizing process can be observed in changes to the use and design of the dwelling.

Beyond this broad conceptual framework there are a number of unresolved questions which lend themselves to empirical research. These largely (but by no means exclusively) concern the masking of corporeal dirt.

The 'masking' of corporeal dirt is a well-established dimension of the civilizing process. Visual pollutions of corporeal dirt are masked through the movement of elimination and sexual activities off-stage. The strict regionalization of the off-stage is accomplished, for example, through the locking of doors, the introduction of frosted glass, and net curtains, etc. Olfactory pollutions are masked, for example, through household deodorizers and fragrances. Aural pollutions are masked, for example, through running taps or placing toilet tissue in the bowl to mask the sound of fecal matter impacting on static water. These techniques of body management are integral to the civilizing process as it is played out in the home. Variations in social class, ethnicity, gender, age and sexuality in the deployment of these techniques might reveal important differences in the way bodily taboos and corporeal dirt are socially constructed. A study of conflicts between teenage children's sexuality and middle-aged parents' attempts to manage and control asexual bodies or a study of conflicts between younger children's leaky embodiment and their parents' attempts to create a clean and fragrant home would seem to offer further insights into the masking of corporeal dirt in the embodied home.

Thinking about the home as a theoretical sensuous space and writing about this using empirical evidence are quite different things however. Elsewhere, Morgan and Scott (1993: 1) have suggested that a self-regulatory 'puritan legacy' prevents sociologists from researching bodily taboos (such as defecation, menstruation or death for example) for fear of arousing accusations of sensationalism or poor taste. The researcher or student who chooses to pursue the questions raised here might, therefore, need a thick skin. However, the very existence of such taboos in contemporary western culture are insightful in revealing the very scale of the negative associations between the body and 'dirt'. Precisely because they are taboos such bodily processes are managed as discreetly and as privately as possible. And of course, the space wherein this management usually takes place is, as this chapter has shown, the home. To overlook the accommodation of bodies because of a puritan legacy which makes our embodiment a source of embarrassment or shame seems to be as misguided as it is repressive.

Acknowledgements

I am indebted to Maggie Gregory for her suggestions for further reading and for lending me so many of her books. Thanks also to Linda McKie – who has proved to have the patience of a saint – and to Chris Allen, Liz Kenyon and Julie Rugg for some inspirational e-mails. This research was unfunded and all usual disclaimers apply.

Notes

1   These include lavatory colourants and fresheners, liquid bleach, multi-purpose cleaners, bathroom and kitchen cleaners, lavatory blocks, cleaning liquids and powders, disinfectants, carpet cleaners and window cleaners (Mintel 1997a).
2   These include odour-neutralizing, odour-masking and perfumed products including aerosols, disposable and refillable slow-release dispensers, 'plug-in' products and anti-bacterial sprays, but exclude pot pourri, scented candles and scented aromatherapy (etc.) oils (Mintel 1997b).
3   It is a misnomer to talk, even in the most general terms, about the existence of an identifiable sociology of housing. Whilst there is a tradition of sociologists writing about housing and housing researchers making contributions to sociology, it remains difficult to point with any certainty towards a sociology of housing in the same way as, say, an identifiable sociology of the family might be said to exist. Kemeny (1992) and King (1996) argue that this is because of the continued policy-driven pragmatism of the subject area.

4   This chapter is primarily concerned with the organization of the living body in the home. This is not to imply, of course, that there are not important questions to be asked in relation to the organization of dying and death at home.

5   See Gurney (1996, 1997, 1999) for a full account of this research.

6   The 'new' sociology of the body refers to the embodied turn discussed in the introduction as distinct from the work of earlier authors such as Simmel (1908) or Berger and Luckman (1967) who Largey and Watson (1972: 1023) regarded as 'just about the only sociologists who even mention the possibility of a sociology of the senses, or "sociology of the body"'.

7   I am grateful to Jacqueline Howard for pointing this out to me.

8   These panics about bacteria at home were accompanied with panics about infestation in institutional homes (e.g. Legionnaires' disease).

References

Allan, G. 1989. 'Insiders and Outsiders: Boundaries Around the Home', in G. Allan and G. Crow (eds.), *Home and Family: Creating the Domestic Sphere*, Basingstoke: Macmillan, 141–58.

Allan, G. and Crow, G. (eds.) 1989. *Home and Family: Creating the Domestic Sphere*. Basingstoke: Macmillan.

Allen, C. 1997. 'Reclaiming the Body: From the Biological Essentialism of Housing and Illness to a Physiological Sociology of Home and Health'. Paper presented to the conference *Housing and Health: Key Issues and Future Directions*. University of Glasgow, 21 November.

Altman, I. and Werner, C. (eds.) 1985. *Home Environments*. New York: Plenum Press.

Appleyard, D. 1979. 'Home'. *Architectural Association Quarterly* 2: 4–20.

Barrett, M. and Mcintosh, M. 1991. *The Anti-social Family*, 2nd edition. London: Verso.

Benjamin, D. with Stea, D. (eds.) 1995. *The Home: Words, Interpretations, Meanings and Environments*. Aldershot: Avebury.

Berger, P. and Luckmann, T. 1967. *The Social Construction of Reality*. London: Allen Lane.

Bell, D. and Valentine, G. (eds.) 1995. *Mapping Desire: Geographies of Sexuality*. London: Routledge.

Best, G. 1979. *Mid Victorian Britain 1851–75*. London: Fontana.

Bowlby, S., Gregory, S. and Mckie, L. 1997. '"Doing Home": Patriarchy, Caring and Space', *Women's Studies International Forum* 20: 343–50.

Cartland, B. 1972. *Barbara Cartland's Book of Etiquette*. London: Arrow.

Comfort, A. 1993. *The Complete Joy of Sex: The Classic Joy of Sex and More Joy of Sex in One Volume*. London: The Chancellor Press.

Cooper Marcus, C. 1995. *House as Mirror of the Self: Exploring the Deeper Meanings of Home*. Berkeley, Ca.: Conari Press.

Corbin, A. 1986. *The Foul and the Fragrant: Odor and the French Social Imagination* (trans. by M. Kochan) Cambridge, Mass.: Harvard University Press.

Crow, G. and Allan, G. 1989. 'Constructing the Domestic Sphere: The Emergence of the Modern Home in Post-war Britain', in H. Corr and L. Jamieson (eds.),

Politics of Everyday Life: Continuity and Change in Work and the Family, Basingstoke: Macmillan, 11–36.

Darke, J. 1994. 'Women and the Meaning of Home', in R. Gilroy and R. Woods (eds.), *Housing Women*. London: Routledge, 11–30.

Darke, J. 1996. 'The Englishwoman's Castle, or Don't You Just Love Being in Control?', in C. Booth, J. Darke, and S. Yeandle (eds.), *Changing Places: Women's Lives in the City*. London: Paul Chapman Publishing, 61–71.

Després, C. 1991. 'The Meaning of Home; Literature Review and Directions for Future Research and Theoretical Development', *Journal of Architectural and Planning Research*. 8: 97–115.

Douglas, M. 1966. *Purity and Danger: An Analysis of Concepts of Pollution and Taboo*. London: Routledge and Kegan Paul.

Dovey, K. 1978. 'Home: An Ordering Principle in Space', *Landscape* 22 (2): 27–30.

Duncan, H. 1962. *Communication and Social Order*. London: Oxford University Press.

Duncan, J. (ed.) 1981. *Housing and Identity: Cross-Cultural Perspectives*. London: Croom Helm.

Duncan, N. 1996. 'Renegotiating Gender and Sexuality in Public and Private Spaces', in N. Duncan (ed.), *Bodyspace: Destabilizing Geographies of Gender and Sexuality*. London: Routledge, 127–45.

Dupius, A. and Thorns, D. 1998. 'Home, Home Ownership and the Search for Ontological Security', *Sociological Review* 48: 24–47.

Egerton, J. 1990. 'Out but not Down: Lesbians' Experience of Housing', *Feminist Review* 36: 75–88.

Elias, N. 1978. *The History of Manners: The Civilising Process*, Volume 1 (trans. E. Jephcott). New York: Pantheon.

Engen, T. 1982. *The Perception of Odor*. Reading, Mass.: Addison-Wesley.

Euromonitor 1998. 'Air Fresheners', *Market Research Europe* 30 (April): 1–29.

Euromonitor 1999. *International Marketing Data and Statistics*, 23rd edition. London: Euromonitor.

Furnival, J. 1998. *Suck, Don't Blow!: The Gripping Story of the Vacuum Cleaner and Other Labour Saving Devices Around the House*. London: Michael O'Mara Books.

Goffman, E. 1959 [1971 imprint]. *The Presentation of Self in Everyday Life*. Harmondsworth: Penguin Books.

Good Housekeeping Institute 1981. *Good Housekeeping Home Hints*. London: Ebury Press.

Gregory, M. and Gurney, C. 1999. 'Oriental, Occidental or Accidental?: Some Diverse Thoughts on *Feng Shui* and the Meaning of Home'. Paper presented to Housing Studies Association Conference: *Housing Diversity*. Newcastle, 6–7 September. Unpublished.

Gurney, C. 1990. *The Meaning of Home in the Decade of Owner Occupation: Towards an Experiential Perspective*. SAUS Working paper 88. Bristol: School for Advanced Urban Studies, University of Bristol.

Gurney, C. 1996. 'Meanings of Home and Home Ownership: Myths, Histories and Experiences'. Unpublished PhD. thesis. Bristol: School for Policy Studies, University of Bristol.

Gurney, C. 1997. '... "Half of me was Satisfied": Making Sense of Home through Episodic Ethnographies', *Women's Studies International Forum* 20: 373–86.

Gurney, C. 1998. 'The Neighbours Didn't Dare Complain: Some (Taboo) Thoughts on the Regulation of Noisy Bodies, the Myth of the Back-region and the Disembodied Housing Imagination'. Paper presented to European Network for Housing Research conference: *Housing Futures: Renewal, Sustainability and Innovation*. Cardiff, 7–11 September.

Gurney, C. 1999. 'Pride and Prejudice: Discourses of Normalisation in Public and Private Accounts of Home Ownership', *Housing Studies* 14: 163–83.

Gurney, C. 2000. 'Transgressing Private–Public Boundaries in the Home: A Sociological Analysis of the Coital Noise Taboo', *Venereology* 13: 39–46.

Henderson, J. and Karn, V. 1987. *Race, Class and State Housing: Inequality and the Allocation of Public Housing in Britain*. Aldershot: Gower.

Jackson, D. 1993. *Do Not Disturb: Giving Our Children Room to Grow*. London: Bloomsbury.

Johnston, L. and Valentine, G. 1995. 'Wherever I Lay my Girlfriend that's my Home: The Performance and Surveillance of Lesbian Identities in Domestic Environments', in D. Bell and G. Valentine (eds.), *Mapping Desire: Geographies of Sexuality*. London: Routledge, 99–113.

Jupp, P. and Howarth, G. (eds.) 1997. *The Changing Face of Death*. Basingstoke: Macmillan.

Kemeny, J. 1992. *Housing and Social Theory*. London: Routledge.

King, P. 1996. *The Limits to Housing Policy: A Philosophical Investigation*. London: Middlesex University Press.

Kira, A. 1974. *The Bathroom* (revised edition). Harmondsworth: Penguin Books.

Kuper, L. 1953. 'Blueprint for Living Together', in L. Kuper (ed.), *Living in Towns: Selected Research Papers in Urban Sociology of the Faculty of Commerce and Social Science, University of Birmingham*. London: Cresset Press, 1–203.

Largey, G. and Watson, R. 1972. 'The Sociology of Odors', *American Journal of Sociology* 77: 1020–34.

Lawless, P. and Brown, F. 1986. *Urban Growth and Change in Britain: An Introduction*. London: Harper and Row.

Lawrence, R. 1984. 'Transition Spaces and Dwelling Design', *Journal of Architectural and Planning Research* 1: 261–71.

Lawrence, R. 1987. *Housing, Dwellings and Homes: Design Theory, Research and Practice*. Chichester: John Wiley & Sons.

Lee, T. 1976. *Psychology and the Environment*. London: Methuen.

Longhurst, R. 1995. 'The Body and Geography', *Gender, Place and Culture* 2: 97–105.

Madigan, R., Munro, M. and Smith, S. 1990. 'Gender and the Meaning of Home', *International Journal of Urban and Regional Research*. 14: 625–47.

Madigan, R. and Munro, M. 1996. ' "House Beautiful": Style and Consumption in the Home', *Sociology* 30: 41–57.

Malos, E. and Hague, G. 1997. 'Women, Housing, Homelessness and Domestic Violence', *Women's Studies International Forum* 20: 397–410.

Mintel 1996. *Deodorants and Bodysprays*. Product Report December 1996. London: Mintel.

Mintel 1997a. *Household Cleaning Products*. Product Report May 1997. London: Mintel.

Mintel 1997b. *Household Fresheners and Insecticides*. Product Report September 1997. London: Mintel.

Morgan, D. J. H. and Scott, S. 1993. 'Bodies in a Social Landscape', in S. Scott and D. J. H. Morgan (eds.), *Body Matters: Essays on the Sociology of the Body*. London: Falmer Press, 1–21.

Munro, M. and Madigan, R. 1993. 'Privacy in the Private Sphere', *Housing Studies* 8: 29–45.

Newton, C. and Putnam, T. (eds.) 1990. *Household Choices*. London: Futures Publications.

Phillips, D. 1986. *What Price Equality?: A Report on the Allocation of GLC Housing in Tower Hamlets*. GLC Housing Research and Policy Report 9. London: GLC.

Pizzey, E. 1978. *Scream Quietly or the Neighbours Will Hear*. Hillside, NJ: Enslow Publications.

Porteous, J-D. 1985. 'Smellscape', *Progress in Human Geography* 9: 356–78.

Rodaway, P. 1994. *Sensuous Geographies: Body, Sense and Place*. London: Routledge.

Rugg, J. 1998. ' "A Few Remarks on Modern Sepulture": Current Trends and New Directions in Cemetery Research', *Mortality* 3: 111–28.

Rybczynski, W. 1986. *Home: A Short History of an Idea*. New York: Viking Penguin.

Saunders, P. and Williams, P. 1988. 'The Constitution of the Home: Towards a Research Agenda', *Housing Studies* 3: 81–93.

Scott, S. and Morgan, D. J. H. (eds.) 1993. *Body Matters: Essays on the Sociology of the Body*. London: Falmer Press.

Shilling, C. 1993. *The Body and Social Theory*. London: Sage.

Sibley, D. 1995. *Geographies of Exclusion*. London: Routledge.

Simmel, G. 1908. *Sociologie*. Leipzig: Duncker and Humbolt.

Sixsmith, J. 1986. 'The Meaning of Home: An Exploratory Study of Environmental Experience', *Journal of Environmental Psychology* 6: 281–98.

Smailes, J. 1994. ' "The Struggle has Never Simply Been about Bricks and Mortar": Lesbians' Experience of Housing', in R. Gilroy and R. Woods (eds.), *Housing Women*. London: Routledge, 151–72.

Stretton, H. 1976. *Capitalism, Socialism and the Environment*. Cambridge: Cambridge University Press.

Somerville, P. 1992. 'Homelessness and the Meaning of Home; Rooflessness or Rootlessness?', *International Journal of Urban and Regional Research* 16: 529–39.

Somerville, P. 1997. 'The Social Construction of Home', *Journal of Architectural and Planning Research* 14: 226–45.

Stretton, H. 1976. *Capitalism, Socialism and the Environment*. Cambridge: Cambridge University Press.

Sudjic, D. 1984. *The House Style Book: New Directions in Design and Decorating for Every Room in the Home*: London: Mitchell Beazley.

Synott, A. 1993. *The Body Social: Symbolism, Self and Society*. London: Routledge.

Turner, B. 1992. *Regulating Bodies: Essays in Medical Sociology*. London: Routledge.

Walter, J. A. 1982. *The Human Home: The Myth of the Sacred Environment*. Tring, Herts.: Lion.

Watson, S. 1991. 'The Restructuring of Work and Home: Productive and Reproductive Relations', in J. Allen and C. Hamnett (eds.), *Housing and Labour Markets: Building the Connections*. London: Unwin-Hyman, 136–54.

Wilkinson, S. (ed.) 1994. *Good Housekeeping Complete Book of the Home: The Ultimate Home Reference Guide*. London: Book Club Associates.

Wright, L. 1960. *Clean and Decent: The Fascinating History of the Bathroom and the Water Closet and of Sundry Habits, Fashions and Accessories of the Toilet Principally in Great Britain, France and America.* London: Routledge and Kegan Paul.

Part II

Institutions Constructing and Representing Bodies

5
Moving Bodies/Still Bodies: Embodiment and Agency in Schools

Tuula Gordon, Janet Holland and Elina Lahelma

Introduction

The task which society requires of the school is dual: regulation and emancipation. The 'citizen-to-be', the student, comes under the regulation and control of the school, through its ethos, practices and processes, in order to produce the future citizen with the requisite 'adult' characteristics. Through this control and regulation, the school can also be seen as producing and reproducing the social divisions which are apparent in any given society – those of social class, gender and 'race' being the most obvious. The task of producing 'citizens', then, itself entails contradictions in the light of these divisions; and that is a focus of this study. But a continuous historical strand in educational thinking has emphasized schools as sites of emancipation, ensurers of social justice and channels for furthering social change (Davies 1990; Green 1990; Donald 1992). The tensions and contradictions between regulation and emancipation in educational politics and policies are manifested in the everyday life at school, in the coexistence of control and agency. We can see these tensions at the level of the school reflected in the contradictions inherent in the construction of identity and subjectivity at the level of the individual. In this chapter our focus is on how embodiment is implicated in these processes.

The body is embedded in the processes and practices of schools both in terms of the exercise of control and in the search for autonomy and agency. Schooling can be understood as practice on the body. Nancy Lesko (1988) has suggested that schools have 'a curriculum of the body' and we have expanded this to include the pedagogy of the body. We trace the curriculum and pedagogy of the body in three intertwined layers of the school: the official, the informal and the physical school.

By the official we mean the curriculum, lessons, formal hierarchies and disciplinary apparatus; the informal school consists of informal hierarchies, the application and interpretation of rules and social interaction; the physical school refers to spatiality and embodiment. In this chapter we analyse the ways in which bodies are present in the different layers of the school and examine the tensions between regulation/control and emancipation/agency in these manifestations. The construction of gendered difference and sexuality are themes that link the layers of the school in the following discussion (Gordon 1996).

The research project on which the discussion that follows draws is 'Citizenship, Difference and Marginality in Schools: With Special Reference to Gender'.[1] This is a comparative, cross-cultural, ethnographic study of four secondary schools, two in Britain (London) and two in Finland (Helsinki). In each city one school is predominantly middle-class in catchment and one predominantly working-class. The broader study is contextualized in a discussion and critique of New Right politics and policies in education, still largely holding sway despite government changes in both Finland and Britain, and the changes these have wrought in the two countries. While government policy in Britain moved to take more control over the curriculum, and in Finland, control was relinquished, none the less many similarities, particularly in terms of marketization of education (and its accompanying rhetoric), are apparent. We trace national policies and curricula through into school-level curricula, and then move to the micro-level, to focus on the practices and processes of the school. In the study we employ a range of methods: documentary analysis, observation, participant observation, formal and informal interviews, and questionnaires.[2] Here we take data from school observations and interviews with 12–14-year-old students and their teachers.[3] In comparing the two countries we draw attention to differences, but when the processes in the schools are similar, we do not make such a clear distinction between the countries.

In the official school the body is muted, and when it does appear this is often in terms of technical descriptions of its nature and functions (in biology, health or sex education). The official school places bodies in time–space paths (Giddens 1985), moving from station to station, or sitting at their desks, upright, facing the teacher. Bodies recreate the abstracted citizen-to-be, the solitary individual; a school student has to learn to be alone in a crowd (Jackson 1968). In the informal school bodies make contact. Students slap each other on the shoulders, clap hands, tap arms, make faces and hand signs, groom, hug, collide, poke, block, grope, push and shove, hit, kick; bodies include and exclude, move to the centre or shift to the margins. When we consider the layer of the physical school we analyse tensions between students' movement and immobility, and discuss the bodily aspects of regulation/control and emancipation/agency in schools.

We have used a metaphor of dance (Gordon Holland and Lahelma 2000) to illustrate the way in which the three layers of the school – the physical, the official and the informal – are analytically distinct, yet intertwined. In the dance of the school, the physical/social space of the school, the buildings and classrooms, sets limits for bodily movement, regulated or transgressive; the official school stipulates and regulates the appropriate movement and steps; and the informal school sees students creating their own steps, individually or collectively, and so exercising agency in the face of the control exercised by the school. We look first at the body in the official school.

Bodies in the Official School

Western educational thought is based on a dichotomy between mind and body. Bodies and embodied desires or fears do not belong in the official school; they disturb, like thirst in the lesson below:

> *Lasse*: Teacher, can I get a drink of water?
> *Teacher*: Are you terribly thirsty, or can you wait for a moment?
> *Lasse*: I'm terribly thirsty!
> *Jyri*: Me too! [other students shout]
> *Teacher*: Look now, others are saying 'me too', 'me too' . . . Now I have forgotten where I was. Please, do not interrupt the lesson! (ObsH)

In this extract, the layers of physical and informal school are also involved. Perhaps Lasse was not dying of thirst, but wanted to break the compulsory immobility of the physical school, and Jyri and the other boys wanted to join him and have an informal chat in the corridor. In this section we try to analyse how bodies are present in the official school when they are not regarded as disturbance.

Mind and Body/Head and Hand: Still Bodies in Lessons

Sara Delamont and Maurice Galton (1986) argue that the cultural assumption about lessons where children will be relatively stationary is not quite true and total immobility is rare. In most lessons movement of students' bodies is not totally forbidden; but bodies and movement are regulated and surveyed. School rules, distributed and explained to the students in their first days in school, include norms about movement

(Lahelma and Gordon 1997). The traditional teaching, 'teaching-as-usual' (Davies and Hunt 1994), is based on students sitting at their desks, listening to the teacher, raising hands, answering questions and conducting exercises or copying texts from the blackboard/overhead into their exercise books. Our data from observations of hundreds of lessons suggest that this is often still the prevalent mode of pedagogic practice (cf. also Norris et al. 1996, on Finnish schools).

The activity valued by teachers in these lessons is mental activity taking place in the heads of students, and the routine activity of hands – writing and raising them. A teacher may sigh to the researcher that 'the content of the book does not stay in their heads', and the metaphor of knowledge that sticks or does not in one's head often occurs in students' interviews:

> Mathematics doesn't stick in the head...I don't like to learn really, because I'm afraid that it will suddenly vanish from there [knowledge from the head]. And you have to remember such a lot all the time. And there's the pressure that you should do well, and such difficult tests. And then, some teachers think that their subject is the most important...I get tired, so much knowledge that I must get in my head each day. And I am afraid that I will forget it, it's so frustrating.
> (Auli)

> It kind of doesn't stay in one's head, when one writes at the same time.
> (Manu)

Manu's remark suggests, moreover, that activity in the head might exist in contrast to activity of the hand. Students are often aware of this dichotomy:

> *Jukka*: Well, I don't know, my father is a plumber, and it's not bad, that he's also handy.
> *Tuula*: Yes, aren't you quite handy yourself?
> *Jukka*: Yes.
> *Tuula*: Yes, so you find practical subjects much easier?
> *Jukka*: Yes, and others are good at reading, like they can keep all the words in their mind.
> *Tuula*: Do you have the feeling that they don't stay in your mind?
> *Jukka*: I suppose they would if I read.

Jukka's last reply indicates that he does not see himself as someone who cannot learn, but someone who does not read. Jukka is a working-class boy who respects the male manual work of his father. The hand/head dichotomy is related to the mental/manual division of labour, institutionalized in a division of the curriculum. Ivor Goodson shows how this division emerged in Britain in the eighteenth century as a division of mentalities; 'higher-order' mentalities were intellectual, abstract and active, whereas for the 'lower orders' they were sensual, concrete and passive (Goodson 1992). This dichotomy involves an ambivalence that is revealed in the language used in one of the London schools in our research: the term 'bod' is used for swot, or a 'brain'. Does it come from 'body', so providing an interesting subversion of mind/body duality?

Today, these links are not openly stated. Rather than saying that students are not achieving academically, it is considered more encouraging to say that they are 'practically talented'. A teacher, who has been in the profession since before comprehensive school reform in Finland, remembered at that time a division between 'those who went to the secondary school and those who stayed in the general school, who were good with their hands'. Teachers of practical subjects often challenge the hand/head dichotomy. One teacher argued in the interview that you do not know what to do unless you have 'the track of movement from the head to the hands'. Another urged the students to 'put eyes into their fingertips' when they were modelling an animal from clay. While this type of challenge is supported by learning theories, the emphasis might be related to teachers' attempts to raise the status of their subjects.

Some low-achieving boys constructed another body/mind dichotomy: when asked about their plans for the future, they expressed the desire to be sports professionals, ice hockey or football heroes. Media publicity about their fantastic salaries produces an alternative ambition when academic achievement seems impossible (Parker 1996).

It is no coincidence that those who challenge the norm of still bodies and the hierarchy of mind over body in the extracts above, are boys. Mind/body dualism has often been equated with a male/female dichotomy in western cultural thought. While in this case 'male' is related to mind, in the school context it is often boys who are expected to be (and in general are) more physically active, and girls more concerned with using their 'heads'. One boy argued: 'But boys, they all mess around and hit out at others, but girls just look and sit.' In another study on sexuality a similar paradox emerged:

The young men did express doubts and uncertainties about their physical attributes and performance, but they presented themselves as unproblematically embodied, in marked contrast to the alienation from their bodies found in the young women's accounts.

(Holland, Ramazanoglu, Sharpe and Thomson 1998)

Janet Holland and her colleagues (1998) argue that nothing could seem more embodied than the female reproductive function: menstruation, fertilization, the growth of the foetus within the body, birth. And young people make sense of their bodies through a discourse of difference that is rooted in the binary thinking of male–social–mind as opposed to female–nature–body. But there is a paradox in this binary thinking, since the interdependence and interlocking of the two to which deconstruction has alerted us, dissolves the dualism of male/female in favour of the male. In the social construction of heterosexuality it is the male who is embodied, in his body, and the female who is disembodied. (See also Martin 1989 on the fragmentation of women's bodies.)

Moving Bodies in Lessons

In physical education, sports, drama and dance, students are required not to sit still, but to move their bodies. 'Talented hands' are particularly important in handicrafts (in Finland) or design and technology (in England/Wales). Some movement takes place in home economics and science lessons. For these lessons silence and immobility are regarded as passivity – no matter what mental activity is taking place in the head (Gordon, Holland, Lahelma and Tolonen 1997).

This bodily movement or use of hands is not unrestricted; it is controlled by strict rules – sometimes as strict as the regulation of 'sitting still' for example in language or mathematics lessons. Science laboratories and technology classrooms have detailed rules on how to move around and handle equipment and machines. Hanging from his neck on the wall of one technical handicraft classroom was a little wooden man, painted as if he were covered in blood, with a note: 'This man ignored the rules of conduct.' The message is clear: lessons in which you use your hands and/or bodies are fraught with danger (cf. Delamont and Galton 1986). Your clothing can be at risk too. The periods when students are supposed to move their bodies in lessons are also those when they are expected to wear special clothing, for example in sports. In home economics and science lessons, the transition when 'theory' ends and 'practice' begins is often marked by the teacher telling students to put on protective clothing and headgear.

Although there are norms and regulations in lessons when movement is allowed, there is an overall feeling that students have more freedom. Raija said that she likes textile work, adding:

> and those subjects when you don't have to sit quietly in your place all the time, and when you don't have to know a lot of stuff by heart, where you can do a bit of your own work, and also those when you can do something in pairs or in a group.

Boys often named physical education (PE) and technical handicrafts as their favourite subjects because they were allowed to decide more independently what they did. Pete said:

> In technical handicrafts you have more freedom, and there isn't someone behind your back all the time telling you to do something. You can have a little break now and then. PE lessons are also quite nice 'cos we have quite a lot of freedom.

Our observation notes do not reveal many instances when we have seen enjoyment or desire in relation to the official school. Shrieks of pleasure or cheeks flushed with excitement were not usual when students were absorbed in the tasks of the official school; in lessons when they were moving their bodies, however, we did observe moments of enjoyment. One example was a rounders game in a London school. During this game, the teacher had to leave the gymnasium and control continued smoothly in her absence, with a student taking her role calling out scores and making decisions about play. The fact that students enjoyed the game and were playing with sheer physical gusto contributed to the lack of disruption. In this instance, male and female bodies were undertaking the same task, the differentiation was around skill and ability, so that the teams were constructed at the beginning of play by choosing first the most skilled and capable, regardless of sex; a male/female twin pair (large, powerful and good at games) were chosen first in turn to go into each team.[4]

In our research schools in Helsinki there were very few male teachers, and many of them taught 'moving bodies' subjects: PE, technical handicrafts, sciences or arts. Some of the lessons commonly taught by male teachers (PE and technical handicrafts) are normally taught in male groups. Physical power can frequently be made an issue in these lessons, and boys seem to admire their teachers' physical competence. In a technical lesson, for example, a male teacher showed his physical strength to the boys in a friendly, humorous way:

> Teacher notices that Matti is trying to wind a handle open but cannot manage it, teacher comes to help, says: 'Many people think that you need strength for this . . . [winds the handle open] . . . and that's true.'
>
> (ObsH)

The image of a gendered dichotomy between mind and body is reiterated here.

Learning about Bodies

The students whom we followed and interviewed in our schools were aged 12–14. For the dominant discourses, in for example the school textbooks studied by Sinikka Aapola (1997), adolescence is an age when bodies are changing dramatically, often causing 'emotional turmoil'. 'Puberty' frequently cropped up in teachers' interviews as some mysterious change, and was used as an explanation for behaviour:

> Jatta . . . she has kept it up [her good progress] . . . no signs of puberty can be seen yet. She's never late, no, she is kind of a very friendly girl.
>
> . . . during the eighth grade it seems that, suddenly, whoops, they have reached puberty, I have not even been conscious of it, it has happened in two months. I have to start from scratch.

Despite teachers' perceptions of the importance of bodies for adolescent students, there is relatively little about human bodies in the content of teaching for this age group. It is dealt with in biology, but normally not before the 9th grade, at age 14–15. Health education and sex education support some aspects of learning about bodies, but these subjects are in a marginal position in schools in both countries (Thomson 1995). Human bodies do come into focus, however, during other lessons. In home economics students are taught to make and consume healthy foods; in handicrafts they make themselves clothes, try them on, and measure their own and each others' bodies; in music lessons they are given detailed information on the mechanics of the ear to teach them that loud music can destroy their hearing, or learn to breathe effectively; and in art students are taught to draw or design bodies and feelings, as described in the observation notes below:

Teacher explains how you can express your feelings with the head, the angle of your skull, with your position. 'Think about the neck, jaw', demonstrates with his own head.

(ObsH)

Bodies are always gendered, as is learning about bodies. In a foreign languages classroom, the project work of two girls was hanging on the wall. It depicted a naked woman with arrows pointing to specific parts of the body and the danger of being too fat was described in the words of this particular language. In Finland it is girls who make themselves clothes, since boys seldom choose to do needlework. In a biology lesson, muscles were discussed and a bicep illustrated in a drawing. The muscle depicted left no doubt that it was that of a man, a strong man moreover, representing a particular type of masculinity. These examples indicate that if the 'gender-neutral' body is too fat or dressed beautifully it is female, and if physically strong, it is male.

Bodies in the Informal School

The informal school is often considered to be 'lurking' in the interstices of the official school. Student cultures and mutual interaction are seen to be points of vulnerability for teaching and learning. The informal school, however, is characterized by complex processes and multifarious alliances. Students make connections amongst each other; but they are also active in processes of differentiation. Diversity is constructed as hierarchical difference in the layer of the informal school as well as in the official school, although the hierarchies and positions afforded to students in the informal school may be different from those established by the official school.

Presentation of Bodies

The presentation of bodies is constructed through dress, and there is a substantial difference between British and Finnish schools in this regard. Uniforms stipulated by formal dress codes are typically worn in British schools, as in our research schools in London. In Finland there are no uniforms or formal dress codes. It is interesting in this context to explore processes of differentiation and normalization, as well as the desire to stand out or to be typical.

We describe the uniforms in our London schools in more detail elsewhere (Gordon, Holland and Lahelma 2000). Here our main focus is on ways in which formal and informal dress codes differentiate between genders. We speculate whether the differences are linked to notions of individuality and citizenship in Britain and Finland. In London the students were constantly trying to establish the difference through informalizing their clothing. In Helsinki informal dress codes operate to produce sameness.

In the London schools the uniform differentiated the genders: for example skirts for girls only (in both schools) and blazers for boys only (in one school). Girls were allowed to wear trousers in both schools; length of skirt and height of shoe heel was specified in each school for girls. Sports clothing were gender-differentiated. Apart from small studs or sleepers in the ears, earrings and particularly multiple earrings were disallowed, as were other items of jewellery. Make-up was against the rules.

In Helsinki both girls and boys tended to wear trousers (often loose) or jeans, and flannel shirts or big tops. Students themselves tend not to emphasize gender difference and sometimes the dress of girls and boys could be almost identical; for example, one boy commented that 'girls wear almost the same clothes as boys, loose trousers and all that'.

T-shirts were used to indicate difference. Boys often wore T-shirts with images and names of popular bands on them, and joking slogans. Girls also wore T-shirts, but with more decorative motifs. Many girls and boys arrived at school wearing tracksuits on days when they had PE, but some wore them at other times. Despite wearing similar clothing with little gender differentiation, the students were able to make fine distinctions on the basis of (for example) the width of trousers, looseness of tops and colours chosen.

In the London schools some girls feminized their uniforms. They made changes in terms of length of skirt (very short) and height of shoe heel (higher than regulation) and wore make-up and jewellery. The make-up could be very obvious, for example highly coloured nail varnish, but there was also very subtle use of make-up, often hard to detect.

Less feminine styles are prevalent in Finnish gender cultures than in Britain. Equality of opportunity politics and policies emphasizing uniformity and sameness promoting the notion of social citizenship may have had an effect in neutralizing sexual difference to a greater extent than in Britain. Young girls repeatedly emphasized comfort and practicality when they talked about their clothing in interviews. Cold winters discourage the wearing of skirts. Girls particularly dislike wearing pink, frills or lace – insignia of the feminine style of clothing in which they had often been dressed when younger (Tolonen 1998). Many girls suggested that they wanted to wear clothes they could relax in, and argued about this with their parents.

But whilst girls do not dress in a particularly feminine way, and they appreciate the comfort of trousers and simple tops, they also desire to be typical and normal. To stand out amongst the others is a potentially dangerous position; visibility renders a student open to comment. Henna explains:

> I like to dress differently from others. But when you come to school everybody says, 'why are you wearing those trousers?', you get comments like that.

fixing limit, + ing line

At times demarcation addresses femininity and what is interpreted as active display of heterosexuality, as Milla's comment suggests: 'I don't wear any crop tops – that doesn't suit my brainy style.' For 13-year-old girls gendered adulthood is a demarcation line; being too childish is not good, but being considered too precocious is also a subversion of typicality and normality.

Although informalization of the uniform was against the rules in the London schools, feminization was an option for young women and did not incite much comment or disciplinary procedures from teachers. The changes which the girls made to their uniforms, which pushed against its constraints and the rules to varying degrees, are associated with presenting a feminine and a sexual image: higher heels, shorter skirts, jewellery, a feminine hair style and adornment. But Annette presents a more threatening and individualistic use of her body:

> [She] has no desire to conform to the 'look' [approved presentation of femininity in the group, a modern, fashionable style; the other girls see her as emulating 1970s fashion, label her a 'hippie'; the boys label her a 'tart'] she threatens the boys and girls simultaneously. Annette produces anxiety because her 'bad taste' look reveals a femininity that is not natural but a hyper-femininity that is performed rather than embodied. In performing camp, Annette threatens masculinity [and femininity] because she reveals how arbitrary the sex/gender equation can be.
>
> (ObsL)[5]

Young women are under pressure more generally in society to construct their material bodies into a culturally coded model of femininity which is inscribed on their bodies through dress, make-up and dietary regimes.

LIT REVIEW + analysis

They need to manage their appearance carefully so that they do not breach the boundary between being acceptably attractive and overtly sexualized. Differences in cultural codes of femininity are demonstrated in formal codes of dress in London schools differentiating between girls and boys; where such formal codes are absent, the girls in Helsinki schools were less femininely dressed. In London, excess boyishness among girls was noted and controlled; in Helsinki, informal dress codes drew attention to heterosexual femininity in dress. Overtly sexual styles were controlled formally in London and informally in Helsinki.

Bodies in Contact

Bodies in contact are gendered bodies. Girls' embodied actions often appear more inclusive and collaborative than the actions of boys. Girls are more likely to touch each other in an evident attempt to make contact and are not likely to be challenged when they make contact. Girlhood and femininity are seen as interpersonal and intimate (Gordon, Holland and Lahelma forthcoming; Hey 1997).

Girls often groomed each other and themselves in the classroom. Teachers did comment on this, but not always. Much of the grooming takes place between lessons (in break and registration) but sometimes in lessons, including the use of hair spray and nail varnish.

Boys, on the other hand, do seem to be making a difference when their bodies are in contact. There is a great deal of pushing and shoving. But often in the slapping of backs and shoulders they are making embodied contact in a way that is considered acceptable in that it does not offend conceptions of appropriate masculinity. In field notes one of us commented on a boy who did transgress appropriate forms of touching:

> When girls started making a point of cuddling and hugging each other, giving each other a massage, doing each other's hair, etc., I saw Tero standing with two boys in his class, and stroking one boy's arm. 'Queer'...they called him. He moved away.
>
> (ObsH)

Anoop Nayak and Mary Kehily (1997) suggest that the ranges of homophobic displays utilized by boys in schools are part of the process of negotiating coherent masculinity. They are also bound up with attempts to negotiate particular positions in the hierarchical order among boys. Sexual cultures are implicated in the shaping of relations of schooling. The intensity of the homophobic displays results, Nayak and Kehily

women are against each (Competition in transup?)
Given against this that girls show more for each other

suggest, from the fraught nature of gender and sexual relations within school, as well as from the uncertainties and vulnerabilities of boys.

Mairtin Mac an Ghaill (1994: 4) suggests that dominant definitions of masculinity 'are affirmed within schools, where ideologies, discourses, representations and material practices systematically privilege boys and men'. A range of masculinities are contesting in this quest for dominance. Robert W. Connell (1989) notes that social power is accessible to those boys who are academically successful. Such a boy may, like Peter Redman, find a solution in 'muscular intellectualness'; a way of taking and making space by 'pushing people around intellectually' rather than physically (Redman and Mac an Ghaill 1997). Tarja Tolonen (1996) argues that it is difficult for boys to step aside from the social order of violence, though they can develop different stances in relation to it. Those male students who are less successful in gaining recognized spaces in the official school do so by claiming other sources of power resorting to aggression, sports and (hetero)sexism (Connell 1989). Bodies are constantly implicated in interaction among boys; some bodies are more successful than others in claiming their spaces and places. Those boys who are not successful in embodied contestation may find support from their position in the official school (as academically successful); they may step aside in various ways, possibly by making a joke of themselves to pre-empt others from doing so; or they may end up occupying a lonely, marginal position.

Bodies in the Physical School

Many of the school rules and regulations focus on aspects of bodily comportment; appropriate bodily control is a crucial element in the progress from unruly child/adolescent to responsible adult, from pupil to citizen. For school and society the most efficient way of producing the necessary 'docile bodies' is for the external surveillance and control to become internalized (Foucault 1980). Students learn what is acceptable and appropriate in relation to their bodies, voice and movement in school contexts, 'sit up straight', 'don't use that tiny voice, like a mouse', 'you do not talk when I am talking', 'I will wait for you to be quiet', 'walk, don't run', 'wipe that smile off your face'. Their bodies are constrained in time and space, they must learn the time-space paths that dictate their trajectory through the school day, which spaces they can and cannot be in at particular times, when and how they must be in and pass through the spaces of the school. Time-space paths are descriptions of how physical space is socially organized, and the school (and individual) timetables are maps to this temporal, spatial and social domain.

New students represent potential chaos in the context of the school's desired ordering of social space, and particular effort is put into imbuing them with the necessary disciplines through information, training, control and compulsion. (See Lahelma and Gordon 1997 and Gordon et al. 1999, for discussions of these processes in the first school day and the first two weeks of school.) This process is not entirely unwelcome to the students; many describe the school as huge and overwhelming when they first arrive compared with their often very small primary schools. But spatial habituation and routinization makes the size and space more manageable, and in this way students begin the process of becoming professional pupils, even smooth operators on their own patch (Gordon and Lahelma 1996).

As they become more experienced in the ways of their particular school, students may also challenge and play with the time-space paths. The physical space of the school may provide opportunities for inappropriate movement, taking the longest and most tortuous route to arrive at the next lesson for example, or the shortest but forbidden. On one occasion the researcher followed a group of giggling students to a music lesson, only to discover later that they had led her through a seriously forbidden area. Her desire to get to the correct room in time and ignorance of both where it was and spatial prohibitions, provided them with the opportunity to demonstrate both good manners (in helping her out) and transgression. Further examples of challenge include bodily removal from the school when compelled to be there. In one school a group of girls slipped out of school through an open window to engage in 'illicit' activities. At another, an announcement was made prohibiting students from sneaking out through a hole in the perimeter fence and visiting a nearby shop. The fence was repeatedly repaired only for the hole to be reopened by students. They were told that dire consequences would follow any further transgressions of this type, and accused of the crime of destruction of school property. If they were caught, their parents would be called upon to pay for repairs.

For the outsider, entering a school during a break between lessons without knowledge of the time-space paths, the impression can be one of chaos, of movement and sound, with a strong sense of embodiment and the physicality of relatively large numbers of young people walking, running, playing, talking, shouting, laughing. This sound and movement is stilled when the students return to their classrooms for lessons; sounds are muted, controlled within the individual classroom, rendered as distant shouts from the sports field, snatches of music, song or voice as doors open and close. Once within the space of the classroom the bodily constraints can fall heavily on young people; they must sit still, work quietly, follow instructions and subdue bodily needs or desires. Some teachers employ methods which allow movement and noise in the classroom and are able to maintain their overall control in this context; others may lose control as students refuse to accept the constraints the teacher wishes to impose on them (Gordon et al. 1999).

The body is a major site of regulation and control in the school; but the school also provides multiple spaces and contexts for the exercise of agency through the deployment of the body, often in the same moment of regulation and control. Girls might use the requirements of the formal school to escape peer-based pressure for gender differentiation, for example, using the space provided by the 'abstract pupil'. Alternatively, the attempts of the school to 'normalize' pupils (Ryan 1991), for example by controlling the expression of their sexuality, may be subverted (in this instance) by the student using the body as an expression of sexual identity (through very 'masculine' or 'feminine' behaviour or presentation). In one class, for example, a group of girls is described as the 'girls gang'; 'six of the girls who often sit together, and act as "girls" publicly in the class, blushing, giggling, gossiping, often look at me [the researcher] in the class but never speak' (ObsL). Other girls adopt 'girlie' actions and tactics. In one science class where the group, both boys and girls, had hated wearing goggles, the teacher finally allowed them to take the goggles off row by row. The first row of boys sighed, 'Thank God'; the second row of girls squealed with delight (ObsL) (see Measor 1983).

It has been argued that the school is a prime site for the construction of gender difference and normative heterosexuality (Delamont 1990; Epstein 1994; Connell 1995; Epstein and Johnson 1998) and while displays of masculinity or femininity might transgress the requirement for the muting of the behaviour or display of sexuality, it paradoxically might meet the requirement for support of gender differentiation and normative heterosexuality. But the representation of femininity and masculinity can also be a space for the expression of agency – it can be played with: in a science lesson, the teacher brought a dead lizard in a specimen tray to a table of girls, who squealed and pulled away at the sight. But the observer later saw them calmly inspecting and touching the dead reptile as they wrote up their notes for the lesson. 'Hyper'-femininity might be deployed in such a way as to present a threat to the normative femininity of 'squeamishness', grooming and the relatively subtle, or at least acceptable, use of style.

In a more extreme case, one girl seemed to fall foul of what Lesko has seen as the sexualization of deviance where the lower-status girl is seen as 'loose', 'wild' and 'hard' and this is equated with sexual pollution (Lesko 1988). The teachers perceived Mandy as a major disruption in the classroom, displays a range of severely undesirable traits, all of which involved inappropriate deployment of the body. She was well known as a truant, who smoked during breaks and in between classes, refused to do her work, talked continuously through lessons, walked around the classroom, chewed gum, wore make-up and long black boots, combed her hair during class, drew pictures and sang songs. They objected to her deep, husky voice which she defended, arguing that 'the teachers don't like the way I act like a boy. I've been sent to a child psychologist but there is nothing wrong with me, my voice is normal, it's a cockney accent.' She was characterized by others as being like her mother, 'promiscuous' (ObsL). ~~Characterized by having transient sexual partners/unselected~~

Girls might also be adumbrating a version of femininity, not so highly sexualized, but somewhat at odds with acceptable, normative femininity – boldly taking up space (as in the case of a group of 'big, bold, beautiful girls' in Finland) or being boisterous and noisy (acting in ways which might be more expected of boys). In one instance the teacher reported the whole class, but particularly the girls, for being noisy and misbehaved, when, from the observer's perspective, the boys had been very noisy, active, practically ignoring the lesson whilst developing an elaborate game with science equipment. The girls, however, had been 'a bit punchy today, lively, talkative' (ObsL).

This gendered display may be seen more usually in support of appropriate gender behaviour. In the following extract, the researcher is surprised to see almost a parody of male/female embodied differentiation:

> One whole class enacted embodied masculinity and femininity whilst waiting for a science lesson. The classroom opened onto a courtyard between two separate sections of the school buildings. The girls stood quietly, talking softly, in an orderly row outside the door of the classroom. The boys leapt up to and swung on girders that formed part of the structure of the courtyard. The separation in space, and the bodily deployment was extreme in its stereotypical gendered display, so much so that the teacher commented on it on coming upon the girls waiting at the door 'What, have I got an all-girls class today?'
>
> (ObsL)

Sport provides a space in the official school where bodies are central, and movement is allowed, prescribed. Here again students can grasp opportunities for agency, and use the symbols and associations of sport as part of their identity construction. Two boys in particular, as new-comers to a school, took their space and place through self-definition as the skilled, athletic, sporting, male body. In each case they carried that self-definition into non-sporting spaces in the school, one spinning a basketball, instrument and symbol of his skill, on his finger in corridors and classrooms. The other, amongst many examples, miming a range of potential sporting situations involving a ball, with great skill, physical dexterity and grace, using as the ball a piece of dough from which he was supposed to be making a pie in a cookery lesson.

Students were allowed to eat the product of their efforts in cookery lessons (part of Design and Technology), but eating was another bodily activity severely constrained in what could be eaten when and where in the school. One researcher felt a *frisson* at the transgression of the norm when two boys arrived very late for a lesson, and explained that they had had to have a drink. Surprisingly, the teacher let this go with a sarcastic rejoinder. But chewing gum was not a light matter; it was in fact a serious ongoing struggle in all the schools to stop students chew-ing gum in class. Students were skilled at chewing without appearing to do so, and even, as one demonstrated to a researcher, slipping the gum back into the throat should a teacher go so far as to search their mouth for the gum to prove their guilt on denial. This can be seen as an invasion of the student's personal space (and body) by teachers, and an extreme response in developing new skills of bodily concealment for the student.

We have argued that in the process of producing the abstract pupil, the school and the pupil together can produce the professional pupil (Lahelma and Gordon 1997). In the following instance, chewing gum forms the centre piece of an exchange between a professional teacher and a professional pupil. The students entered the classroom and went to their desks. The teacher, seated at her desk at the front, caught the eye of a girl, a look passed between them, and the girl walked to the front of the class and spat out her chewing gum into the waste bin. Not a word had been spoken. This teacher was in fact expert in the use of the gaze to control, and employed amongst others the admonishing, accusatory and regretful gaze in her skilful control of the class. In a similar instance in another school, a boy's immediate response to the requirements of the teacher's gaze led another boy to comment to him: 'What have you got, a secret eye language?' This teacher also used more dramatic techniques, banging a board cleaner (or a ruler, whatever came to hand) on the desk with a loud noise to call the class to a halt and silence. He also moved students around physically when they did not do as he wished – 'Move, there, now, take only your book' – pointing to the front of the class (ObsL).

Conclusions

We have argued that education systems are required to produce the future citizens of the nation-state, and in that process they are expected to both regulate – maintain stability and the status quo, and to emancipate – promote social change and individual mobility. The 'citizen' is a neutral, universal term that denotes individuals who are equal and abstracted from their social locations. But human beings are embedded in social relations in diverse ways and diversity becomes difference when it is hierarchically organized. Socially, culturally and sexually some positions are invested with more privilege than others. We have seen in our analysis of the body in the everyday life of the school, that all elements of the school, the official, the informal and the physical, play their part in producing difference, particularly in the examples we have given, gender difference. Embedded in the curriculum, materials and regulations of the official school are 'naturalized' gender differences in descriptions, portrayals and expectation of the body and its dress and decoration. Entwined around the official school, the informal school produces its own differentiation, if the official dress code is uniform, then it is subtly or more openly transformed to display gender, masculinity and femininity. If there is no formal dress code, even more subtle pressures may be brought to bear for students to produce the acceptably covered male or female body. The ways that bodies are deployed in the informal school is gendered, certain types of bodily movement and contact is acceptable and appropriate for girls and for boys, and transgression of the normative across the gender divide, or even in dramatizing movement and display, or performing hyper-sexuality within gender, can bring opprobrium. And these constraints of dress, movement and voice are incorporated into the regulations of the school, and the gendered expectations of participants. Girls take up less space and move less than boys in lessons where immobility is expected; 'boisterous' girls, who take up their space, are noticed, whereas boisterous boys are the norm.

Within these multifaceted layers of bodily constraint and control, however, we see from the examples above that individual students exercise agency, selecting modes of deploying their bodies to create their subjectivity, using compliance with and/or transgression of both official and informal requirements in that process.

To return to the metaphor of the dance, if we imagine the dance of the school as a ballet taking place in a theatre, the physical school is the stage, with its constraints of space, lighting and curtains, which provides the possibilities and limits for taking both official and informal steps. The official school can be seen as the formal dance with the corps de ballet moving in unison, without soloists, doing their best to adhere to the steps they have been taught. In the informal school some of the dancers change their steps, moving their bodies in ways that create new types of interaction, or new individual, solo performances. These new steps may be interesting and imaginative, pleasurable and engaging, but they are not, in the specific predetermined context, acceptable. It is through these new steps, however, these variations and novel interactions that subjectivity and identity can be constructed.

Notes

1 The other members of the Finnish research team were Pirkko Hynninen, Tuija Metso, Tarja Palmu and Tarja Tolonen. Janet Holland worked with Nicole Vitellone and Kay Parkinson.
2 The study is described in detail in Gordon, Holland and Lahelma 2000.
3 Field note observations in the text are designated ObsL for London and ObsH for Helsinki. The names of participants in the research have been changed.
4 We should not forget, of course, the effects on individuals of not being chosen for the team.
5 Interpretation and comments on observation notes in this school, Vitellone 1995. See Butler 1990; Holland et al. 1994.

References

Aapola, S. 1997. 'Mature Girls and Adolescent Boys? Deconstructing Discourses of Adolescence and Gender', *Young* 5: 50–68.

Butler, J. 1990. *Gender Trouble: Feminism and the Subversion of Identity.* London: Routledge.

Connell, R. W. 1989. 'Cool Guys, Swots and Wimps: The Interplay of Masculinity and Education', *Oxford Review of Education* 15: 291–303.

Connell, R. W. 1995. *Masculinities.* Cambridge: Polity Press.

Davies, B. 1990. 'Agency as a Form of Discursive Practice: A Classroom Scene Observed'. *British Journal of Sociology of Education* 11: 341–61.

Davies, B. and Hunt, R. 1994. 'Classroom Competencies and Marginal Positionings'. *British Journal of Sociology of Education* 15: 389–408.

Delamont, S. 1990. *Sex Roles and the School*. London: Routledge.

Delamont, S. and Galton, M. 1986. *Inside the Secondary Classroom*. London: Routledge & Kegan Paul.

Donald, J. 1992. *Sentimental Education: Schooling, Popular Culture and the Regulation of Liberty*. London: Verso.

Epstein, D. 1994. *Challenging Lesbian and Gay Inequalities in Education*. Buckingham: Open University Press.

Epstein, D. and Johnson, R. 1998. *Schooling Sexualities*. Buckingham & Philadelphia: Open University Press.

Foucault, M. 1980. *Power/Knowledge*. London: Harvester Wheatsheaf.

Giddens, A. 1985. 'Time, Space and Regionalisation', in D. Gregory and J. Urry (eds.), *Social Relations and Spatial Structures*. London: Macmillan.

Goodson, I. F. 1992. 'On Curriculum Form: Notes Toward a Theory of Curriculum', *Sociology of Education* 65: 66–75.

Gordon, T. 1996. 'Citizenship, Difference and Marginality in Schools: Spatial and Embodied Aspects of Gender Construction', in P. F. Murphy and C. V. Gipps (eds.), *Equity in the Classroom*. London & Washington: Falmer Press.

Gordon, T., Holland, J. and Lahelma, E. 2000. *Making Spaces: Citizenship and Others in Schools*. London: Macmillan.

Gordon, T., Holland, J., Lahelma, E. and Tolonen, T. 1997. 'Hidden from Gaze: Problematising Action in the Classroom'. Paper presented at the British Sociological Association Annual Conference, York, 7–10 April 1997.

Gordon, T. and Lahelma, E. 1996. ' "School is like an Ants' Nest" – Spatiality and Embodiment in Schools', *Gender and Education* 8: 301–10.

Gordon, T., Lahelma, E., Hynninen, P., Metso, T., Palmu, T. and Tolonen, T. 1999. *Learning the Routines: Professionalisation of Newcomers to Secondary School. Qualitative Studies in Education*.

Gordon, T., Holland, J. and Lahelma, E. forthcoming. 'Friends or Foes? Interpreting Relations between Girls in School. 'Gender and Sexualities', *Studies in Educational Ethnography*, Vol. 3.

Green, A. 1990. *Education and State Formation: The Rise of Education Systems in England, France and the USA*. London: Macmillan.

Hey, V. 1997. *The Company She Keeps. An Ethnography of Girls' Friendships*. Buckingham & Philadelphia: Open University Press.

Holland, J., Ramazanoglu, C., Sharpe, S. and Thomson, R. 1994. 'Power and Desire: The Embodiment of Female Sexuality', *Feminist Review*, 46: 21–38.

Holland, J., Ramazanoglu, C., Sharpe, S. and Thomson, R. 1998. *The Male in the Head: Young People, Heterosexuality and Power*. London: The Tufnell Press.

Jackson, P. 1968. *Life in Classrooms*. New York: Holt, Reinhard and Winston.

Lahelma, E. and Gordon, T. 1997. 'First Day in Secondary School: Learning to be a "Professional Pupil"'. *Educational Research and Evaluation* 3: 119–39.

Lesko, N. 1988. 'The Curriculum of the Body: Lessons from a Catholic High School', in L. G. Roman and L. K. Christian-Smith with E. Ellsworth, *Becoming Feminine*. London: Falmer Press.

Mac an Ghaill, M. 1994. *The Making of Men*. Buckingham: Open University Press.

Martin, E. 1989. *The Woman in the Body*. Milton Keynes: Open University Press.

Measor, L. 1983. 'Gender and the Sciences: Pupils Gender-based Conceptions of School Subjects' in M. Hammersley and A. Hargreaves (eds.), *Curriculum Practice: Some Sociological Case Studies*. Lewes: Falmer Press.

Nayak, A. and Kehily, M. J. 1997. 'Masculinities and Schooling: Why are Young Men so Homophobic?', in D. L. Steinberg, D. Epstein and R. Johnson (eds.), *Border Patrols: Policing the Boundaries of Heterosexuality.* London: Cassell.

Norris, N., Aspland, R., Macdonald, B., Shostak, J. and Zamorski, B. 1996. *An Independent Evaluation of Comprehensive Curriculum Reform in Finland.* National Board of Education. Helsinki: Yliopistopaino.

Parker, A. 1996. 'The Construction of Masculinity within Boys' Physical Education', *Gender and Education* 8: 141–15.

Redman, P. and Mac An Ghaill, M. 1997. 'Educating Peter: The Making of a History Man', in D. L. Steinberg, D. Epstein and R. Johnson (eds.), *Border Patrols: Policing the Boundaries of Heterosexuality.* London: Cassell.

Ryan, J. 1991. 'Observing and Normalizing: Foucalt, Discipline and Inequality is Schooling', *The Journal of Educational Thought*, 25: 104–19.

Thomson, R. 1995. 'Unholy Alliances: The Recent Politics of Sex Education', in L. Dawtrey, J. Holland and M. Hammer with S. Sheldon, *Equality and Inequality in Education Policy.* Clevedon: Multilingual Matters in association with The Open University.

Tolonen, T. 1996. 'Väkivaltaa ja sosiaalista järjestystä' (Violence and Social Order). In T. Hoikkala (ed.), *Miehenkuvia: Välähdyksiä, nuorista miehistä*, Suomessa. Helsinki: Gaudeamus.

Tolonen, T. 1998. 'Ideal Boys and Ideal Girls: Youth Cultural Descriptions of Embodiment'. Paper presented at the BSA Annual Conference Making Sense of the Body: Theory, Research and Practice, Edinburgh, April.

6
Feared and Revered: Media Representations of Racialized and Gendered Bodies – A Case Study

Sarah Neal

Introduction

This chapter examines how the newspaper media chose to represent two individuals who were involved, in very different ways, in a particularly tragic event in the early 1990s. Central to the chapter is a concern as to what extent certain notions of race and gender shaped those representations. In November 1992 Christopher Clunis, a young man severely mentally ill with schizophrenia, walked onto the platform at Finsbury Park tube station in North London and approached Jonathan Zito, a young man, completely unknown to him, who was waiting for a train with his brother. Christopher Clunis fatally stabbed Jonathan Zito three times in the face piercing his eye. Christopher Clunis, who made no attempt to leave the scene of the killing, was immediately arrested. Jonathan Zito's death and the circumstances which led to it were to dominate populist and policy debates around mental health care provision throughout the early and mid-1990s. During this period a six-month NHS inquiry into the care and treatment of Christopher Clunis was set up and the published report of the inquiry appeared in 1994. This chapter argues that a number of reasons can be identified as contributing to placing Jonathan Zito's death at the heart of public concern. First, and most obviously, was Jonathan Zito himself, an innocent victim who was killed in a horrific manner both in terms of the actual injuries and because the attack took place in the daytime in the 'everyday' urban location of a tube station platform. Second, Jonathan Zito's widow, Jayne Zito, a beautiful[1] and articulate young white woman who had been married to Jonathan Zito for just three months became an increasingly public figure. (Importantly, Jayne Zito was herself knowledgeable and experienced in the field of mental health care.)

Third, Christopher Clunis was a young African/Caribbean who was also of 'considerable height and powerful build' (Ritchie et al. 1994: 8). Finally, widespread public anxiety as a response to an individual tragedy does not usually occur in a social vacuum and the extent of concern over Jonathan Zito's death can be linked to broader issues of mental health care systems. The passing of the 1990 NHS and Community Care Act had signalled a significant shift in public policy on mental health care. This shift saw the move away from the old and established strategy of containing mentally ill people in institutions towards the practice of care in the community. Anxieties about the proximity of madness and its associations with danger occupy a specific place in both the individual and the collective pschye. Unsurprisingly, the care in the community policy heightened populist concern as to what extent the public could be protected from madness. The events of December 1992 powerfully symbolized the apparent inability of the new system of care in the community to protect the public.

Clearly the body in a variety of interpretations underpins these variables. The gendered, feminized body of Jayne Zito; the ultimately vulnerable body of Jonathan Zito; the racialized, dangerous body of Christopher Clunis and the sane/healthy (public) body ever threatened by the mad/diseased (Other) body. The cogency of the combination of these themes, packaged by the media, resulted in an NHS inquiry and, seven years later, it retains a highly evocative place in populist and policy agendas. For example, whilst writing broadly in defence of the care in the community programme, Professor Ray Rowden acknowledges flaws in the implementation of the policy, but highlights public anxieties about safety: 'in recent years . . . high-profile cases of killings by mentally ill people, *most notably Christopher Clunis*, have conspired to fragment consensus and undermine public confidence' (*Guardian*, 9 March 1998; my emphasis). Similarly in media reporting of the present government's decision to review the care in the community system it is the Christopher Clunis case which is consistently used as the primary example of the failure of the care in the community policy (see, for example, *Guardian*, 25 July 1998). The media's coverage of the Zito/ Clunis story involved the articulation of a range of anxieties which, drawing on postcolonial notions race and gender, came together to offer particular frameworks for public understanding. It is this process that the chapter now examines. However, before doing so it is crucial to clarify that the commentary offered here is about media representations of bodies (for, as Dyer notes, 'to represent people is to represent bodies': 1998: 14) and the ways in which historical notions of race and gender inform those representations in contemporary settings. It is not about Jayne Zito or Christopher Clunis as private individuals. Although in asserting this, it is necessary to recognize that such a distinction can (and did) become uncomfortable when the site of sociological analysis is of media coverage of named people who have been tragically involved in an event of immense horror, personal loss and private grief. This discomfort does not detract from the legitimacy of investigating the media coverage and sense-making, but it does (and must) act as a sensitizing voice at the shoulder of the investigator.

Media, Representation and Methodology

The relationship between the media, race, representations, cultural myths and common-sense stereotypes has been extensively commented on elsewhere (Hartmann and Husbands 1974; van Dijk 1991; Fiske 1994; Campbell 1995; Fergason 1997; Gabriel 1998) and there is insufficient space to rehearse these debates in depth here. However, it is important to refer briefly to some of the key themes which have occupied the literature. Perhaps the most obvious of these is the way in which the media and the representations which it offers are heavily anchored to the wider socio/economic/political contexts in which it operates. It is the specific contexts which allow the particular representations and/or stereotypes their potency, their ability to construct forms of (common) sense and encourage particular interpretations. As Fergason notes:

> media representations of issues of race are a structured part of evolving, socially based epistemologies. They also relate to material relations and lived existence. Media discourses about race and normality are shared and circulate amongst media producers, public figures and members of the public constituted as audiences.
>
> (1998: 174)

In his focus on the ways in which discourses of whiteness appear in, and via, various forms of media Gabriel similarly argues:

> media representations are part and parcel of everyday culture including the material fabric of institutional culture. Media do not merely 'report' economic restructuring, political upheavals, environmental crises, migration and displacement ... They have done so in ways which have enhanced the experience of dilution, loss, pursposelessness

and imminent catastrophe. The media has thus played a key role in buttressing whiteness with selective versions of national culture: by mobilising deep-seated anxieties and insecurities.

(1998: 11)

The media coverage of the death of Jonathan Zito and the circumstances of the tragedy linked directly into a particular set of public anxieties over a changed mental health care system that were being expressed during the early 1990s. The media representations of the individual bodies involved further nourished these anxieties by tapping into the broader 'discursive reserves' (Fergason 1998) of race and gender. This is not to argue that race or gender were openly named issues in the media reporting of the events surrounding Jonathan Zito's death, but rather to argue that within the visual and written media text it is possible to track a systematic, but coded, *invitation* to make a raced and gendered sense of the Clunis/Zito incident, an invitation to make what Hall (1990) has called 'a racist chain of meaning'. Pictorial images, headlines and captions are crucial elements of this invitation process as these act as 'cueing devices' which are able to invoke certain discursive reserves (Fergason 1998: 130). When Butler (1993: 16) argues, in relation to the Rodney King video, that 'seeing' is not necessarily only an 'act of direct perception but the racial production of the visible, the workings of racial constraints on what it means to "see"'' this is applicable to the reporting of the Clunis/Zito tragedy and the wider landscapes of media (covert and overt) representations of race and gender.

Transported into the public (populist) gaze via the media it is the coverage of the three interconnected events of Jonathan Zito's death, Christopher Clunis's trial, Jayne Zito and the campaign for a public inquiry that provides the focus for the primary data collection and analysis of this chapter. In other words, my task is to interpret the media interpretations of these events which took place between December 1992 and July 1993 and examine the 'cultural meaning-making' (Campbell 1995) that the media reporting gave these events. I examined five newspapers – *Daily Mirror, Evening Standard, Daily Mail, Guardian, Independent* – for each of the three key moments: Jonathan Zito's death in December; Christopher Clunis's trial in June 1993; Jayne Zito and the campaign for a public inquiry in July 1993. Commonality of the central themes which the media chose to highlight, in both the written and the visual text in its coverage of these events, was my primary framework of analysis.

Racialized and Gendered Bodies

Black Dangerousness

Within racialized and gendered discourses the black[2] (male and female) body represents a number of fantasies which ambiguously veer between fascination and fear, desire and danger, attraction and repulsion (Gil man 1985; Young 1994; Pieterse 1997; Nwekto-Simmonds 1997). However, the historically constructed link between the black male body and the notions of threat and danger has more overtly dominated white imaginations. One of the most recent and bizarre examples of this domination was been the 1992 acquittal of the Los Angeles Police Department Officers in the Rodney King verdict in which a member of the jury claimed that King 'was in complete control' and 'directing all the action' (cited in Williams, 1993: 51). In seeking to offer an explanation of the verdict and the position of that juror, Butler persuasively argues that the black male body is fundamentally associated with menace and threat within 'white paranoia'. Within this context, then:

> the police are thus structurally placed to protect whiteness against violence, where violence is the imminent action of that black male body. And because within this imaginary schema, the police protect whiteness, their own violence cannot be read as violence; because the black male body, prior to any video, is the site and source of danger, a threat, the police effort to subdue this body, even if in advance, is justified regardless of the circumstances. (1993: 18)

It is possible to apply Butler's analysis to the death of Winston Rose in London in 1981. Winston Rose was a young African/Caribbean who was suffering from mental crisis. The family doctor decided a period of compulsory hospitalization was needed and called in Social Services, psychiatrists and the police for the sectioning. Winston Rose, who had no history of violent behaviour and who was not displaying any violent tendencies, was actually sitting in his garden shed reading when, executing the Section Order, the police officers jumped on him and restrained him in an illegal neck-hold which choked him to death. Explaining the reasons for the type of extreme action used, one of officers stated: 'all I knew was that he was big and coloured' (cited in Francis 1993: 192). The apparent simplicity of the racism of this statement is significant in itself because it obscures the complexity of the connections between physicality and race. Both the death of Winston

Rose and the Rodney King verdict demonstrate the extent to which the black male body, irrespective of its actions, occupies a consistent place as a signifier of danger (requiring pre-emptive violent containment) within white racial phobias (Hawkins and Thomas 1991).

Winston Rose is also important here as he raises the spectre of madness. While the rapist and the mugger are racialized folk devils who continue to stalk contemporary urban landscapes, more recently these have been joined by another folk devil – the violent schizophrenic. In the 1990s the potent fusion of insanity and blackness has secured a place within populist racialized discourses and the practices of various state-sponsored agencies such as the police and the psychiatric systems. For example, African Caribbean people are diagnosed with a major psychotic illness at five times the rate of the general population, and 60 per cent of those black people who do enter the psychiatric system do so via Section 136 of the 1983 Mental Health Act. Yet only 10–15 per cent of the general population enter psychiatric care through this compulsory route (Sashidaran 1994: 3).[3] As a result, Francis argues that in the late twentieth century 'madness has become synonymous with blackness' (1993: 179), which echoes Gilman's assertion that 'the mad black is the nexus at which all [white] fears coalesce' (1985: 136). This process has meant that discourses surrounding mental illness and dangerous/violent behaviour, as with discourses around immigration and law and order, evoke notions of race without directly identifying race as an issue (Gilroy 1987; Barker 1991; Gillborn 1995). Media coverage and interpretations of Christopher Clunis and his killing of Jonathan Zito occurred very much within this *racialized* process, effectively evoking race rather than explicitly naming race as the basis of an explanatory framework of the event.

As the story of the muddled and ad hoc care given to Christopher Clunis by the psychiatric services began to come to light, the crucial question for the media became why a schizophrenic with a past history of violence was being cared for within the community. This was, of course, a legitimate question, but it is not possible to divorce it from the wider social relations in which it is inevitably placed. Given this, what was significant in the media's presentation of this question was its formulation around and evocation of the concepts of freedom and imprisonment. For example, the *Daily Mail* (29 June 1993) devoted a whole page to the trial of Christopher Clunis and, in an apparent echo of Jayne Zito, headlined its coverage with 'Why was he *set free* to kill my husband?' The sub-heading below the visuals accompanying this story continued the freedom theme: 'Widow's question as psychotic knifeman is *locked away at last*' (my emphasis). The concept is employed again by the *Mail* a month later when it detailed Virginia Bottomley's (then Minister for Health) order for an investigation into the case: 'Inquiry ordered into *freed* schizophrenic who killed musician' (22 July 1993; my emphasis). For the *Evening Standard* (30 June 1993) too, Christopher Clunis was the 'killer who *roamed free*' (my emphasis). Similarly the *Independent* (19 July 1993) used its front page to state: 'The tragic scandal of a schizophrenic killer that *nobody stopped*' (my emphasis).

In foregrounding the question of the freedom of Christopher Clunis rather than, or as well as, the question of the care and treatment he was receiving it is possible to identify an agenda which is actually questioning how a situation had arisen in which a large, young, black, mad man had not been contained within either the mental health care or the criminal justice systems. In other words, there is a certain degree of incredulity that is expressed in the media coverage which is not only about the failings of a psychiatric system to treat a severely mentally ill person, but also about the failings of a psychiatric system to detain/ contain an individual who appeared to be the very embodiment of a *visible* and *traditional* source of danger and menace in white imaginations.

The media used the concepts of size, blackness and madness to evoke the obviousness of Clunis as a social danger. It was this obviousness which fed directly into the expressions of incredulity as to Christopher Clunis's 'freedom' and his being cared for in the community. For example, the *Independent* devoted a whole inside page detailing its own in-depth investigations of 'events that led to a random killing' (19 July 1993). The theme of the investigation was that responsibility for Christopher Clunis was constantly transferred, with little or no co-ordination between geographical areas, or between doctors, social workers and psychiatrists. It is a theme which is reflected in its headline: 'Passing the buck until an innocent man died'.

Importantly, Christopher Clunis's body is drawn for the reader at a very early stage of the article (second paragraph). Describing the scene at Finsbury Park tube station minutes before Jonathan Zito was attacked, the article notes that 'several passengers became alarmed by his size [he was more than 6ft tall and weighed 18 stone], sloppy appearance and erratic, unnerving behaviour'. Race is the unspoken variable here, but a small head-and-shoulders picture of Clunis is located directly to the side of this information. Through a working of written and visual text the article immediately foregrounds the *obviousness* of Clunis as a figure of danger and menace: large, black, disturbed. There is a colonial undertow within the language used to describe why Clunis alarmed passengers on the tube station platform – his physicality ('size', 'sloppy appearance') and his demeanour ('erratic, unnerving behaviour') evoke notions of primitiveness, wildness and, ultimately, of the uncivilized. Similar themes are evident in the *Mail*'s reporting of Christopher Clunis's trial. The *Mail* tells the reader how 'eighteen stone Clunis, from North London, had been discharged from at least nine mental units over five years despite deteriorating psychosis and a long history of violence involving a fascination for knifes'. Again it is possible to see here a fusion of physicality, insanity and danger which is connected to, and framed by, the notions of race. The suggestion or evocation of racially embodied black madness and danger is made via the incorporation, as in the *Independent*, of the visual text. Placed significantly *between* photographs of Jayne Zito on one side and Jonathan and Jayne Zito on their wedding day on the other, a head- and-shoulders picture of Christopher Clunis stares solemnly out, directly above the sub-headline which identifies him as the 'psychotic knifeman'.[4]

What dominates the media coverage of the death of Jonathan Zito is the presentation of Christopher Clunis as a symbol which evokes historically based racial stereotypes relating to Otherness, insanity and social danger. For the media, the issue is not only the inability of a mental health care system to protect the (sane) public from the insane, but the inability of the mental health care (and criminal justice) systems to protect the public from such an obvious figure of threat and menace. For the media Christopher Clunis was much more than a severely mentally ill person in need of appropriate care which was not made available to him with ensuing terrible and tragic consequences. Placed within the public gaze Christopher Clunis operated within a racialized landscape in which he embodied, at both a literal and a symbolic level, postcolonial anxieties about blackness and madness.

Given this, the high-profile media campaign for a public inquiry into the care and treatment of Christopher Clunis has a duality to it. In part it represents legitimate concerns over the quality and competence of mental health care provision, but in part it also represents a wider, more complex raced agenda in which fear and fascination are central, 'for the ill as well as the black have a fascination for Western culture' (Gilman 1985: 148). This duality is best illustrated in the illustration accompanying the *Independent* (23 July 1993) 'Comment' article headlined 'Clunis: the wider failures', in which the psychiatrist for the defence in the Clunis case argues the need for a full public inquiry. This visual takes the form of a collage in which the three lines of repeated head and shoulders shots of Christopher Clunis, Jonathan Zito and Jayne Zito form the background to superimposed roughly torn newspaper clippings which scream a variety of headlines relating to mental illness, violence (rape, attacks, killings) and failures in mental health care policy. The seeming chaos of the illustration belies a coherent fusion of populist anxieties which blend concepts of race, gender, mental illness and safety. However, the extent to which Christopher Clunis, in himself, symbolized the mythologized nexus of western anxieties involved the representation of his antithetical cultural construction – white feminine vulnerability. It is on the racialized body of Jayne Zito that I now focus.

White Feminine Vulnerability

The academic focus on whiteness has emerged as a relatively new area of analysis and although the analysis of whiteness has tended to come from the areas of gender (Ware 1993: Frankenburg, 1993), class (Roediger 1991; 1994) cultural and lesbian and gay studies (Morrison, 1992; Davy 1995; Dyer, 1997) the unifying notion behind such the focus is an interrogation of the meaning of whiteness and the place of whiteness within ideas of race and racialized discourses. As Frankenburg crucially notes: 'any system of differentiation shapes those on whom it bestows privilege as those whom it oppresses. White people are raced just as men are gendered. And in a social context where white people have too often viewed themselves as non-racial or racially neutral it is crucial to look at the racialness of the white experience' (1993: 1). Similarly Dyer argues that 'we may be on our way to genuine hybridity, multiplicity without (white) hegemony and it may be where we want to get to – but we aren't there yet, and we won't get there until we see whiteness, see its power, its particularity and limitedness, put it in its place and end its rule. This is why studying whiteness matters' (1997: 4). The work of theorists such as Morrison (1992) and Said (1978) has examined the ways in which white discourses place the racialized (black) Othered subject into a space which operates to emphasize the hierarchical difference with the white subject. However, some caution is required when relocating the analytical gaze onto whiteness, especially when exploring representations of bodies which are constructed against each other. In other words, care is needed to avoid invoking an analytical framework in which 'whiteness is only white, or only matters, when it is explicitly set against non-white . . . whiteness reproduces itself as whiteness in all texts all of the time' (Dyer 1997: 13). Solomos and Back warn too that 'there is a danger of reifying whiteness and reinforcing a unitary idea of "race". In order to avoid doing this it is crucial to locate any discussion of whiteness in a particular empirical and historical context' (1996: 24).

Looking at the ways in which the media selected to represent Jayne Zito it is possible to see a process in which racialized bodies are placed (in visual and written text) so as to emphasize not simply the horror of what happened on Finsbury Park tube station, but also to relate that horror to an historical and cultural hegemonic discourse whereby constructions of black masculine violent insanity/danger depend on and revolve around white feminine vulnerability (Ware 1993). However, looking at the representations of Jayne Zito it is also possible to see a process in which whiteness is able to reproduce itself as whiteness *without* being '*explicitly* set against non-white' (Dyer 1997: 13; my emphasis). For example, when the *Evening Standard* (19 July 1993) covered the story of the failures of the mental health care and criminal justice systems to detain Christopher Clunis – 'A catalogue of blunders' – the accompanying visual is simply a single large picture of Jayne Zito, although the actual report has very little direct relevance to her.

In examining the configurations of both these processes what I became aware of as I read and re-read the media coverage in the six months following Jonathan Zito's death was, in many ways, the peripheral position which Jonathan Zito was allocated. While it is not unusual for such a shift in the public gaze from the victim, to those that surround the victim and while there were certain factors which can be seen to encourage this shift – the failures to provide appropriate care and treatment to Christopher Clunis – this shift is significant in this particular context because of its relation to broader hegemonic discourses. For example, on the front page of the *Independent* (19 July 1993) which bore the headline 'The tragic scandal of a schizophrenic killer that nobody stopped' the written text is 'bookended' by two head-and-shoulders pictures: on the left Jayne Zito and on the right Christopher Clunis. Not only is Jonathan Zito visually absent, but what the visual text emphasizes is the juxtapositioning, the antithetical positioning of the white subject and the black/non-white subject. This absence is again apparent in the same issue on the full-page investigation *Independent* journalists conducted into the events surrounding Jonathan Zito's death. The written text is completely dominated by a head-and-shoulders photograph of Jayne Zito which covers at least a quarter of the page. While there are photographs of both Christopher Clunis and Jonathan Zito, these are very small and buried within the text. Similarly, in its full-page coverage of the trial of Christopher Clunis, the *Daily Mail* (29 June 1993) uses three pictures to accompany the text, the largest of these is a photograph of Jonathan and Jayne Zito, on their wedding day, next to this is a picture of Christopher Clunis and next to this is the third picture which is not of Jonathan Zito, but of Jayne Zito. It is then the image of Jayne Zito that is repeated and thereby emphasized at a visual level. As Jonathan Zito is allocated a decentred position then, Jayne Zito comes to occupy an increasingly centred location within the public gaze. This centred location is set explicitly against Christopher Clunis *and* inhabits its own place as a site in which the racialized gendered body is reproduced. For example, after the trial, the *Evening Standard* (30 June 1993) ran a full-page interview with Jayne Zito in the Caroline Phillips Interview (a regular feature in the *Standard*). Both the visual and the written texts (the outcome of the dialogue between two white women) reproduce a racialized (white) and gendered (feminized) body without any visual reference to Christopher Clunis. A large head-and-shoulders picture of Jayne Zito with the headline 'I don't know who I am any more. I feel lost and exposed' occupies a significant proportion of the page. What is important to note here is the way in which Jane Zito's expressions of loss and grief are selected (and thereby highlighted) as headlines. The construction of these emotions as public statements of vulnerability and frailty works here to obscure Jane Zito as a pro-active figure.[5] It is in this same *Standard* article that the written text fore-grounds what has only been supplied visually previously. The reader is told early on in the article of how 'Jayne, whose courage has touched the nation, is beautiful, tanned and with long blonde hair'. In this way the text provides an immediate connection between moral quality (courage) and a specific and idealized white beauty (tanned and blonde). In his discussion of whiteness, gender and cinematic and photographic light-ing, Dyer argues that 'idealized white women are bathed in and per-meated by light. It streams through them and falls on them from above. In short, they glow' (1997: 122). Blonde hair can be an important element in the construction of this glow, which is as much about sign-posting internal moral superiority as it is a particular physical beauty. Indeed Dyer makes the point that these glowing constructions of white femininity draw on and evoke images of angels. That Jayne Zito was beautiful, compassionate and forgiving were crucial components in the media sense-making of the events surrounding Jonathan Zito's death. As with other white women who have, at various points in their lives, occupied a high-profile place in the public gaze (Elizabeth Hurley, Nicole Simpson Brown, Princess Diana) their beauty has been an impor-tant aspect of their raced whiteness (Ware 1993; Gabriel 1998; Neal, 1999). Sadness and tragedy and moral dignity all serve to emphasize further this specific form of feminized, idealized beauty. It is within these arenas that Jayne Zito, as a public body, worked perfectly: she effectively operated at the intersection between a specific, idealized beauty, moral superiority and tragedy. Just as Christopher Clunis symbolized the racialized and gendered figure of fear in the white pschye so too Jayne Zito symbolized the raced and gendered figure of femininized vulnerability and dignity which also inhabits that same white pschye. Lurking at the heart of the media's use of these symbols are the older notions of the civilized and the uncivilized. These notions have been deracialized and coded in order to operate in more contemporary discursive contexts. For example, the media's emphasis on Jayne Zito's compassion for Christopher Clunis and her knowledge of mental health care served to centre the notion of forgiveness in the face of savagery and thereby mined a neocolonial theme of civilization. So while Jayne Zito is the 'dignified widow who bears no hatred' (*Independent*, 19 July 1993), Christopher Clunis is the 'psychotic knifeman' (*Evening Standard*, 30 June 1993; *Mail*, 28 June 1993), the 'freed schizophrenic' (*Mail*, 22 July 1993) and the 'schizophrenic killer' (*Independent*, 19 July 1993; *Evening Standard*, 19 July 1993).

For the media the configurations of race and gender were grounded in ideas of masculinized black dangerousness and feminized white vulnerability. Dichotomously racialized and gendered bodies provided a platform from which the need to investigate not only the death of Jonathan Zito but also the care (and failed containment) of Christopher Clunis could be effectively and evocatively argued and transferred to the social policy arena. In other words, it was the media's implicit racialization and gendering of the events surrounding Jonathan Zito's death which was highly influential in creating a climate which necessitated a public policy response. For example, it was the coverage in the *Independent* which had a direct impact on the eventual commissioning of an NHS inquiry and the newspaper is cited and acknowledged in the Report of the inquiry: 'at the beginning of our Inquiry we were greatly helped . . . by an article in the 19th July 1993 edition of the *Independent* Newspaper, which set out their investigations into the case' (Ritchie et al. 1994: 1).[6]

Conclusion

Within the public and populist gaze the death of Jonathan Zito, stabbed through the eye while waiting for a train in the heart of London on a December afternoon, represented one of the ultimate horrors of late twentieth-century urban life. Consequently, the circumstances and figures surrounding this death were all transferred from the private sphere of grief and loss and relocated to a raced landscape in which gendered and racialized bodies were represented in ways which promoted particular frameworks with which to make (constructed) sense of events within the populist context. Within this process Jayne Zito and Christopher Clunis moved from private individuals to public symbols, to embodiments of racialized (feared) demons and racialized (revered) icons. The media's foregrounding of incomprehension at Christopher Clunis's 'freedom' effectively worked a deracialized discourse in which the (angelicized) figure of Jayne Zito (rather than Jonathan Zito) was pivotal in order to offset the extent of the (white) tragedy and to fuel the campaign for the circumstances surrounding it to be publicly investigated. Placed within a wider political context in which anxieties as to the proximity of madness via the care in the community policy (NHS and Community Care Act 1990) were being voiced, the media speculation and representations surrounding the Clunis/Zito event were influential in the setting up of the NHS Inquiry into the care and treatment of Christopher Clunis. Although the chapter has argued that this media coverage was framed by polemicized populist representations which drew on particular discursive reserves, it has also argued that those representations were not totally dependent on the other for their effectiveness, which is to return to Dyer's argument that whiteness reproduces itself as whiteness and that whiteness 'has been about maintaining traditions, representing culture and anchoring identities' (Gabriel 1998: 187). Similarly, it is important to emphasize that the media constructions of dichotomous bodies is, of course, a process which obscures the complexities of events and distorts the individuals involved. Finally, the chapter has argued that although media representations of bodies within racialized and gendered contexts have traditionally been relatively crude, increasingly they rely on a more coded invitation to construct certain meanings. As Fergason (1998: 153) notes: 'it is clear that some of the excesses of the 1970s and 1980s' reportage of issues of race have been tempered over the decades. This does not mean that such representations have simply become so innocuous as to be of little consequence.'

Notes

1   The term 'beautiful' is of course problematic. The concept of who and what is beautiful is not aesthetically neutral but socially constructed. Idealized ver-

sions of feminine beauty have been inextricably linked to whiteness both historically and contemporarily (Ware 1992; Young 1996).

2 The term black is being used in this chapter to refer to people of African and African/Caribbean/American descent.

3 Section 136 of the 1983 Mental Health Act grants the police powers to arrest anyone in a public place whom they deem to be a threat to themselves or others and compulsorily remove that person to psychiatric care.

4 This image is reminiscent of the media coverage of Winston Silcott after his (subsequently quashed) conviction for the murder of PC Blakelock in the mid0-1980s. For example the *Sun* (20 March 1987) used a head-and-shoulders picture of Winston Silcott with the caption 'Face of Monster' (Jordan and Weedon 1995).

5 Six years later Jayne Zito was the winner of the Politics and Public Service category of the *Cosmopolitan* magazine's 'Women of Achievement Awards' which described her as a 'relentless campaigner for the mentally ill' (*Cosmopolitan*, May 1998).

6 For an examination of the findings of this Report and particularly its engagement with the issues of race, see Neal (1998).

References

Butler, J. 1993. 'Endangered/Endangering: Schematic Racism and White Paranoia', in R. Gooding-Williams (ed.), *Reading Rodney King: Reading Urban Uprising*. London: Routledge.

Campbell, C. 1995. *Race, Myth and the News*. London: Sage.

Coid, J. W. 1994. 'The Christopher Clunis Enquiry', *Psychiatric* Bulletin, 18: 449–452.

Dijk,T. van 1991. *Racism and the Press*. London: Routledge.

Dyer, R. 1997. *White*. London: Routledge.

Fiske, J. 1994. *Media Matters: Everyday Culture and Political Change*. Minneapolis: University of Minnesota.

Fergason, R. 1998. *Representing 'Race', Ideology, Identity and the Media*. London: Arnold.

Francis, E. 1993. 'Psychiatric Racism and Social Police: Black People and the Psychiatric Services', in W. Harris and C. James (eds.), *Inside Babylon: the Caribbean Diaspora in Britain*. London: Verso.

Frankenburg, R. 1993. *The Social Construction of Whiteness*. London: Routledge.

Gabriel, J. 1998. *Whitewash: Racialized Politics and the Media*. London: Routledge.

Gilman, S. L. 1985. *Difference and Pathology: Stereotypes of Sexuality, Race and Madness*. London: Cornell University Press.

Gordon, P. 1990. 'A Dirty War: The New Right and Local Authority Anti-racism', in W. Ball and J. Solomos (eds.), *Race and Local Politics*. Basingstoke: Macmillan.

Hall, S. 1990. 'The Whites of Their Eyes: Racist Ideologies and the Media', in M. Alvarado and J. Thompson (eds.), *The Media Reader*. London: British Film Institute.

Hartmann, P. and Husbands, C. 1974. *Racism and the Mass Media*. London: Davis-Poytner.

Hawkins, H. and Thomas, R. 1991. 'White Policing of Black Populations: A History of Race and Social Control in America', in E. Cashmore and E. McLaughlin (eds.), *Out of Order? Policing and Black People*. London: Routledge.

Law, I. 1996. *Racism, Ethnicity and Social Policy*. London: Harvester Wheatsheaf.

Littlewood, R. and Lipsedge, M. 1982. *Aliens and Alienists: Ethnic Minorities and Psychiatry*. London: Routledge.

Morrison, T. 1992. *Playing in the Dark: Whiteness and the Literary Imagination*. Harvard, Mass.: Harvard University Press.

Neal, S. 1998. 'Embodying Black Madness, Embodying White Femininity – Populist Representations and Public Policy Responses: The Case of Christopher Clunis and Jayne Zito', *Sociological Research Online*, Volume 3, Issue 4, <www.socresearchonline.org>

Neal, S. 1999. 'Populist Configurations of Race and Gender: The Case of Hugh Grant, Liz Hurley and Divine Brown', in M. Hickman and A. Brah (eds.), *Thinking Identities and Ethnicities*. London: Macmillan.

Nkweto-Simmonds, F. 1997. 'My Body, Myself: How does a Black Woman Do Sociology?', in H. Mirza (ed.), *Black British Feminism: A Reader*. London: Routledge.

Pieterse, J. N. 1992. *White on Black: Images of Africa and Blacks in Western Popular Culture*. London: Yale University Press.

Ritchie, J. H., Dick, D. and Lingham, R. 1994. *The Report into the Care and Treatment of Christopher Clunis*. HMSO.

Roediger, D. 1991. *The Wages of Whiteness: Race and the Making of the American Working Class*. London: Verso.

Sashidaran, S. and Francis, E. 1993. 'Epidemiology, Ethnicity and Schizophrenia', in W. Ahmed (ed.), *Race and Health in Contemporary Britain*. Buckingham: Open University Press.

Said, E. 1978. *Orientalism*. London: Routledge and Kegan Paul.

Smaje, C. 1995. *Health, 'Race' and the Evidence*. London: Kings Fund Institute.

Solomos, J. and Back, L. 1996. *Racism and Society*. London: Macmillan.

Soothill, K. and Walby, S. 1991. *Sex Crime and the News*. London: Routledge.

Ware, V. 1993. *Beyond the Pale, White Women, Racism and History*. London: Verso.

Young, R. 1995. *Colonial Desire: Hybridity in Theory, Culture and Race*. London: Routledge.

7
The Body's Second Skin: Forming the Protective Community of Grand Prix Motor Racing

Alex Twitchen

Introduction

Over the last 30 years Grand Prix Formula One motor racing has undergone a process of dramatic transformation. Whereas the sport was once the almost exclusive preserve of a European-based gentlemanly elite, it has now become a global spectacle which in terms of commercial exploitation rivals the soccer World Cup and Olympic Games (Henry 1991). However, the transformation of Grand Prix Formula One motor racing, since the late 1960s, does not just reflect a process of intense commercialization, since during this period the sport has also been transformed into a much less hazardous and life-threatening occupation as well. This development has primarily stemmed from the progressive introduction, and on-going refinement, of increasingly rigorous, far-reaching and more stringently enforced rules and regulations. Furthermore, this process has not just been specific to Grand Prix Formula One racing, the pinnacle formula of motor racing, as all categories of motor racing have similarly become observably less dangerous and hazardous. In this respect the introduction of safety-oriented rules and regulations by the sport's governing organization can be conceptualized, as I shall demonstrate, in terms of a 'second skin', which enhances the protection of the body against the hazards of motor racing by acting as a supplementary skin to the body's own skin. In this way the body does not just have one skin but has what Douglas and Calvez (1992) term a 'double skin', its own and that of its community. Consequently, the focus of this chapter will explore how the introduction of safety-oriented rules and regulations in Grand Prix Formula One motor racing illustrates how communities may act as a protective secondary skin against hazards which threaten the bodily well-being of individuals.

The Hazards of Motor Racing

Through its constitutive structure motor racing is an inherently hazardous sport. This is because the sport involves driving a motorized vehicle to the limits of both human ability and mechanical performance. As such, mistakes and mechanical failure, which can lead to potentially hazardous accidents, are a frequent occurrence. However, the extent to which such accidents actually result in injury or death is not just a consequence of the ferocity or violence of the accident, an important contributory factor is also the effectiveness of the safety standards that are in place at the time. Since the late 1960s, through a more intensive process of introducing safety-oriented rules and regulations, the vehicles, the drivers' clothing and the circuits on which they race, have gradually come to incorporate a higher standard of protection which has enabled the rate of injuries and deaths to decline noticeably. Watkins (1996), for example, calculates that between 1963 and 1982 there were 12 driver fatalities in 262 Grand Prix, whilst between 1983 and 1995 there were two fatalities in 208 Grand Prix. This equates to one fatality for every 22 Grand Prix for the period 1963–82, but only one fatality for every 104 Grand Prix for the period 1983–95. The analysis also reveals a marked reduction in the number of serious injuries. In the same periods the frequency of a serious injury occurring in a Grand Prix Formula One event fell from an average of one serious injury every two and half Grand Prix to one every 20 Grand Prix. In all, between 1963 and 1982 Watkins documents 106 serious injuries to competitors in Grand Prix Formula One motor racing, whereas between 1983 and 1995 there were five.

However, the statistical decline in the number of fatalities and serious injuries sustained in Grand Prix Formula One motor racing does not explain why the sport has become safer. What appears to explain such a development is a change in the perceptions and attitudes of individuals towards accidents that cause fatal and serious injuries to competitors in motor racing, whether it be in Grand Prix Formula One racing or any other category of the sport. That is, it now appears that fatal and serious accidents in motor racing are much less acceptable as an unavoidable element of the sport than they were in the past. For example, Russell Davies, writing in *The Sunday Telegraph* (8 May 1994) following the death of Ayrton Senna at Imola during the San Marino Grand Prix, observes:

> We are much more bothered about all this than we used to be, even as little as a quarter of a century ago. When Jim Clark, the British

driving hero and two times World Champion, was killed in a Formula Two race at Hockenheim in 1968, the event was front page news, to be sure. But if you look at *The Daily Telegraph* of those times, you do not find the prolonged analysis of the crises in motor racing or leader page articles agonising over the future of the sport, or enthusiasts pleading for its continued autonomy.

Davies' view reflects how the depth of public feeling, the sense of shock and a reaction to the deaths of two competitors (an Austrain competitor Roland Ratzenberger was killed in practice the day before Senna) as a terrible tragedy provoked the feeling of crises within the racing community. In the past such an event may not have generated the same degree of intense feeling because the public's response would not have been so acute or dramatic. Instead, more people would have accepted such accidents as an unfortunate but inevitable consequence of participation in motor racing. The development of a more widespread sensitivity to accidents that cause fatal or serious injuries is also conveyed by Henry (1994: 6) when he expresses his view, again following Senna's death, that:

> Clark's death was largely regarded as simply a legitimate consequence of competing in a hazardous sport. The post-mortems were limited and, to a large extent, shrugged aside. A generation later, we live in a very different environment where the freedom of the individual to make a personal choice as to how, or indeed whether he risks his life, is very much hemmed in by wider social constraints.

Henry's comments, like those of Davies, reflect a sense in which the fatalities at Imola transgressed the collective social threshold of what constitutes an acceptable level of hazardous risk in Grand Prix Formula One motor racing. Consequently, not only has the imposition of more stringent rules and regulations helped to lessen the risk of a serious or fatal injury occurring in Grand Prix Formula One motor racing, but the introduction and continuous refinement of such rules and regulations have been prompted by a significant change in the tolerance and acceptability of accidents that result in such injuries being sustained. However, this development would not seem peculiar or specific to motor racing, for as Furedi (1997) suggests, a more acute sensitivity to risk and harmful accidents has become dominant in late twentieth-century society generally. In Furedi's view, risk-taking has become less acceptable and discourses of safety, risk avoidance and the promotion of risk-adverse attitudes now dominate a whole range of social activities. This has meant that taking precautions against potentially injurious accidents has become a fundamental cultural value. It would seem, then, that motor racing is not exceptional and reflects a more general trend in modern societies towards minimizing the risks of unnecessary harm and injury. Consequently, safety in Grand Prix Formula One motor racing is now an important and high-priority issue since a fatality rate similar to that experienced in the 1960s and before would threaten the high-profile status the sport has developed. Indeed such is the extent of the transformation in the safety of motor racing that it would be possible to suggest, by adapting the words of Baudrillard (1993: 126) when he writes that 'today, *it is normal to be dead*, and this is new', that today it is not normal to die, or be severely injured, when competing in Grand Prix Formula One, or any other category of motor racing, and this is also new. However, an explanation of why such a change has occurred and why serious and fatal injuries in motor racing now generate such a greater sense of shock and remorse lie outside the scope of this chapter. My aim instead is to address how the implementation of a variety of safety-oriented rules and regulations can in effect contribute to, and be understood as, a 'second skin' which supplements the protective capacity of the body's own skin.

The Community as 'Second Skin' for the Body

I have drawn the idea of communities acting as another protective 'second skin' for the body from the work of Mary Douglas and Marcel Calvez (1990). From fieldwork conducted in northern France regarding HIV infection, Douglas and Calvez distil four predominantly different beliefs that individuals hold about the body. One of these is the belief that the body is strong because it has two protective layers: its own and that of the community. For Douglas and Calvez the belief which individuals hold about the skin of the community stems from a view that communities can be a source of immunity, and a means of preventing threats from entering the body, by stopping the threat from entering the community in the first instance. In connection with the threat of the HIV virus this means communities may repress or expel members of the community who do not adhere to the dominant standards of acceptable behaviour. Communities may also repel strangers from entering the community and 'call home' wandering members who have left the community in order to ensure further that the threat does not enter the community. Thus for Douglas and Calvez the foundation of a community's protective capacity, which enables individuals to believe in the community as an extra source of immunity, predominantly lies in controlling the boundaries of the community by controlling which individuals inhabit, enter and leave the community. That is, a threat such as the HIVs virus can be contained by monitoring and limiting the movements of community members to the extent that contact between individuals is ideally restricted to only the accepted members of the community. In this way members of the community can lessen the danger of the threat by avoiding contact with unknown strangers and come to believe in their community as a 'second skin' because of the confidence instilled by controlling membership of the community.

Douglas and Calvez have usefully demonstrated in this respect how communities may act in the face of potential threats. Yet their work principally reflects how communities may deal with threats that exist outside of the community and have yet to infiltrate the community, and secondly, are threats that already reside in the body of an individual and are passed on by bodily contact with other individuals, so making the control of entry and exit to the community a primary and important consideration. This relates clearly to the nature of the threat posed by the HIV virus, but the idea of communities acting as a 'second skin' can be developed to understand how, by introducing safety measures, communities can similarly protect the bodies of individuals from threats and potential harm. By this I mean that a community undertakes the protection of its members' bodies by not only controlling the physical movements of individuals but also by introducing rules, regulations and legislation that compel the introduction of specific safety precautions. Consequently the standards of protection and safety adopted by the community can help to protect the body from the harm potentially sustained by exposure to a variety of threats and hazards. Thus it is through the mechanism of a regulatory structure that a community also acts as a 'second skin' and so becomes a supplement to the protection offered by the body's own skin. Sometimes, however, as the study of motor racing reveals, individuals may perceive that their community, in adopting ever more stringent safety standards, may over-protect their body.

In regard to the introduction of rules, regulations and legislation that may help to protect individuals from harm it is also useful to draw on the analysis of modern society undertaken by Baudrillard. For Baudrillard (1993) a key aspect of modern society is the increasingly pervasive extent to which individuals are subjected to forms of control that are intended to protect them from a 'premature' accidental death. In

Baudrillard's view such a situation emerges out of modern society's growing obsession with avoiding preventable and avoidable death, thereby enabling individuals to live out their lives to the end of their 'biological clock'. This aspiration is not derived from an essentialist desire simply to let individuals live for as long as possible, but in contrast stems from how 'premature' accidental deaths dramatically highlight the limitations of 'objective' rational human control over nature. That is, the body is a vulnerable biological organism which can be all too easily fatally wounded in a way that is beyond human control. Consequently, the desire to protect individuals from harm reflects a quest central to the ethos of modernity which is to gain omnipotent control over nature by subjecting nature to human reason. In Baudrillard's (1993: 161) words: 'the Accident as persecution, as the absurd and spiteful resistance of a matter or a nature that will not abide by the "objective" laws with which we have pursued it.'

For Baudrillard, then, the introduction of rules, regulations and legislation which serve to protect individuals, emanates from the particular political economy of modern society in which death in accidental circumstances escapes the logic and reason of human science and rationality. Accidental death, therefore, represents the power of untamed nature and the failure of human rationality to subject its mastery over everything.

However, in Baudrillard's view, the overwhelming plethora of rules, regulations and legislation that now govern and control the behaviour of individuals effectively consigns individuals to a living death since the freedom to self-determinate behaviour is increasingly limited. As Baudrillard writes (1993: 174): 'from birth control to death control...the essential thing is that the decision is withdrawn from them, that their life and death are never freely theirs, but they live and die by a social visa.' Indeed Baudrillard goes further and likens the regulatory constraints of a modern society, which are directed at preventing accidents, to a sarcophagus that surrounds the body like a steak under shrink-wrap (1993: 177). For some this might suggest that Baudrillard too pessimistically understands the evolution of rules, regulations and legislation, which are intended to protect individuals from harm, as a development that denies a sense of freedom. I believe, however, that more importantly his analysis illustrates the process whereby modern societies have taken an increasingly more interventionist role in protecting individuals from threats and dangers. For example, the growing volume of health and safety legislation, which exerts an impact on all aspects of modern life, succinctly highlights this trend. As a consequence, it is likewise possible to conceive this process as one in which modern societies have tried to form an increasingly resilient skin around individuals. In such a way I believe that it would be possible to determine, following on from the work of Douglas and Calvez, whether individuals believe that the body is strong because their society protects them in relation to the many types of threats posed by living in a modern industrial world. For example, I believe it would be interesting to examine how individuals perceive the actions of the government in banning certain foods over concerns about public health. Would this reveal that individuals understand their bodies to be protected by the actions of government and derive from this a further sense of comfort and potential immunity from the threat? However, I also believe that Baudrillard's analysis is closer to my own understanding of communities functioning as 'second skin' than that which may be derived from the work of Douglas and Calvez, in so far as I view the regulatory structure of a community, as a means of protecting the body, as equally important to that of policing entry and exit to a community. Yet I would not want to go so far as to suggest that the regulatory structure that facilitates the protective skin of a community is a burden on the freedom of individuals, or represents a detrimental advance of the social into all aspects of individual life.

So far I have suggested that it is possible to view the actions of a community, when implementing increasingly protective measures, as conceptually understandable by way of a 'second skin'. In this way communities like motor racing or societies in general can, through the introduction of various rules, regulations and legislation, protect the bodies of individuals from various threats and hazards. Consequently the skin of the community is not just formed by 'sealing off' the boundaries of a community by controlling entry and exit to the community, as the analysis of Douglas and Calvez highlights. Instead the skin of community can be conceived as deriving from the safety measures developed by the community to protect the body from harm. To illustrate this point more fully I shall now analyse the development of Grand Prix Formula One motor racing since the late 1960s.

Motor Racing and Safety: The 'Milk and Water' Debate

In his autobiography, Juan Manuel Fangio (1986) laments the number of fellow competitors who lost their life whilst competing in motor racing events. In Fangio's estimation during his ten year European racing career between 1949 and 1959 30 of the best racing drivers lost their lives.

Similarly former English Grand Prix driver Tony Brooks recounts that when he competed in the 1950s three or four top-line drivers were killed each year (personal interview, 10 February 1997) However, in the face of such a fatality rate, little seems to have been attempted to reduce the hazards and make the sport safer for competitors. In my view this was because the dominant belief at the time considered motor racing competitors to be brave, and heroic young men who espoused a deferential attitude to the dangers of the sport and lived an idealized image of masculinity by competing in a sport that was inherently hazardous. As such, the death of a competitor was much mourned but made meaningful and legitimated as the consequence of competing in a hazardous activity in which individual competitors knew the hazards and accepted those hazards as a risk of participation. Consequently, improving the safety of competitors was an issue that was little discussed or considered necessary. In such circumstances the motor racing community hardly acted as another protective skin for competitors since the hazards of motor racing were viewed as inherent and unavoidable and an integral part of the challenge. Rather, the motor racing community was more concerned with protecting spectators at events since this was an issue that threatened the continued existence of the sport as the aftermath of the Le Mans disaster in 1955, when at least 92 spectators were killed, testifies.

Motor racing's early past from the inception of the sport in the late nineteenth century to the 1960s can therefore be characterized in terms where little was done to protect competitors from the hazards of the sport. Safety was not considered a problematic issue and as such few rules or regulations were imposed that attempted to enhance the safety of competitors. Furthermore, such a disinterested attitude towards safety appears to have been a view that was held by the majority of individuals within the community of motor racing. As Stirling Moss suggested to me (personal interview, 15 December 1996) not even the competitors themselves thought about making the sport safer. Consequently, the community of motor racing offered little protection to competitors and concerned itself solely with the safety of spectators.

During the course of the 1960s the issue of safety in motor racing gradually became more significant and the loss of talented drivers such as Jim Clark in 1968 began to heighten concern about the hazards of motor racing. Initial developments in safety were mostly promoted by competitors themselves. Les Leston, for example, pioneered the development and use of fireproof protective clothing. Similarly, towards the end of the 1960s, drivers began to wear seat belts as research increasingly suggested that in the event of an accident it is safer to be strapped into a vehicle rather than, as the previous orthodoxy had suggested, be thrown clear. The magnitude of change that took place in the 1960s and the role of competitors in this process can be understood by recalling the words of the late Bruce McLaren who, in his regularly weekly column wrote:

> We are all doing our utmost to make the sport safer, and we've come a long way over the years doing this. When I first drove at Monaco I wore a short sleeved blue sports shirt, now it's fireproof Nomex underwear and overalls. Drivers didn't wear crash helmets not long ago and when they were first suggested as a safety measure there were those who thought they were 'cissy'.
>
> (*Autosport* 26 May 1967)

Increased attention was also given to improving the medical facilities available to help injured drivers at motor racing events. Organizers and promoters of motor racing events were not obliged by regulations to provide sophisticated medical support and often only provided very rudimentary facilities, sometimes consisting of not much more than a tent staffed by basic first aiders. For the 1967 season Louis Stanley, owner of the British Racing Motors (BRM) team, set up the Grand Prix Medical Service (GPMS). This was essentially an articulated truck that could attend Grand Prix and other races in Europe and provide emergency care at the trackside. It was equipped with the most sophisticated intensive care facilities available which could sup port immediate life-saving surgical operations and was staffed by fully qualified surgeons.

As well as improving the standard of safety equipment used by competitors and improving trackside medical facilities, the rules pertaining to the design and construction of racing cars was also subject to increased scrutiny. In Britain the governing organization of the sport the Royal Automobile Club (RAC) stipulated that racing cars should be built with fireproof bulkheads, be fitted with fire extinguishers and possess flexible fuel tanks to reduce the risk of a fire starting on impact. Similarly, circuit owners, and in particular John Hugenholtz the pioneering manager of the Zandvoort track in the Netherlands, began to equip tracks with metal 'armco' barriers and 'catch fencing' which offered a more effective form of protection, to both competitors and spectators, than straw bales.

Such developments do not represent an exhaustive list of safety changes that took place, however they do reveal the extent of the transformation that occurred during the 1960s. As such, in comparison to the past, much had changed and the safety of competitors had become a central and important consideration within the sport.

However this process was far from uncontested, as a number of individuals clearly felt that enhancing the safety of motor racing represented an unwelcome emasculation of the sport. As the leading English motor racing journalist Denis Jenkinson wrote:

> I have always thought that one of the enduring features of a Grand Prix driver was that he had GUTS and would accept a challenge that normal people like you and I would not be brave enough to face; now I'm not so sure.
>
> (*Motor Sport* May 1969)

Likewise the editorial of the monthly magazine *Motor Sport* suggested in August 1968: 'Let us hope that top rank Formula One drivers have not become namby-pamby in recent times.'

The questioning of a competitor's courage was the central tenet around which the 'milk and water' debate, a phrase coined by Jenkinson himself in response to the drivers' boycott of the 1969 Belgium Grand Prix at Spa, revolved. And whilst Jenkinson himself may have been the most prominent and vociferous objector to the implementation of more widespread safety measures, as a process that was removing much of the essential challenge to participation in motor racing, his was not a lone voice. As Geoffrey Charles highlighted when writing in *The Times* (11 June 1968), even the competitors themselves were divided over the merits of the safety campaign. As Charles wrote:

> against this there is a hard and steady stream of criticism from other drivers, particularly the younger set of Grand Prix drivers, who argue that, however well intentioned the advocates of greater safety may be, they are slowly eroding one of the basic elements and attractions of the sport for both drivers and spectators – namely the built in danger. Give the mis-guided safety fanatics any more freedom ... and every circuit will become a harmless watered down nursery track on which only completely protected drivers will dare to race. Remove the dangers from racing and you destroy its appeal and challenge.

Similarly at the end of 1968 Charles wrote (*The Times* 19 December 1968):

> When the campaign for circuit safety was launched, its backers were criticised in some quarters for being 'over-protectionist' in their

attitude, which, it was suggested, could remove all the dangers and, therefore, much of the spectacle from motor-sport.

An examination of the letter pages in *Autosport*, the popular weekly motor racing magazine, also revealed the depth of feeling which the process of improving the safety of motor racing generated, as a number of letters both strongly advocated and resisted the safety campaign, to the extent that, in September 1970, the editor of *Autosport* commented on 'the "milk and water" controversy... that [has] raged in our Correspondence columns.'

In response to the criticisms that motor racing was becoming too safe, the leading competitor Jackie Stewart wrote (1970: 112), those

> who write about drivers boycotting a Grand Prix and imply we are spoiled or cowards... do not enjoy writing about drivers being killed and whilst one respects their right to be critical, it is hard to understand anyone who thinks that Grand Prix drivers are a lot of cowards, just because they do not much enjoy the idea of racing under conditions they consider unsafe.

The resistance to the safety campaign was also expressed in the reluctance of many organizers and track owners to enhance the safety measures at their meetings and circuits as well as an ideology that improving safety measures over-protected competitors. As Louis Stanley recounts (1994: 103) in his memoirs, the GPMS truck was moved from its position at Silverstone on the day of the 1968 British Grand Prix by an official who suggested:

> We have never had this type of vehicle before. If a driver gets injured, he will just have to take his chances like anybody else. I don't believe in mollycoddling any fellow.

As this historical evidence suggests, the increasing prominence of safety measures and the greater attention that was being given to protecting competitors was not a process that was uncontested. Clearly there were those, with some degree of influence and power within the community of motor racing, who felt that the changes the sport was pursuing in the late 1960s and early 1970s represented a detrimental emasculation of the sport as well as an unnecessary economic burden. Yet such views became increasingly marginalized as motor racing became increasingly commercialized and broader social processes developed, which also mitigated against the views of those who expressed regrets about motor racing becoming safer.

Motor Racing and Safety in the 1980s and 1990s

The process of making motor racing safer did not end, or reach a point of static progress, in the early to mid-1970s. Rather, there has been a continuing programme of measures taken to ensure that the hazards of motor racing are further minimized or at least maintained at a now acceptable level. Some of these measures extend to occasionally redrafting the rules of Grand Prix Formula One motor racing, and other categories of motor racing, to ensure that improvements in the performance levels of racing cars do not significantly heighten the hazards of motor racing. Similarly, medical care and the provision of medical facilities has been greatly extended such that the sophistication of mandatory provision now enables a wider range of surgical operations to take place at the circuit (Cranston, 1998). Consequently, through the continuous refinement of the rules and regulations of motor racing the sport has been able to maintain a level of safety that is unprecedented in the sport's history. In this case it has been the community of Grand Prix Formula One, and motor racing generally, which, via the implementation of more rigorous safety measures, has functioned as a supplementary 'second skin' to the bodies of individual competitors. So whereas in the past individual competitors had only the protective capacity of their own body to protect them from the hazards of the sport, the implementation of more rigorous safety standards, a process undertaken by the community of motor racing and not one imposed by outside agencies, has added an additional layer of protection. However, there are limits and unintended consequences associated with this process.

Despite the introduction of many measures that have helped to lessen the risks of bodily injury in motor racing, injuries, some serious and causing permanent disfigurement and disability, still occur. The burns sustained by Formula One World Champion Niki Lauda in 1976, the paralysis of Clay Regazzoni caused by injuries sustained in an accident during the United States West Grand Prix in 1980 and the career-ending injuries suffered by Martin Donnelly during practice for the Spanish Grand Prix in 1990 highlight how the body is still prone to harm by the inherent hazards of competing in Grand Prix Formula One motor racing. Clearly whilst the implementation of more extensive safety measures has lessened the risks of severe and fatal injuries being sustained, and in this way the community of Grand Prix Formula One motor racing has helped to protect the body, this 'second skin' is not a skin that is entirely resilient or one that guarantees protection from injury. Instead the skin of the motor racing community helps, but motor racing is a sport in which severe and fatal injuries are still a potentially prominent consequence of participation. In this case the deaths of Ayrton Senna and Roland Ratzenberger forcibly reminded the Grand Prix Formula One motor racing community that the sport is still, despite all the precautions now taken, a hazardous occupation. Yet whilst the shock of these two deaths prompted the International governing organization, the Fédération Internationale d'Automobile (FIA) to take further action to try to prevent such incidents re-occurring, some of the measures introduced have not been met with uniform approval.

During 1997 when the FIA was proposing a series of measures to 'slow' the performance capability of Grand Prix Formula One cars the Canadian competitor Jacques Villeneuve (whose father Gilles was killed during practice for the 1982 Belgian Grand Prix) spoke out as he believed the changes potentially took the excitement out of motor racing. Villeneuve argued that the FIA's-obsession with controlling the rules and regulations of Grand Prix Formula One to ensure the safety of competitors had extended to the point that the sport was becoming 'too safe'. Instead Villeneuve made it clear that whilst he did not want the sport to become significantly life-threatening again, he did feel that the changes would 'slow' the cars enough to remove the excitement of driving. Villeneuve's argument, which was supported by others, highlights how the extent of communal regulation can be seen to impinge on the personal choice of individuals. That is, it would appear that there is a limit beyond which a communal 'second skin' is perceived as being constructive and helpful or constraining and over-protective.

Another perceived unintended consequence of introducing more rigorous safety measures into motor racing is the belief that current competitors take more risks in their driving behaviour than previous competitors. Several well-reported incidents in Grand Prix Formula One racing have led many individuals to suggest that because competitors have become increasingly better protected so they can afford to take risks that heighten the chance of an accident occurring. Therefore, whilst there may be fewer actual injuries stemming from accidents it may be the case that competitors are engaging in behaviour that causes more accidents to occur, and so an accident that causes a severe or fatal injury may stem from an instance of unnecessary and unruly driving behaviour. Some have gone further and suggested that because of the safety measures introduced, some drivers are now prepared to 'take out' another competitor deliberately by driving into him. This perception and belief highlight a rather paradoxical and unintended consequence of making motor racing safer; that is, by introducing more rigorous rules and regulations competitors may actually be exposing their bodies to a greater degree of potential harm by taking greater risks.

This observation corresponds to the observations made by Adams (1995), who has demonstrated that the introduction of safety measures does not necessarily produce a decline in the rate of injury because individuals take greater risks. Adams theorizes his observations by way of a 'risk compensation' theory which suggests that individuals adjust their behaviour to how safe they feel. Consequently Adams (1995: 155) suggests that if the government wishes to reduce the number of fatalities sustained in road accidents for example, it should consider making the fitting of a long metal spike to vehicle steering wheels compulsory and then observe how cautiously and safely motorists drive.

Following this conclusion it may be that the most appropriate course of action to prevent injuries in some circumstances is not to implement further safety measures, but to rely on individuals adapting their behaviour and acting more cautiously in potentially hazardous and dangerous situations.

Conclusion

I have attempted to highlight how the body of competitors in motor racing is additionally protected by the actions of the motor racing community. In this way I have suggested that the body does not only have one skin but two, as the rules and regulations of the community act as a 'second skin'. However, I have shown that this communal skin has not always been present to the same degree throughout the history of motor racing, since it is only in the last 30 years that the rules and regulations of Grand Prix Formula One motor racing, and motor racing generally, have become more focused on protecting competitors. This has also been a process that has witnessed a profound debate about the merits of increasingly protecting competitors in motor racing. It has also been a process that may have initiated, as an unintended consequence, a decline in driving standards to the extent that one of my research participants, a former Grand Prix driver, labelled many young participants 'hooligan drivers' since they exhibit, in his opinion, a complete lack of respect for the hazards of motor racing. Above all though, I have tried to highlight that the regulatory structure of a community is a means of protecting the body from harm and may enable individuals to derive a sense of comfort and security from their community. In this regard perhaps, attention should be directed to the importance of communities generally and the collective *we* as a foil against the individualism and beloved *I* of market democracies.

References

Adams, J. 1995. *Risk*. London: UCL Press.

Baudrillard, J. 1993. *Symbolic Exchange and Death*. London: Sage.

Charles, G. 1968. *The Times*. 11 June.

Charles, G. 1968 *The Times*. 19 December.

Cranston, D. 1998. Motor Sport *NSMI News* No. 13.

Davies, R. 1994. *The Sunday Telegraph*. 8 May.

Douglas, M. and Calvez, M. 1990. 'The Self as a Risk Taker: A Cultural Theory of Contagion in relation to Aids', *Sociological Review*, Vol. 38, No. 3, 445–64.

Fangio, J. 1986. *Fangio: My Racing Life*. Yeovil: Patrick Stephens.

Furedi, F. 1997. *Culture of Fear*. London: Cassell.

Henry, A. 1991. *Williams: The Business of Grand Prix Racing*. Yeovil, Patrick Stephens.

Henry, A. 1994. 'The Darkest Hour', *Autocourse*, Vol. 44. London, Hazelton Publishing.

Jenkinson, D. 1969. *Motor Sport* May.

McClaren, B. 1967. *Autosport* 26 May.

Stanley, L. 1994. *Grand Prix: The Legendary Years*. Harpenden: Queen Anne Press.

Stewart, J. and Dymock, E. 1970 *Jackie Stewart: World Champion*. London, Pelham Books.

Watkins, S. 1996. *Life at the Limit* London: Macmillan.

8

Social Death as Self-fulfilling Prophecy: David Sudnow's *Passing On* Revisited

Stefan Timmermans

Introduction

The purpose of resuscitative interventions is to reverse the dying process and preserve human lives. In most resuscitative efforts, however, the final result is a deceased patient (Eisenberg et al. 1990). When this result is the likely outcome of the resuscitative attempt, the staff's task is to avoid prolonged and unnecessary suffering and prepare for the patient's impending death. How do the staff – as gatekeepers between life and death (Pelligrino 1986) – decide in the relative short time span of a resuscitative trajectory (Glaser and Strauss 1968) to resuscitate aggressively or to let the patient go with minimal medical interference?

In the early 1960s, social scientists demonstrated that those apparently moral questions rest on deep social foundations (Fox 1976). Sociologists argued that the fervour of the staff's intervention depends mostly on the patient's perceived social worth (Glaser and Strauss 1964; Sudnow 1967). In one of the first studies of resuscitative efforts in hospitals, Sudnow provided appalling insights into the social rationing[1] of the dying process. He argued that depending on striking social characteristics – such as the patient's age, 'moral character' and clinical teaching value – certain groups of people were more likely than others to be treated as 'socially dead'. According to Sudnow (1967: 74), social death is a situation in which 'a patient is treated essentially as a corpse, though perhaps still "clinically" and "biologically" alive'. The most disturbing aspect of Sudnow's analysis was his observation that social death becomes a predictor for biological death during resuscitative attempts. People who were regarded as socially dead by the staff were more likely to die a biological death sooner as well.

Zygmunt Bauman has questioned whether Sudnow's observations are still relevant. Bauman (1992: 145) postulated that because resuscitative efforts have 'lost much of their specularity and have ceased to impress, their discriminating power has all but dissipated.'[2] Biomedical researchers and legislators appear to agree by omitting social rationing from a vast medical, legal and ethical resuscitation literature.[3] The rationalization of medical knowledge was supposed to turn the 'art' of medical practice into a 'science' (Berg 1997) and eliminate the social problems of a still experimental medical technology. After countless pilot and evaluation studies, national collaborations, and international conferences, medical researchers created uniform and universally employed resuscitation protocols supported by a resuscitation theory (CPR-ECC 1973; 1992). Health care providers reach decisions during lifesaving efforts by simply following the resuscitation protocols until they run into an endpoint. The data taken into consideration consist solely of observable clinical parameters and biomedical test results. In lifesaving, social factors should be irrelevant and filtered out.

In addition, in the United States legislators instituted extensive legal protections against any form of discrimination, including social rationing. Legislators made it obligatory for health care providers to initiate cardiopulmonary resuscitation (CPR) in all instances in which it is medically indicated (CPR-ECC 1973). Paramedics and other health care providers have the legal duty to respond and apply all professional and regional standards of care, that is, they should follow the protocols to the end. Consent is implied for emergency care such as resuscitative efforts. To encourage further resuscitative measures, first-aid personnel are immune from prosecution for errors rendered in good faith emergency care under the Samaritan laws.[4] Failure to continue treatment, however, is referred to as abandonment that 'is legally and ethically the most serious act an emergency medical technician can commit' (Heckman 1992: 21).

Did these scientific and medicolegal initiatives remove the social rationing in sudden death exposed by Sudnow? I will show that biomedical protocols and legal initiatives did not weaken but reinforced inequality of death and dying. In the emergency department (ED), health care providers reappropriate biomedical theory and advance directives to justify and refine a moral categorization of patients. Furthermore, although the legal protections indeed result in prolonged resuscitative efforts, this does not necessarily serve the patient. The goal of lifesaving becomes subordinated to other objectives. The result is a more sophisticated, theoretically supported and legally sanctioned configuration of social discrimination when sudden death strikes.

Methodology

This article is based on 112 observations of resuscitative efforts over a 14-month period in the EDs of two Midwestern hospitals. I focused my observations on medical out-of-hospital resuscitative efforts. This research was approved by the institutional review board of the two hospitals and by the University of Illinois. I was paged with the other resuscitation team members whenever a resuscitative effort was needed in these EDs. I attended half of the resuscitative efforts that occurred in the two EDs during the observation period.

In addition to the observations, I interviewed 42 health care providers who work in EDs and routinely participate in resuscitative efforts. This group includes physicians, nurses, respiratory therapists, nurse supervisors, emergency room technicians, social workers and chaplains. These health care providers came from three hospitals: the two hospitals in which I observed resuscitative efforts and one bigger level-1 trauma centre and teaching hospital. All responses were voluntary and kept anonymous. The interviews consisted of 15 open-ended, semi-structured questions. The interview guide covered questions about professional choice, memorable resuscitative efforts, the definition of a 'successful' reviving attempt, patient's family presence, teamwork, coping with death and dying, and advanced cardiac life support protocols.

Social Viability

The ED staff's main task is to find a balance of care that fits the patient's situation (Timmermans and Berg 1997). Based on my observations, whether care providers will aggressively try to save a life still depends on the patient's position in a moral stratification. Certain patient characteristics add up to a patient's presumed social viability, and the staff ration their efforts based on the patient's position in this moral hierarchy (Glaser and Strauss 1964; Sudnow 1967). A significant number of identity aspects that signify a person's social status and overall social worth in the community (e.g. being a volunteer, good speaker, charismatic leader or effective parent) are irrelevant or unknown during the resuscitation process.[5]

During reviving efforts, *age* remains the most outstanding characteristic of a patient's social viability (Glaser and Strauss 1964; Sudnow 1967; Kastenbaum and Aisenberg 1972; Roth 1972; Iserson and Stocking 1993). The death of young people should be avoided with all means possible. Almost all respondents mentioned this belief explicitly in the interviews. One physician noted: 'You are *naturally* more aggressive with younger people. If I had a forty year old who had a massive MI [myocardial infarction], was asystolic for twenty minutes, or something like that, I would be very aggressive with that person. I suppose for the same scenario in a ninety-year-old, I might not be.' A colleague agreed: 'When you have a younger patient, you try to give it a little bit more effort. You might want to go another half-hour on a younger person because you have such a difficult time to let the person go.' Although respondents hesitated uncomfortably when I asked to give an age cut-off point, the resuscitation of young people triggered an aggressive lifesaving attempt.

A second group of patients for whom the staff was willing to exhaust the resuscitation protocols were patients *recognized* by one or more team members because of their position in the community. During the interview period in one hospital, a well-liked, well-known senior hospital employee was being resuscitated. All the respondents involved made extensive reference to this particular resuscitative effort. When I asked a respiratory therapist how this effort differed from the others, he replied: 'I think the routines and procedures were the same, but I think the sense of urgency was a lot greater, the anxiety level was higher. We were more tense. It was very different from, say, a 98-year-old from a nursing home.' A nurse explained how her behaviour changed after she recognized the patient:

> The most recent one I worked on was one of my college professors. He happened to be one of my favourites and I didn't even realize it was him until we were into the code and somebody mentioned his name. Then I knew it was him. Then all of the sudden it becomes kind of personal, you seem to be really rooting for the person, while as before you were just doing your job...trying to do the best you could, but then it does get personal when you are talking to them and trying to...you know...whatever you can do to help them through.

Staff also responded aggressively to patients with whom they *identified*. One nurse reflected: 'incidentally, anytime there is an association of a resuscitation with something that you have a close relationship with – your family, the age range, the situation...there is more emotional involvement.' Another nurse explained how a resuscitative effort became more difficult after she had established a relationship with the patient by talking to her and going through the routine patient assessment procedures.

How do these positive categorizations affect the resuscitation process? Basically, when the perceived social viability of the patient is high, the staff will go all out to reverse the dying process. In the average resuscitative effort, four to eight staff members are involved. In the effort to revive a nine-month-old baby, however, I counted 23 health care providers in the room at one point. Specialists from different hospital services were summoned. One physician discussed the resuscitative effort of a patient she identified with: 'I even called the cardiologist. I very seldom do call the cardiologist on the scene, and I called him and asked him, "Is there anything else we can do?"'

How does a resuscitative effort of a highly valued patient end? In contrast with most other reviving attempts, I never saw a physician make a unilateral decision. The physician would go over all the drugs that were given, provide some medical history, mention the time that had elapsed since the patient collapsed and then turn to the team and ask, 'Does anybody have any suggestions?' or 'I think we did everything we could. Dr Martin also agrees – I think we can stop it.'

At the bottom of the assumed moral hierarchy are patients for whom death is considered an appropriate 'punishment' or a welcome 'friend'. Death is considered a 'friend' or even a 'blessing' for *seriously ill* and *older patients*. For those patients, the staff agree that sudden death is not the worst possible end of life. These patients are the 'living dead' (Kastenbaum and Aisenberg 1972). The majority of resuscitation attempts in the ED were performed for elderly patients (Becker et al. 1991). Often these patients resided in nursing homes and were confronted with a staff who relied on deeply entrenched ageism. For example, one nurse assumed that older people would want to die. 'Maybe this eighty-year-old guy just fell over at home and maybe that is the way he wanted to go. But no, somebody calls an ambulance and brings him to the ER where we work and work and work and get him to the intensive care unit. Where he is poked and prodded for a few days and then they finally decide to let him go.' According to a different nurse, older people had nothing more to live for: 'When people are in their seventies and eighties, they have lived their lives.'

The staff considered death an 'appropriate' retaliation for *alcohol-* and *drug-addicted people*. For example, I observed a resuscitative attempt for a patient who had overdosed on heroin. The team went through the resuscitation motions but without much vigour or sympathy. Instead, staff members wore double pairs of gloves, avoided touching the patient, joked about their difficulty inserting an intravenous line and mentioned how they loathed to bring the bad news to the belligerent 'girlfriend' of the patient. Drunks are also much more likely to be nasally intubated rather than administered the safer and less painful tracheal intubation.

These negative definitions affect the course and fervour of the resuscitative effort. For example, patients on the bottom of the social hierarchy were often declared dead in advance. In a typical situation, the physician would tell the team at 7:55 a.m. that the patient would be dead at 8:05 a.m. The physician would then leave to fill out paperwork or talk to the patient's relatives. Exactly at 8:05, the team stopped the effort, the nurse responsible for taking notes wrote down the time of death and the team dispersed. In two other such resuscitative efforts, the staff called the coroner before the patient was officially pronounced dead.

Even an elderly or seriously ill patient might unexpectedly regain a pulse or start breathing during the lifesaving attempt. This development is often an unsettling discovery and poses a dilemma for the staff: are we going to try to 'save' this patient or will we let the patient die? In most resuscitative efforts of patients with assumed low social viability, these signs were *dismissed or explained away* (Timmermans 1999). In the drug overdose case, an EKG monitor registered an irregular rhythm, but the physician in charge dismissed this observation with, 'This machine has an imagination of its own.' Along the same lines, staff who noticed signs of life were considered 'inexperienced', and I heard one physician admonish a nurse who noticed heart tones that 'she shouldn't have listened'. Noticeable signs that couldn't be dismissed easily were explained as insignificant 'reflexes' that would soon disappear (Glaser and Strauss 1965). In all of these instances, social death not only preceded but also led to the official pronouncement of death.

Even after 25 years of CPR practice, Sudnow's earlier observations still ring true. The social value of the patient affects the fervour with which the staff engage in a resuscitative effort, the length of the reviving attempt, and probably also the outcome. The staff ration their efforts based on a hierarchy of lives they consider worth living and others for which they believe death is the best solution, largely regardless of the patient's clinical viability. Children, young adults and people who are able to establish some kind of personhood and overcome the anonymity of lifesaving have the best chance for a full, aggressive resuscitative effort. In the other cases, the staff might still 'run the code' but 'walk it slowly' to the point of uselessness (Muller 1992).

Legal Protections?

One of the aspects of resuscitation that has changed since Sudnow's ethnography is the drop in the prevalence of DOA or 'dead on arrival' cases. Sudnow (1967: 100–9) noted that DOA was the most common occurrence in 'County' hospitals' emergency wards. Ambulance drivers would use a special siren to let the staff know that they were approaching the hospital with a 'possible', shorthand for possible DOA. At arrival, the patient was quickly wheeled out of sight to the far end of the hallway. The physician would casually walk into the room, examine the patient, and – in most cases – confirm the patient's death. Finally, a nurse would call the coroner. Twenty-five years later, I observed DOA only when an extraordinarily long transportation time occurred in which all the possible drugs were given and the patient remained unresponsive. For example:

> Dr Hendrickson takes me aside before the patient arrives and says, 'Stefan, I just want to tell you that the patient has been down for more than half an hour [before the paramedics arrived]. They had a long ride. I probably will declare the patient dead on arrival.' When the patient arrives, the paramedic reports, 'We had asystole for the last ten minutes. We think he was in V-fib for a while but it was en route. It could have been the movement of the ambulance.' The physician replies, 'I declare this patient dead.'

The DOA scenario has now diminished in importance for legal reasons. When somebody calls 911 (the US emergency number), a resuscitative effort begins and is virtually unstoppable until the patient is examined in the ED by a physician. After the call, an ambulance with Emergency Medical Technicans (EMTs) or paramedics is dispatched. Unless the patient shows obvious signs of death,[6] the ambulance team start the advanced cardiac treatment as prescribed by their standing orders and protocols. The patient is thus transported to the ED, where the physician with the resuscitation team takes over. Legally, the physician again cannot stop the lifesaving attempt, because the physician needs to make sure that the protocols are exhausted. Stopping sooner would qualify as negligence and be grounds for malpractice. These legal guidelines, more than any magical power inherent to technology, explain the apparent technological imperative and momentum of the resuscitation technology (Koenig 1988; Timmermans 1998).

Patients who in Sudnow's study would be pronounced biologically dead immediately are now much more likely to undergo an extensive resuscitative effort. These patients cluster together in a new group of already presumed low-value patients. They are referred to as *pulseless nonbreathers, goners* or *flat-liners*. Most of these patients are elderly or suffer from serious illnesses. Sudden infant death syndrome babies and some adults might fulfil the clinical criteria for pulseless nonbreathers, but because they are considered valuable and therefore viable, the staff do not include them in this group.

A respiratory therapist described her reaction to these patients: 'If it comes over my beeper that there is a pulseless nonbreather, then I know they were at home, I know that they were down a long time...I go and do my thing, [but] it's over when they get here.' Some respondents added that this group does not leave a lasting impression: 'they all blend together as one grey blur.'

Instead of prompting health care workers to provide more aggressive care, the legally extended resuscitative effort has created a situation in which the staff feel obligated to go through some useless motions and they spend the time for other purposes. I observed that while they were compressing the patient's chest and artificially ventilating him or her, the staff's conversation would drift off to other topics such as birthday parties, television shows, hunting events, sports, awful patients, staffing conflicts and easy or difficult shifts.

In addition, instead of attempting to save lives with all means possible, the process of accurately following the protocols became a goal in itself. A resuscitative effort could be rewarding for the staff based on the process of following the different resuscitation steps, regardless of the outcome of the resuscitative effort. A physician confessed: 'As bad as it sounds, there are many times when I feel satisfied when it was done very well, the entire resuscitative effort was done very well, very efficiently even though the patient didn't make it.' In this bureaucratic mode of thinking, following the legal guidelines *à la lettre* officially absolved the physician of the blame for sudden death. The physician could face the relatives and tell them sincerely that the staff did everything possible within the current medical guidelines to save the life of their loved one.

Finally, the staff used the mandated resuscitation time to take care of the patient's relatives and friends instead of the patient. A physician explicitly admitted that the current resuscitation set-up was far from optimal for the patient or relatives. He saw it as his responsibility to help the family as best he could:

Even when I am with the patient for the sixty or ninety seconds, if that, I almost don't think about the patient. I prepare myself for the emotional resuscitation or the emotional guidance of the family in their grief. The patient was gone before they got there [in the ED]. In a better world, they wouldn't be there because there is nothing natural or sanctimonious about being declared dead in a resuscitation. It is far more natural to be declared dead with your own family in your own home. We have now taken that patient out of their environment, away from their family, brought that family to a very strange place that is very unnatural only to be served the news that their loved one has died.

The 'resuscitation' of the relatives and friends of the patient became more important than the patient's resuscitation attempt. The staff used the resuscitation motions and prescriptions as a platform to achieve other values. They might turn the resuscitative effort into a 'good death' ritual in which they prolong the lifesaving attempt to give relatives and friends the option to say goodbye to their dying loved one (Timmermans 1997).

The legal protections guaranteeing universal lifesaving care have not resulted in qualitatively enhanced lifesaving but instead have created a new set of criteria that need to be checked off before a patient can be pronounced dead. In Sudnow's study, social death often preceded and predicted irreversible biological death. The staff of 'Cohen' and 'County' hospitals did not stretch the lifesaving effort unnecessarily. Once patients of presumed low social value showed obvious signs of biological death, the staff would quickly pronounce them officially deceased. Currently, many patients of presumed low social value in resuscitative efforts are already biologically dead when they are wheeled into the ED. The time it takes to exhaust the resuscitation protocols has created a new temporal interval with *legal death* as the endpoint. This management of sudden death does not reduce any social inequality. The same situational identity features that marginalized certain groups of patients still predict the intensity of lifesaving fervour. Social death now also becomes a predictor of legal death

Resuscitation Theory

Not only do the staff use legal guidelines to perpetuate existing views of social inequality, but health care providers also reappropriate the accumulated medical knowledge about resuscitations to justify withholding care of *new groups with presumed low social value*. For a technique that is not really proved to be effective with national survival rates, the field of resuscitation medicine has a surprisingly high level of agreement as to what constitutes the best chances for survival.[7] From physician to technician to chaplain in the ED, almost all respondents provided a more or less complete reflection of the dominant theory. The basics of resuscitation theory are very simple: the quicker the steps of the 'chain of survival' are carried out (Cummins et al. 1991), the better the chances for survival. The chain consists of four links: early access to emergency care, early CPR, early defibrillation and early advanced care. A weakness in one step will reverberate throughout the entire system and impair optimal survival rates.

The chain of survival is intended as a simple tool for educators, researchers and policy makers to evaluate whether a community obtains optimal patient survival. In the ED, however, the same theoretical notions underlying the chain of survival serve as a rationalization for *not* trying to resuscitate particular patient groups. The professional rescuers in the ED are acutely aware of their *location* in the chain of survival's temporal framework. The ED is the last link of the survival chain, and many elements need to have fallen in place before the patient reaches the hands of the team. Anything that deviates from the 'ideal' resuscitative pattern and causes more time to elapse is a matter of concern for the staff. One technician estimated how important every step in the resuscitation process is for the final outcome:

> One of the most important things would be the time between when the patient actually went down until the first people arrive. That is like, I'd say, 30 per cent and then the time that a patient takes to get to the hospital takes another, probably, 30–40 per cent. Sixty to 70 per cent of it is pre-hospital time.

The consequence of this acute awareness about their location in the chain of survival is that the emergency medical hospital staff feel only limited control over the outcome of the resuscitative effort. A physician reiterated: 'for a lot of these people, their outcome is written in stone before I see them.' A colleague added: 'there are certainly many, many instances of cardiac arrest where the end result is predestined, where the chance of resuscitation is very slim.' Most respondents echoed the nurse supervisor who remarked: 'I think there are always factors involved whether a resuscitation is successful or not. But I don't know if there is any personal or even physical control.'

Because of this perceived lack of control, health care providers were less willing to resuscitate patients aggressively who deviate from the ideal scenario. Often such a consensus was reached even before the patient arrived in the ED. I observed how the nurse in charge sent a colleague back to the intensive care unit when paramedics radioed that a patient was found with an unknown downtime, saying, 'We will not need you. She'll be dead.' Sometimes only the name of the patient's town was sufficient for the staff to know that it probably would be 'a short exercise'. The town would give an indication of the transportation time and the available emergency care.

The staff interprets the official theory of reviving as a justification for only lukewarmly attempting to resuscitate patients who did not fit the ideal lifesaving scenario. This rationing rests not on biological but on social grounds. Underneath the staff's reluctance to revive patients who deviate from the ideal resuscitative scenario lies the fear that the patient would be only partially resuscitated and suffer from brain damage. According to the dominant resuscitation theory (CPR-ECC 1973), irreversible brain damage occurs after less than five minutes of oxygen deprivation. The staff are concerned that if they revive a patient after this critical time period, the patient might be severely neurologically disabled or comatose. When a nurse got a patient's pulse back, she exclaimed: 'Oh no, we can't do that to him. He must be braindead by now.' A physician stated: 'There have been situations where after a prolonged downtime we get a pulse back. My first feeling is, "My God, what have I done?" It is a horrible feeling because you know that patient will be put in the unit and ultimately their chances of walking out of the hospital without any neurological deficits are almost zero.' Health care providers generally consider this the ultimate 'nightmare scenario', an outcome that will haunt them for years to come.[8] The patient survived in a permanent vegetative state, continuously requiring emotional and financial resources of relatives and society in general.

With those 'excesses' in mind, several respondents made thinly veiled arguments in favour of passive euthanasia. A nurse stated that she felt that in many cases attempting to resuscitate patients meant 'prolonging their suffering'. A technician asserted that 'with an extensive medical history it is inhumane to try'. Another technician reflected: 'Sometimes you wonder if it is really for the benefit of the patient.' A chaplain even made a case for suicide (or euthanasia, depending on who the 'them' are in his sentence): 'I feel a bit of relief knowing that if a person couldn't be resuscitated to a productive life, that it is probably just as well to have them have the right to end life.' The principle that guides the rescuer's work is that a quick death is preferable to a lingering death with limited cognitive functioning in an intensive care unit. A nurse said this explicitly: 'The child survived with maximum brain injury and has become now, instead of a child that they [the parents] can mourn and put in the ground, a child that they mourn for years.'

Although health care providers again hesitated to define a criterion for a quality of life they would find unacceptable, I found implicit in both interviews and observations a view that such lives were not worth living. Drawing from the dominant resuscitation theory, the *prospect* of long-term physical and mental disabilities was reason enough to slow down the lifesaving attempt to the point of uselessness. In an age of disability rights, health care providers reflect and perpetuate the stereotypic assumptions that disability invokes (Zola 1984; Fine and Asch 1988; Mairs 1996). People with disabilities are associated with perpetual dependency and helplessness; they are viewed as victims leading pitiful lives, 'damaged creatures who should be put out of their misery' (Mairs 1996: 120). Disability symbolizes a lack of control over life, and health care providers fall back on the outcome over which they have the most control. The *possibility* of disability is considered worse than biological death. In a survey of 105 experienced emergency health care providers (doctors, nurses and EMTs), 82 per cent would prefer death for themselves over severe neurological disability (Hauswald and Tanberg 1993).

Along with the dominant resuscitation theory, health care providers support the view that people with disabilities should not be resuscitated. To be fair, the same theory is also invoked as a warning about giving up too soon. Several respondents mentioned that one can never be sure whether a report about downtime and transportation time is accurate. Even if there was a long transportation time, one cannot be certain when the patient went into cardiac arrest. Exactly because there exists this margin of uncertainty, many respondents considered it worthwhile at least to attempt to resuscitate and follow the protocols. In most observed resuscitative efforts, however, it appeared that the expectations were clearly set and became self-fulfilling prophecies.

Social Rationing and the Medicalisation of Sudden Death

In the conclusion to *Passing On*, David Sudnow discussed the ways in which dying became an institutional routine and a meaningful event for the hospital staff. He emphasized that the staff attempted to maintain an attitude of 'appropriate impersonality' toward death and how the organization of the ward and the teaching hospital favoured social death preceding biological death. In ethnomethodological fashion, Sudnow (1967: 169) underscored how 'death' and 'dying' emerged out of the interactions and practices of health care providers: 'what has been developed is a "procedural definition of dying," a definition based upon the activities which that phenomenon can be said to *consist in.*'[9]

My update of Sudnow's study indicates that with the widespread use of resuscitation technologies, health care providers now have to make sense of engaging in a practice with the small chance of saving lives and the potential to severely disable patients. They cope with this dilemma by deliberately not trying to revive certain groups of patients. These groups are not distinguished by their clinical potential but by their social viability. The staff reappropriates biomedical protocols and legal guidelines to refine further a system of implicit social rationing. The bulk of resuscitative efforts are still characterized by a detached attitude towards patients. In most reviving efforts, the staff feels defeated in advance and reviving becomes an empty ritual of going through mandated motions. It is only when patients transcend anonymity and gain a sense of personhood that the staff will aggressively try to revive them.

With regard to the broader institutional context, resuscitation is less than in Sudnow's study, marked by the health care provider's desire to 'obtain "experience," avoid dirty work and maximize the possibility that the intern will manage some sleep' (Sudnow 1967: 170) as well as by the requirements of defensive medicine and managed care. With the gradual erosion of physician autonomy because of peer review and utilization boards, the wave of cost-effectiveness in medicine, the proliferation of medical malpractice suits and the patient rights movement, physicians' practices have become more externally regulated. As several respondents commented, a resuscitative effort is as much an attempt to avoid a lawsuit as an endeavour to save lives. Health care providers try to manoeuvre within the boundaries of the law, professional ethics and biomedical knowledge to maintain lives worth living and proper deaths for their patients. Every resuscitative effort becomes a balancing act of figuring out when 'enough is enough' based on the clinical situation and prognosis, legal and ethical guidelines, the wishes of the patient and relatives, and – most importantly – the preferences and emotions of the resuscitation team. The latter are in charge, so ultimately their definitions of the situation and their values will prevail.

Instead of concluding that such rampant social inequality is an inevitable part of the interaction between the patient and the care provider, I suggest that the policy changes of the last decades did not address the broader societal foundations of social inequality. Unfortunately, the attitudes of the emergency staff reflect and perpetuate those of a society generally not equipped culturally or structurally to accept the elderly or people with disabilities as people whose lives are valued and valuable (Mulkay and Ernst 1991). As the need for and problems with an Americans with Disabilities Act show, the disabled and seriously ill are not socially dead only in the ED but also in the outside world; this is the original sense in which Erving Goffman first introduced social death (1961). The staff have internalized beliefs about the presumed low worth of elderly and disabled people to the extent that more than 80 per cent would rather be dead than live with a severe neurological disability. As gatekeepers between life and death, they have the opportunity to execute explicitly the pervasive but more subtle moral code of the wider society. Just as schools, restaurants, and modes of transportation became the battlegrounds and symbols in the civil rights struggle, medical interventions such as genetic counselling, euthanasia and resuscitative efforts represent the sites of contention in the disability and elderly rights movements (Fine and Asch 1988; Schneider 1993).

Rationalizing medical practice or providing legal accountability only accentuated the medicalization of the dying process and social inequality. The biomedical protocols are part of the problem of the medicalization of death because they promote aggressive care instead of providing means to terminate a reviving attempt (Timmermans 1999), and the staff rely on those theories to justify not resuscitating people who might become disabled. Legal initiatives mostly stimulated the predominance of resuscitative efforts at the expense of other ways of dying and have been unable to protect marginalized groups.

In the liminal space between lives worth living and proper deaths, resuscitative efforts in the ED crystallize submerged subtle attitudes of the wider society. The ED staff enforce and perpetuate our refusal to let go of life and to accommodate certain groups. Preusely because health care providers implement our moral codes, they are the actors who might be able to initiate a change in attitudes. On a personal level, many health care providers seem to have made up their minds about the limitations of reviving. Medical researchers presented emergency health care providers with a common 48-minute resuscitation scenario with a relatively good prognosis and a reasonable time course. Only 2.9 per cent of the respondents would prefer to be resuscitated for the entire episode (Hauswald and Tanberg 1993). If those who are the most informed and have the most personal experience with resuscitative efforts are reluctant to undergo lifesaving attempts, the solution for social inequality needs to be sought among initiatives which discourage CPR for all.

Acknowledgments

This chapter is a shortened version of a paper published in *The Sociological Quarterly*, 19198 39 (2), 453–72. I thank the University of California Press for their permission to reprint it here. I also thank Sharon Hogan, Norm Denzin, Linda McKie, Margie Towery, and anonymous reviewers for their useful comments.

Notes

1   Social rationing means the withholding of potentially beneficial medical interventions based on social grounds (see Conrad and Brown 1993).
2   Bauman does not argue that resuscitative efforts are not decided on patients' presumed social worth any longer, but that social discrimination has shifted from 'primitive' technologies to more advanced medical technologies such as organ donation and 'the electronic computerized gadgetry'.
3   Sometimes medical critics will discuss the ethical implications of individualized resuscitation scenarios. Part of Sudnow's contribution, however, was to show that social rationing was not an isolated, individualized event, but a widespread, social practice.
4   Massachusetts General Law c.111C, Paragraph 14 states that 'No emergency medical technician certified under the provisions of this chapter... who in the performance of his duties and in good faith renders emergency first aid or transportation to an injured person or to a person incapacitated by illness shall be personally in any way liable as a result of transporting such person to a hospital or other safe place...'
5   In contrast with Sudnow's conceptual preference, I opt for social viability to indicate the grounds of rationing because social worth is too broad to indicate the variations in reviving attempts.
6   Death is obvious when rigor mortis has set in, decapitation has occurred the body is consumed by fire, or there is a massive head injury with parts missing.
7   Partly this is due to the fact that US (and international) resuscitation medicine is dominated by a limited number of research groups who mostly seem to agree with each other. According to Niemann about 85 per cent of all CPR related research articles in the United States come from a community of ten research groups (Niemann 1998: 8).
8   The physician told me this story six years after it happened. My original question was 'Can you give me an example of a resuscitative effort that left a big impression on you?'
9   Although I did not emphasize Sudnow's ethnomethodological legacy in this Chapter, the idea of lifesaving, the technology, and saving lives in itself are jointly accomplished in practice (see Timmermans and Berg 1997). The ironic aspect of resuscitation technology is that resuscitation techniques and practice establish the value of saving lives at all costs while the actual numbers of saved lives remain very low. I discuss this seeming paradox at length in my book (Timmermans 1999). I thank Norm Denzin for drawing my attention to the ethnomethodological importance of Sudnow's study.

References

Bauman, Z. 1992. *Mortality, Immortality and Other Life Strategies*. Stanford, Ca: Stanford University Press.

Becker, L., B. M. P. Ostrander, J. Barrett, and G. T. Kondos. 1991. 'Outcome of CPR in a Large Metropolitan Area: Where are the Survivors?', *Annals of Emergency Medicine* 20: 355–61.

Berg, M. 1997. *Rationalizing Medical Work: A Study of Decision Support Techniques and Medical Practices*. Cambridge, Mass: MIT Press.

Conrad, P. and P. Brown. 1993. 'Rationing Medical Care: A Sociological Reflection', *Research in the Sociology of Health Care* 10: 3–22.

CPR-ECC. 1973. 'Standards for Cardiopulmonary Resuscitation and Emergency Cardiac Care', *JAMA* 227: 836–68.

CPR-ECC. 1992. 'Guidelines for Cardiopulmonary Resuscitation and Emergency Cardiac Care', *JAMA* 268: 2171–95.

Cummins, R., J. P. Ornato, W. H. Thies, and P. E. Pepe. 1991. 'The "Chain of Survival" Concept', *Circulation* 83: 1832–47.

Eisenberg, M., B. T. Horwood, R. O. Cummins, R. Reynolds-Haertle, and T. R. Hearne 1990. Cardiac Arrest and Resuscitation: A Tale of 29 Cities. *Annals of Emergency Medicine*, 19:2:179–86.

Fine, M., and A. Asch. 1988. 'Disability beyond Stigma: Social Interaction, Discrimination, and Activism', *Journal of Social Issues* 44: 3–21.

Fox, R. C. 1976. 'Advanced Medical Technology: Social and Ethical Implications', *Annual Review of Sociology* 2: 231–68.

Glaser, B. G. and A. L. Strauss. 1964. 'The Social Loss of Dying Patients', *American Journal of Nursing* 64: 119–21.

Glaser, B. G., and A. L. Strauss. 1965. *Awareness of Dying*. Chicago: Aldine.

Glaser, B. G., and A. L. Strauss. 1968. *Time for Dying*. Chicago: Aldine.

Goffman, E. 1961. *Asylums: Essays on the Social Situation of Mental Patients and Other Inmates*. New York: Doubleday Anchor.

Hauswald, M. and D. Tanberg. 1993. 'Out-of-Hospital Resuscitation Preferences of Emergency Health Care Workers', *American Journal of Emergency Medicine* 11: 221–4.

Heckman, J. D. (ed.) 1992. *Emergency Care and Transportation of the Sick and Injured*. Dallas: American Academy of Orthopaedic Surgeons.

Iserson, K. V. and C. Stocking. 1993. 'Standards and Limits: Emergency Physicians' Attitudes toward Prehospital Resuscitation', *American Journal of Emergency Medicine* 11: 592–94.

Kastenbaum, R. and R. Aisenberg. 1972. *The Psychology of Death*. New York: Springer.

Koenig, B. A. 1988. 'The Technological Imperative in Medical Practice: The Social Creation of a "Routine" Treatment', in *Biomedicine Examined*, ed. Margaret Lock and Deborah R. Gordon. Dordrecht: Kluwer Academic Publishers, 465–97.

Mairs, N. 1996. *Waist-High in the World: A Life Among the Nondisabled*. Boston: Beacon Press.

Mulkay, M. and J. Ernst. 1991. 'The Changing Position of Social Death', *European Journal of Sociology* 32: 172–96.

Muller, J. H. 1992. 'Shades of Blue: The Negotiation of Limited Codes by Medical Residents.' *Social Science and Medicine* 34: 885–98.

Niemann, J. T. 1993. 'Study Design in Cardiac Arrest Research: Moving from the Laboratory to the Clinical Population', *Annals of Emergency Medicine* 22: 8–9.

Pelligrino, E. D. 1986. 'Rationing Health Care: The Ethics of Medical Gatekeeping', *Journal of Contemporary Health Law and Policy* 2: 23–44.

Roth, J. A. 1972. 'Some Contingencies of the Moral Evaluation and Control of Clientele: The Case of the Hospital Emergency Service', *American Journal of Sociology* 77: 839–55.

Schneider, J. P. 1993. *No Pity: People with Disabilities Forging a New Civil Rights Movement.* New York: Random House.

Sudnow, D. 1967. *Passing On: The Social Organization of Dying.* Englewood Cliffs, NJ: Prentice-Hall.

Sudnow, D. 1983. 'D.O.A', in *Where Medicine Fails*, ed. Anselm Strauss. Lovelorn, NJ: Transaction Books, 275–94.

Timmermans, S. 1997. 'High Tech in High Touch: The Presence of Relatives and Friends during Resuscitative Efforts', *Scholarly Inquiry for Nursing Practice* 11: 153–68.

Timmermans, S. 1998. 'Resuscitation Technology in the Emergency Department: Toward a Dignified Death', *Sociology of Health and Illness.* 20: 144–67.

Timmermans, S. 1999. *Sudden Death and the Myth of CPR.* Philadelphia: Temple University Press.

Timmermans, S. and M. Berg. 1997. 'Standardization in Action: Achieving Local Universality through Medical Protocols', *Social Studies of Science* 27: 273–305.

Zola, I. K. 1984. *Missing Pieces: A Chronicle of Living with a Disability.* Philadelphia: Temple University Press.

Part III
Working Bodies

9
Making Bodies, Making People, Making Work

Lisa Adkins and Celia Lury

Introduction

This chapter explores the labour of identity not simply as the work of self-identity, but also as the work or labour of production, a kind of sub-field in the division of labour.[1] However, we do not presume that these two processes run concurrently; rather we start from the position that just as a person's relation to his or her self-identity cannot be assumed, so the relationship between (different aspects of) personhood and production is not fixed. Indeed, we hope to show that a person's self-identity is a key site of contestation in the political struggle that maps out production. While many recent studies (for example, du Gay 1996) have focused on the self-identity of people in the workplace, we believe (and have argued elsewhere: Adkins and Lury 1996) that such studies have stopped short of considering how the labour of identity contributes to the political organization of production. In the frequently made assumption that it is the self-identity of workers that is the issue, the question of a person's relation to that self-identity is hidden. It is as if while everybody has an identity, and those identities are recognized to be different (and complex and contradictory), every person's relation to their (complex, contradictory) self-identity is the same, that is, a reflexive relation of performance. Everybody, it is implied, is in the same position vis-à-vis their capacity reflexively to perform their identity as part of an employment contract. But is this so? Isn't this to presume the labour of identity, to presume the relationships between self and identity, and of both with the body?

In what follows we illustrate the significance of exploring not simply the kinds of self-identity that are available to workers, but the terms, conditions and effects of their availability, that is, we seek to explicate the mutual interdependence of the performance of identity and the performativity of economies. We will be sensitive to the ways in which the labour of identity is both produced by and helps produce the labour of production, including its organization in hierarchical occupations, regulation in labour markets, spatial distribution and temporal rhythms. In doing so, we foreground issues of the body and gender which we see as important aspects of both identity and the division of labour. We also pay attention to the specific ways in which techniques of the self – of reiteration, of citation, of performance – may or may not be deployed in the creation of workplace identities. However, we do not presume that either the gendering of self-identity or the gendering of the labour of division has precedence over the other. On the contrary, what we hope to show is that one cannot be considered without reference to the other.

Reflexive Accumulation

To do so we turn first to recent social theory, especially that which emphasizes an increasing significance of the aestheticization and emotionalization of social life. Lash and Urry (1994), for example, highlight this process in relation to shifts in the organization of the economy, suggesting that the aesthetic and the emotional components of labour are taking on increasing value in comparison with its 'technical' aspects. They argue that this shift is connected to a process of individualization, which in turn requires a reflexive – that is, a self-monitoring and self-appraising – subject. They link the emergence of this reflexive subject to the

> ongoing process of de-traditionalization in which social agents are increasingly 'set free' from the heteronomous control or monitoring of social structures in order to be self-monitoring or self-reflexive.
>
> (Lash and Urry 1994: 4–5)

A number of workplace techniques are identified as precipitating – or 'forcing' – this shift, including the intensification of the management of employee dress codes and behaviour, and increasing interventions into the emotional lives of employees through therapy, counselling, stress management practices, and self-appraisal and performance review techniques. Many of these techniques, Lash and Urry note, open up and make available the emotional and aesthetic aspects of the worker's self-identity for mobilization as labour market resources.

Like Lash and Urry, a range of feminist writers have noted the increasing emotionalization and aestheticization of labour. But much of this commentary focuses on family labour and has a much longer time frame. So, for example, Game and Pringle (1984) argue that with what they call the shift from production to consumption work, housework has become increasingly emotionalized and aestheticized. As they note, this is a shift that has been underway since *at least* the beginning of the twentieth century. They discuss the ways in which, for example, shopping has developed into a key activity in terms of family labour for women: taking not only progressively more time but also acquiring an increasing symbolic significance. Thus shopping is not simply a straightforward technical or rational activity, but involves selecting the 'right' goods to please and express love for 'husbands, boyfriends, children, even the dog, the cat' (1984: 123). Similarly, they note how, with the rise of full-time 'housewives' performing their work in single-family dwellings (once again implying a much longer-term process than that discussed by Lash and Urry), housework has increasingly taken on emotional value. Indeed so strong is this emotionalization of housework, that to complain is 'tantamount to saying [women] don't love their husbands and children'. Significantly, such emotionalization is not about reflecting, knowing about and acting on one's own emotional requirements/needs, as if such needs could be defined independently of others or of context, rather it is about care for the other and responding to the other within a familial economy in which the self and its needs are continually at issue. It is not an individualizing process; nor one in which aspects of the self – affect, appearance, technical expertise – can be easily separated or detached from the person and are thus not easily made available for self-possession.

Thus Game and Pringle suggest that in the context of family labour both emotionalization and aestheticization have been significant for much of the twentieth century. But what kind of identity is involved in the work of consumption or family labour? Is it the individualized identity required by regimes of reflexive accumulation? Game and Pringle's research suggests that it is not: far from knowing one's self in ways which are self-promoting and self-enhancing, the successful presentation of identity required to be a wife/mother requires a self which is other-directed, and responsive. It is also an identity which is not easily made available to the self in the form of a self-authorized narrative (it is more usually a repetition: I washed up this morning and then I washed up again this evening) and is thus not recognizable in terms of commonly available heroic genres such as adventure or self-discovery. It does not have the developmental – or accumulative – potential of the identities created in such genres. In the context of the family, whilst women/wives may carry out this work of identity they do not 'own' its effects because their work is appropriated through the structuring of marital and familial relations. The context of the family thus provides a set of relations in which the woman is dispossessed of her self-identity through complex, historically changing processes, including those of romanticism, normalization and naturalization (including specific forms of biological or bodily essentialism).

Two points strike us as particularly significant about this research. First, studies such as Game and Pringle's – carried out over 15 years ago now – suggest that emotionalization and aestheticization of work may have a far longer history, and certainly is not as novel, as many commentators on the contemporary labour market suggest. Second, by implication, such research shows that much of the contemporary writing on the labour market only reveals processes of emotionalization and aestheticization in relation to a particular kind of worker, namely an individualized, reflexive worker who has the ability to detach aspects of self-presentation from the context of production and claim them through the performance of identity as a labour market resource.

Accumulating Reflexivity

In order to explore the provenance of this ideal of the individualized, reflexive worker in more detail, let us consider some recent management theory. Our first example is that of the worker who enters into a 'psychological contract'. According to an article in the *European Management Journal*, psychological contracts of employment are defined as 'the understanding people have regarding the commitments made between themselves and their organization.... [they concern] an individual's belief in and interpretation of a promissary contract, whether written or unwritten' (Hiltrop 1995: 287). The author continues:

> Since psychological contracts are, by definition, voluntary, subjective, dynamic and informal, it is virtually impossible to spell out all details at the time a contract is created. The dynamic character of the psychological contract means that individual and organizational expectations mutually influence one another. People fill in the blanks along the way, and they sometimes do so inconsistently. Yet these 'additions' are a reality that has many implications for the success of the organization.
>
> (1995: 287)

In this view, the successful worker is one who not only can make all aspects of self-identity available to the employer (Total Employee Involvement, TEI), but can also freely adapt his or her self-identity to a changing environment: what Hiltrop elsewhere describes as the 'free agency' employment strategy. Implicit here is the neo-social Darwinianism described by Martin in her study of the emergence of the ideal of the flexible body across a range of social domains (1994). It is an understanding of workplace identity linked to an 'achievement culture' in which each worker's ability to enter into an employment contract depends upon his or her ability to survive in increasingly 'ambiguous' workplace 'environments', their progress monitored by regular appraisal and performance reviews. It is a matter of adaptation, people reflexively filling in the blanks along the way.

Further indication of the idealized relation between self and identity assumed in the notion of reflexivity is offered by discussions of how 'feedback' should function in self-appraisal or performance review. In an article in *Human Resource Development Quarterly*, Nickols aims to 'revisit the technical view of feedback and to stimulate its broader, better application' (1995: 289). He does so by outlining his own first encounter with the term: 'as a young US Navy technician working on complex shipboard naval weapons systems' (1995: 289). Drawing a parallel between the worker and military machinery, he identifies two key characteristics of feedback:

> First, the purpose of feedback is *control*. Feedback is used to control the gun mount's position and its movement. Said somewhat differently, feedback is used to obtain results and to shape behaviour. Second, feedback is an integral element of the system itself, not information from outside the system.... And, as we shall see, this self-contained, self-governing aspect of the technical view of feedback has its counterpart in human performance systems.
>
> (1995: 298–9)

Nickol's analogy between human and machinic performance systems makes it possible for him to assert that the defining characteristics of the reflexive individual are those of self-containment and self-government. The labour of identity involved is obscured by the phrase 'as we shall see' and the three further claims that Nickols makes. The first of these assertions is that feedback 'occurs naturally. Contrivance is unnecessary' (1995: 292). The second is that 'Unlike gun mounts, people have minds of their own. Their behaviour is exactly that – *their* behaviour' (1995:

291). While the third, somewhat more complicated, is that while performance is often confused with behaviour, 'it pays to keep the two straight' (1995: 293).

In the first of these claims, Nickols posits the naturalness of feedback, so ignoring the different ways in which self-reflection has been socially organized, making it the abstract ability of the universal individual rather than the outcome of specific social relations. In the second claim, he not only makes behaviour the personal possession of the individual, but also voluntary in so far as the individual sets his or her own goals. The third assertion makes visible how the imposition of such notions of performance may contribute to the creation of occupational resources. As noted above, Nickols makes a distinction between performance and behaviour; crucially, performance includes 'a complex mix of goals, expectations, behavior *and the effects of behavior*' (1995: 293; our emphasis). In claiming ownership of the effects of behaviour evaluated by others as well as oneself as part of one's own individual performance ('Feedback is information about my performance': 1995: 296), the worker is able to appropriate his or her reflexive relation to identity as an occupational resource. In this way, he or she may be able to enhance his or her position within an occupational hierarchy.

In his account, Nickols asserts that feedback is natural. However, he presumes and prescribes a self-possessed and self-transforming subject; indeed, it is only such a subject who could lay claim to behaviours and their effects as occupational resources. Feedback, in Nickols' terms, not only makes available all aspects of the self for management, it does so in terms that are set by the individual himself: 'What is essential to understand here is that the classification of feedback as positive or negative is made by the person receiving it' (1995: 294). This is to ignore the ways in which reflexivity – or feedback – is a key site of contestation between workers. In contrast to Nickols, we suggest that feedback is a strategy that may be more or less successfully operated by workers; workers may be more or less able to classify feedback as positive or negative, to set their own ends. Thus we do not assume that this success – and the survival which success brings – is equally available to all workers. Rather, we believe, and will go on to argue, that some groups of workers are likely to be denied, through specific practices, the ability to perform self-identity (and claim occupational resources) that are recognized positively in practices such as feedback. In short, their behaviour or presentation of self-identity will tend not to be recognized as reflexive and thus, while contributing to the performativity of organizations, is not made worth their while (it does not pay for them individually as a performance). We will further argue that this lack of recognition occurs in gendered practices of naturalization. In other words, our claim is that the notion of reflexivity realized in workplace practices is likely to be gendered and is part of a gendered regime of reflexive accumulation. We shall now try to support this view by considering some recent studies of specific occupations.

Naturalization

In a research project on employment in tourist organizations, Adkins (1995) shows that workplace identities are not universally available as resources and, in particular, that identities are not constituted as the property of the self that all workers are equally free to exchange. She looks at the ways in some service workplaces producing and maintaining a sexualized identity for women is 'part of the job'. Presenting a certain appearance and a sexualized way of being is required, appropriated and simultaneously denied. This paradox arises because of the ways in which the required sexual identity practices cannot be detached from their person, contracted out and freely exchanged; on the contrary, these identity practices are rendered intrinsic to women workers through relations of appropriation. So, for example, the gendered relations of production in these sites ensure that women's labour (including the production of workplace identities) is frequently embodied as part of their selves. Moreover, this embodiment is achieved through a process of naturalization; more specifically, this embodiment is not seen to be a consequence of reflexivity. Rather it is seen to exist – indeed is required to exist – independently of the women's occupational skills. As a consequence, the women in Adkins' study did not 'own' their workplace identities. In this sense, they are not individuals at work; rather, they are gendered workers, that is, the social group 'women workers'.

Men workers in these sites, on the other hand, were more able (although none actually reached, and some were more able than others) to come close to the ideal of the reflexive individual at work. (Clearly, sexual, age, classed and race-related identities are also produced and appropriated in relations of production and thus not all men are equally available to approach the abstract ideal of the individual.) That (some) men were able to do so is because they are not required to have an already fixed or naturalized relationship between self and identity. As a consequence, men as workers are better placed to detach their labour and make use of their identity as a resource. Put simply, because men are not required to have a fixed or natural relationship between self and identity, they are more able to determine there own 'self-hood'. This is true even in many aspects of their workplace relationship to their bodies and self-presentation. Thus, unlike women workers, men workers may claim their workplace identity as their own property, as a self-identity, which they may contract out and exchange, and make use of as a labour market resource, that is they may act as individualized workers, with performable identities.

Hochshild's (1983) work on airline attendants suggests Adkins' findings do not describe conditions specific to tourist organizations. She shows that from the 1950s onwards, emotional servicing became a naturalized and unrewarded requirement of the job for women. Other research on the airline industry by Williams (1988) further shows that the outcome or effects of a naturalized presentation of self – that is, emotionally appeased customers and men co-workers – cannot be claimed through performance as indicators of personal effectivity. Women airline attendants present aestheticized – attractive, desirable – selves and attend to customers' emotional desires. The achievement of this self is not rewarded, yet if women do not carry out this naturalized labour of identity, discipline may follow: 'the minute you don't smile you get a complaint' (Williams 1988: 107). Thus, within the airline industry women do not gain and retain jobs because of the particular occupational resources they possess; rather they are employed as 'women' with an assumed responsiveness. Moreover these terms and conditions of employment for women do not operate for men workers. They may differentiate themselves from each other – that is, achieve a reflexive self-identity – because they are not hired or retained on the basis of being 'men' but rather on the basis of what skills they possess. In this way, men airline attendants can claim their relation to self-identity as an occupational resource. Put another way they can claim to own their selves and achieve a reflexive identity in a way that women attendants cannot.

All this, however, is not to deny that, as a number of recent studies have shown, in an increasing range of jobs, for men as well as for women, there is now an emphasis on the presentation of aestheticized selves. Such changes have been taken by some as an indicator not only of an increasing move to a performative structuring of service economies (see Crang 1997),[2] but also as an indicator that workplace hierarchies may no longer be figured in terms of collective categories such as gender. For instance, it is sometimes claimed that the emphasis on both men and women presenting aestheticized selves is potentially disruptive of traditional techniques of the gendering of work since, for example, it

Discussion

displaces the ideal of the disembodied worker which has been seen as central to the making of women's disadvantage at work. However, we suggest that, rather than simply indicating the disappearance of long-standing techniques of the gendering of work, such presentations make visible new techniques of gendering in reflexive economies and illustrate how the formation of identity that occurs in the workplace is significant for the production of bodies.

The is slight move away from

Although the authors themselves do not analyse their findings in these terms, these conclusions can be drawn from McDowell and Court's study of professional financial service sector workers (McDowell and Court 1994; McDowell 1997). Here particular attention is paid to the corporeal performances of workers because such performances are understood to 'have become an integral element of workplace success' (McDowell 1997: 139). They note, for example, that while many of the men workers performed a traditional, disembodied, patriarchal masculinity, younger men were performing various forms of 'body work' (that is, forms of work which are often associated with the workplace performances of women). These younger men were conscious of the significance of bodily discipline for their work, and paid considerable attention to issues of dress, style and weight. Yet while such men are increasingly performing (and being rewarded for) body work, McDowell and Court found corporeal performances of 'masculinity' for women 'whether through dress or behaviour...to be counterproductive' (McDowell and Court 1994: 745). So, for example, the efforts of those women who adopt a 'feminised version of the male uniform' (McDowell 1997: 146) or who perform as 'honorary men' are shown to be 'doomed to failure' (McDowell 1997: 197).

lit. review

McDowell and Court's evidence on men and women workers' performances shows how self-monitoring and self-appraisal are deployed in relation to the corporeal styles of 'femininity' and 'masculinity' by both groups. What is important from our point of view, however, is that these performances are not equally recognized as reflexive. For example, while men's 'feminized' corporeal performances 'work' in the sense that they are recognized to be a product of reflexivity and are mobilized as workplace resources, women's 'masculinized' performances tend not to be recognized as reflexive at all. On the contrary, they are demeaned and trivialized, defined as inappropriate, unexchangable performances. Far from constituting workplace resources and allowing women to claim a position as workers with a reflexive relation to corporeality, such performances are 'doomed to failure' and usually 'backfire'.

lit

performed without conscious thought

Interestingly, McDowell and Court stress that the difficulties in terms of these more 'masculinized' performances relate to the ways in which a particular mode of corporeality centring on femininity – for instance, presenting a desirable and responsive (hetero)sexed body – tends to be normalized in workplace practices (McDowell 1997: 140). Even though some women set out to subvert this naturalization, nevertheless they felt unhappy in their adoption and exploitation of a parodic femininity which they found demeaning (McDowell and Court 1994: 746). Thus even though a range of (self-monitored) forms of body work are performed by women, they are not conducted in conditions which allow a reflexive relation to corporeality to be claimed.[3] Instead, feminine corporeality is naturalized as part of their selves for women workers.

For men workers, on the other hand, a naturalized relation between body and self is clearly not a problem; rather, in many cases men workers' corporeal acts are recognized as workplace performances. Indeed, not only can they claim their corporeal acts as performances, they may also claim mobility in relation to modes of corporeality. Thus, unlike women where there is a naturalization of the labour of corporeality, these men may 'take on' and 'take off' various modes of corporeality. In this sense, it seems that (some) men may be coming close to reaching the ideal of 'flexible' corporeality – a mode of corporeality, which is adaptable, innovative, continuously adjusting and adjustable in changing workplace environments. And, as Martin (1994) has shown, such flexibility increasingly secures workplace rewards. Indeed, while the ideal of the disembodied worker may well be being displaced in service economies through men's performances of body work, it seems that a new ideal of flexible corporeality is emerging, one which, we suggest, can only be reached through a performative and mobile relation to corporeality. Such an ideal, however, is clearly one from which many women are likely to be excluded.

Accumulating Reflexivity and Reflexive Accumulation

As our introduction indicates, we do not think that the labour of identity is simply determined by the division of labour; rather, we believe it is likely that the labour of identity will also help create the division of labour. To try to explore this, we turn now to Newton's (1995) study of stress management, *Managing Stress*. Here Newton argues that management practices place responsibility on employees for managing and coping with their own stress and emotions and, as a consequence, individualize workers. For example, through psychotherapy and other psychosocial techniques stress management practices can 'treat [problems] as a form of [individual] sickness, curable by means of therapeutic intervention' (1995: 103). Newton finds this process of individualization associated with such therapeutic interventions problematic. He wishes to redefine stress in terms of socially stratified and gender segregated workplaces, and power relations between employer and employee. More specifically, Newton implies that stress and stressed subjects are the product of these workplace divisions.

But we would reverse the terms of his analysis. Rather than simply being the outcome of already given workplace power relations and hierarchies we see stress management and in particular the constitution of the stressed subject – that is the achievement of a manageable stressed identity – as constitutive of new forms of workplace hierarchy and division. We see such practices as part of the restructuring of the labour market in which new resources – such as emotion and style or aesthetics – are being mobilized by workers and are productive of new hierarchies and divisions. In particular, we believe that the issues of whether and how stress can be managed, and whether and how it is seen to be intrinsic to the job or workplace environment, are highly political issues in the organization of occupational hierarchies.

Newton's own study gives us evidence of this. He notes, for example, that there may be an element of (what he terms) coercion involved in stress management practices. Specifically, he argues that job promotion may be consequent on the ready participation of the employee in such programmes. He argues that because such practices are designed to dissipate frustrations and improve job performance, employees who participate and learn to 'manage' their stress are looked on favourably by employers. But rather than seeing stress management as simply a technique to dissipate employee grievances, we would suggest that Newton's evidence is indicative of a far more fundamental shift in the labour market. Specifically, we believe it suggests that becoming an individualized reflexive worker – in this case achieving a stressed identity – is an occupational resource within (some) workplaces. Thus, learning to know one's self (becoming reflexive) and managing one's own stress at work, that is, achieving a stressed, individualized identity, may lead to promotion and other workplace rewards. It suggests that new workplace hierarchies are emerging in which knowledge of and management of the self may be exchanged for labour market remuneration. This leads us to question Newton's assumption that it is their position in lower levels of occupational control and discretion in the workplace that lead women to experience greater stress than men. On the contrary, we suggest, it is women's inability to achieve a stressed identity of their own – and other reflexively individualized forms of identity (because they are workers as women) – which is in part constitutive of 'lower levels of occupational control and discretion'. This inability, we suggest, is a consequence of the fixing of the stress in the workplace environment rather than in the worker as individual.

Newton himself brings up the issue of workplace environment in his suggestion that workplace 'stress' and stress management practices are often particularly at issue in periods of environmental change. For Newton stress management practices reinforce 'the normality of environmental change because it portrays an image of people being able to cope with any kind of change provided they are stress fit' (Newton 1995: 67). But we would argue that what is at issue in relation to workplace 'stress' is not so much a normalization of environmental change, but rather the constitution of subjects who are able to detach and differentiate aspects of themselves from 'stressful' workplace environments. Put slightly differently, being able to be 'stress fit', that is, being mobile, flexible and adaptable in relation to shifting environments, depends on the ability to differentiate a self-managed (reflexive) identity from the workplace context. Yet as we have shown, some workers are unable to differentiate their identities from the environment, that is, to claim their labour of identity as resources for exchange. In particular we have shown how workplace processes often deny women workers ownership of identity. So while, on the one hand, practices such as stress management define workers as requiring reflexive techniques of self-management to succeed, on the other, workplace processes do not allow some workers to own and manage stress because they prevent these workers claiming ownership of their identities. As a consequence workers who are dispossessed of self-identity end up permanently 'stressed out' (that is, permanently caught up in stressful workplace environments) but at the same time unable to claim they can manage this stress because they cannot detach and differentiate their 'selves' from (stressful) workplace contexts. Thus, we suggest, such processes of dispossession may account not only for women's greater levels of stress at work but also their 'lower levels of control and discretion'. Indeed, in these ways we suggest that a worker's relation to self-identity should be recognized to be a technique of gender in the labour market which creates gendered division and hierarchy, and is not simply determined by it.

Speculations/Conclusions

We have shown that a number of techniques – such as self-appraisal, performance review and forms of stress and emotion management – are productive of a new range of identities which are themselves exchanged as resources in the labour market. Thus such techniques are in part constitutive of the reflexive workers currently required for accumulation. But we have also shown just how difficult it is for women workers to achieve such reflexive identities because their labour of identity may be naturalized as part of their selves, and cannot be mobilized as a resource. Whilst, as we have made clear, women's position as workers certainly requires self-monitoring and self-appraisal, this is often carried out in different conditions to men workers who can make use of such self-monitoring as a workplace resource. In contrast to men, women workers cannot claim ownership of their performance and as such men workers are far better placed to fulfil reflexive subjecthood as defined by Lash and Urry. Furthermore, they are better able to use such performances to constitute the social: to create new hierarchies and reward structures within the labour market. This leads us to question just how universal the reflexive worker is in the contemporary economy. Lash (1994) too has considered this issue. Thus he discusses what he terms reflexivity winners and reflexivity losers and in particular the emergence of (new) new reflexive middle classes, a reflexive working class and a (non-reflexive) lower class or underclass. For Lash these classes are defined by access to and exclusion from occupational places which have developed from the new principles of accumulation. However what we have highlighted through our consideration of the performance of identity and the performativity of economies is that achieving reflexive selfhood may not only concern principles of inclusion and exclusion from specific sites, but also the ability to claim ownership of the performance of specific techniques of the self.

Our analysis also suggests that the 'cultural' should not be unproblematically accepted as a universal medium of performance by labour market theorists, for to do so is to fail to see the cultural itself as gendered (Lury 1995). To avoid this, it may be useful to look at what Sedgwick calls 'the representational contract' between one's body and the world (1994: 230). Such a contract can be seen as one aspect of what Pateman (1988) calls 'the sexual contract', those (historically changing) conditions which make it possible for men to enter into the social contract as if they were free-standing individuals. To fail to look at the terms, conditions and effects of a performative relation to the self is, as Sedgwick argues, to render the notion of reflexivity the effect of nothing more than either individual choice or compulsion. We have been concerned not only to show that a reflexive relation to identity is itself the effect of particular social processes but also that these processes are themselves both gendered and gendering. In doing so, we have begun to document the complexity, range and significance of processes such as naturalization, normalization and trivialization in the making of people, of bodies and of work.

What other implications does our analysis have for the emerging regime of reflexive accumulation? Lash and Urry argue that the distinction between subjects (workers) and objects (including commodities and services) is becoming increasingly difficult to make within this new regime (because, for example, of the increasing importance of aesthetics and emotions). But so, we have suggested men are far better placed to achieve reflexive economic identities, that is, to become the subjects of this regime. Tentatively, we would suggest, women (because of their non-ownership of identity) are more likely to be the objects of reflexive accumulation; that is their identity is (often) part of the product or service, that is, appropriated material. In other words, processes of objectification may be as important as processes of commodification in the new regime of reflexive accumulation.

Notes

1 An earlier version of this chapter was presented at the First Annual CSTT Workshop, 'The Labour of Division', Keele University, 23–25 November, 1995. We are grateful for comments made by participants.
2 The notion of performance has been mobilized in a number of different ways in recent analyses of work. At times it is used to refer to the ways in which work is increasingly individualized. Thus Beck (1992) suggests that labour market positions are now constituted less by determinants such as class or gender location, and more by self-design, self-creation and individual performances. At other times 'performance' is mobilized as a metaphor of theatre to refer to the ways in which service work has a dramaturgical structuring, involving the skills of theatre: acting, role-playing, directing, and so on (see Crang 1997 for a discussion of this understanding). And finally, the term is used to refer to the ways in which job criteria increasingly concern issues of appearance, personality, style, and self-presentation (see Crang 1997, McDowell and Court 1994). Although these different understandings clearly overlap, it is the latter understanding of performance we employ here because it is the most germane to the increasing aestheticisation and emotionalisation of social life we are exploring.
3 While evidence is provided to suggest that some women were often uneasy regarding performances of feminine parody, it is also suggested that such parodies may be subversive of ideals of femininity at work and thus may be

mobilized to gain workplace advantage. So, for example, it is suggested that 'older women seem to recognise that a display of overt femininity confers advantages, realising that "feminine" decorativeness may function "subversively" in professional contexts which are dominated by highly masculinist norms' (McDowell 1997: 197). In making this argument McDowell seems to put in place a distinction between 'unconscious' and 'self-conscious' acts of femininity. Thus deliberate performances are termed 'parodies' or 'masquerades' to mark their difference from (what are implied to be) less deliberate acts. However, others have argued that this distinction is difficult to uphold since femininity involves a continuum of 'self-conscious stratagems' (Stern 1997: 186).

References

Adkins, L. 1995. *Gendered Work: Sexuality, Family and the Labour Market*. Buckingham: Open University Press.

Adkins, L. and Lury, C. 1996. 'The Cultural, the Sexual and the Gendering of the Labour Market', in L. Adkins and V. Merchant (eds.), *Sexualizing the Social: Power and the Organization of Sexuality*. Basingstoke: Macmillan.

Beck, U. 1992. *Risk Society: Towards a New Modernity*. London: Sage.

Crang, P. 1997. 'Performing the Tourist Product', in C. Rojek and J. Urry (eds.), *Touring Cultures: Transformations of Travel and Theory*. London: Routledge.

Game, A. and Pringle, R. 1984. *Gender at Work*. London: Pluto Press.

du Gay, P. 1996. *Consumption and Identity at Work*. London: Sage.

Hiltrop, J-M. 1995. 'The Changing Psychological Contract: The Human Resources Challenge of the 1990s', *European Management Journal* 13(3): 286–94.

Hochschild, A. 1983. *The Managed Heart: Commercialization of Human Feeling*. Berkeley: University of California Press.

Lash, S. 1994. 'Reflexivity and its Doubles: Structure, Aesthetics, Community', in U. Beck, A. Giddens and S. Lash (eds.), *Reflexive Modernization: Politics, Tradition and Aesthetics in the Modern Social Order*. Cambridge: Polity.

Lash, S. and Urry, J. 1994. *Economies of Signs and Space*. London: Sage.

Lury, C. 1995. 'The Rights and Wrongs of Culture', in B. Skeggs (ed.), *Feminist Cultural Theory*. Manchester: Manchester University Press.

Martin, E. 1994. *Flexible Bodies*. Boston: Beacon Press.

McDowell, L. 1997. *Capital Culture: Gender at Work in the City*, Oxford: Blackwell.

MCDowell, L. and Court, G. 1994. 'Performing Work: Bodily Representations in Merchant Banks', *Environment and Planning D: Society and Space* 12: 727–50.

Newton, T. with Handy, J. and Fineman, S. 1995. *Managing Stress: Emotion and Power at Work*. London: Sage.

Nickols, F. W. (1995) 'Feedback about Feedback', *Human Resource Development Quarterly* 6(3): 289–96.

Pateman, C. 1988. *The Sexual Contract*. Cambridge: Polity.

Sedgwick, E. 1994. *Tendencies*. London: Routledge.

Stern, K. 1997. 'What is Femme? The Phenomenology of the Powder Room', in *Women: A Cultural Review* 8(2): 183–96.

Williams, C. 1988. *Blue, White and Pink Collar Workers: Technicians, Bank Employees and Flight Attendants*. London: Allen and Unwin.

10
'When a Body Meet a Body...': Experiencing the Female Body at Work

Joanna Brewis

Introduction

This chapter explores women's experiences of their bodies in work organizations, using data from a series of qualitative interviews. Themes considered in the discussion include the ways in which the respondents prepare their bodies for work; their thoughts on what their bodies signify (negatively and positively) to colleagues and clients, and how they manage their bodies at work as a consequence; their comparisons of men's and women's experiences of their bodies in the workplace; and their general sense that their occupations do not 'require' the body in the same way as others (such as modelling) might do.

Analysis of these data suggests that the respondents' bodies have a material reality, but that they can only relate to this and others' materiality through the operations of prevailing discourses around organization, gender, age, and so on. Moreover, a comparison of the ways in which they understand their bodies, and these bodies in relation to those of men, also points to a shared and simultaneously not-shared experience of the body as a physical mass inscribed in different ways by multiple social texts. Hence the title of the chapter, taken from the traditional folk-song 'Coming Through the Rye', which indicates that these women have learnt and continue to learn about their own and others' bodies as a result of meeting other bodies, of interacting in the wider social domain.

Framing the Body at Work

Discussion in this chapter is theoretically informed by the work of Foucault (especially 1977; 1979; 1980; 1982), and his claim that we are exposed to various discourses (temporally and culturally-specific sets of ideas, images, structures, behaviours, institutions and regulations) which allow us to 'know' who 'we' 'are' and what 'we' can 'do'. These discourses, for Foucault, are powerful in so far as we reproduce them through thinking, being and doing in particular ways – thus his reading of identity is performative. We constantly strive 'to reproduce the most perfect replication of the discursive model in everyday life' (Brewis, Hampton and Linstead 1997: 1277), understanding, experiencing, working on and using our bodies' physicality as the result of the operations of discourse. For example, contemporary Western discourse dictates a preference for 'slim' as opposed to 'fat' bodies, so that we may perform what Shilling (1993) calls 'body work' (dieting, say) in order to have the 'right' kind of body (also see Bartky 1988; Featherstone 1991; Gamman and Makinen 1994; Moore 1994).

The above also, however, has the important corollary that discourses are always open to 'rearticulation' (Knights and Vurdubakis 1994). Moreover, there are many discourses available to us – a germane example here being the curvaceous image of female beauty portrayed by Pamela Anderson and Sophie Dahl as opposed to the waif-like bodies of Jodie Kidd and Kate Moss. Foucault therefore argues that the particular way in which individuals will define themselves is unpredictable, given this multiplicity of discourse, and the fact that we, as individual subjects constituted through the operations of these discourses, can resist particular ways of understanding ourselves. None the less, Foucault's resistance does not allow us to escape from the powerful effects of discourse. Rather, he argues that our resistance to one discourse is always overdetermined, based on an alternative understanding of self deriving from the effects of other discourses.

Following this line of reasoning, then, would lead us to expect our 'body knowledge' to be made up of fragments from several discourses, as opposed to deriving from one predominant influence – and to suggest that our relationships with our bodies may be complex, even contradictory. Certainly the Foucauldian understanding of identity is of a disparate collection of subject positions that we constantly work to unify, as Knights and Vurdubakis (1994: 185) point out:

[discourses] are diverse and their demands complex and inconsistent . . . Subject positions are made available in a number of competing discourses . . . Identity is thus of necessity always a project rather than an achievement.

Our sense of our bodies, we might therefore argue, involves the daily accomplishment of a coherent sense of our physical reality.

What is also significant, of course, is that Foucauldian analysis suggests that we not only learn about ourselves and our bodies via exposure to particular discourses, but also understand and evaluate other selves and other bodies in this way. Shilling (1993: 92) argues that:

> the means for managing the self have become increasingly tied up with consumer goods, and the achievement of social and economic success hinges crucially on the presentation of an acceptable self-image.

Featherstone (1991: 171), likewise, emphasizes the importance of maintaining the body's appearance within modern consumer culture – and Butler (1993: 16) identifies a dichotomy between bodies which 'qualify as bodies that matter... ways of living that count as 'life', lives worth protecting, lives worth saving, lives worth grieving...'. Here, the functionality of the body takes a poor second place to its symbolic value, so that our bodily appearance is crucial to our identity *and* to the ways in which other people judge us (indeed the two are inextricably connected). Women are particularly likely to be subject to discursive imperatives concerning their bodies, as Fine and Macpherson's (1994: 229) comment that women's bodies are 'a public site (gone right or wrong), commented on and monitored by others' implies (also see Bartky 1988; Gamman and Makinen 1994; Moore 1994).

However, the late twentieth century discipline of bodily presentation identified above means that individual subjects of whatever gender are unlikely ever to feel that they conform to prevailing ideals of bodily appearance. Foucault (1980: 57) himself argues that there are now fewer restrictions on how our bodies behave – for example, wearing revealing clothes is now fashionable – but, if we do 'undress', we need to measure up precisely to cultural preference to avoid censure.

Foucauldian analysis, therefore, suggests that it is impossible to think about, relate to or use the body outside of discourse – it does not rely on biology as the source of what we know about our bodies, and is thus more encompassing of phenomena that are not easily explicable by reference to, say, biological sex as a component of physical materiality. Indeed, Kerfoot and Knights (1993) suggest that masculinity and femininity are nothing more (and nothing less) than roles created by the powerful operations of contemporary discourses – and that the sexes typically work to make sense of their biological differences by conforming to the 'appropriate' gender roles. However, because gender identity here is seen not to derive from the biological body, this also means that masculinity is not: 'unproblematically what men do and what men are...' (Kerfoot and Knights 1993: 660) – women may work to be masculine as well. Moreover, given unequivocal evidence that the senior positions in organizations are dominated by men, we can conclude that organizations are masculine environments, discursively speaking, designed by and for men. Consequently, working at masculinity, a deliberate underplaying of biological 'femaleness' in the organization, may be a fact of life for working women (Sheppard 1989; Collinson and Collinson 1997). So-called 'power dressing', for example, masculinizes the female body, conveying an image of organizational conformity as opposed to standing out by emphasizing female physique (Williamson 1980; McDowell and Court 1994: 745; Brewis, Hampton and Linstead 1997: 1287–8). Pringle (1989: 177), moreover, notes that: 'to dress in this way is to *feel* like a man does, sexually empowered, an actor rather than an object to be looked at.'

However, working women may not necessarily simply strive to embody masculinity at work. Research findings suggest that, because gender is *discursively* located within biological sex, working women actually have to tread a careful tightrope; 'blending in' (working at masculinity) whilst still retaining aspects of femininity in their bodily/ self-management. Sheppard's (1989: 146, 148) women managers felt they had to work to appear feminine and business-like (masculine) *at the same time* – or run the risk of attracting punitive labels like 'lesbian' and 'castrating bitch' (also see Bartky, cited in Martin 1989: 21; Yount 1991; Gherardi 1995: 135; Brewis 1998; Cassin 1998).

Moreover, the discursively masculine world of the workplace arguably has other repercussions for women, particularly as regards their biology. Martin (1989: 123) suggests that organizations do not make time or space for menstruation, pregnancy and menopause because:

Women are perceived as malfunctioning and their hormones out of balance rather than the organization of society and work perceived as in need of a transformation to demand less constant discipline and productivity.

The discourse of gender, then, appears to be powerful in constituting the ways in which we think about our own and others' bodies, at work and elsewhere. Another discourse through which we 'make sense of' bodies and their differences is age. This Gherardi (1995: 133) identifies as a primary means of social classification in organizations, suggesting that discursive 'rules' concerning age are usually observed at work. Echoing this point, both Bendick, Jackson and Romero's (1996) US research and Walker and Maltby's (1997) European data suggest that age discrimination at work is well established in both contexts.

In general, then, using Foucault means that we can explore the 'outside-in' process through which identities are formed – the ways in which what we encounter around us structures our sense of who we are. Here Foucault differs from more conventional sociological analyses of socialization because he emphasizes that:

> The individual is not to be conceived of as a sort of elementary nucleus, a primitive atom, a multiple and inert material on which power comes to fasten or against which it happens to strike, and in so doing subdues or crushes individuals . . . it is already one of the prime effects of power that certain bodies, certain gestures, certain discourses, certain desires come to be identified and constituted as individuals.
>
> (Foucault 1980: 98)

None the less, we do not experience this process of being exposed to discourse as one which constitutes us but, rather, as one through which we *discover* ourselves. We believe that certain discourses are 'true' – even though these discourses actually only serve to make us reproduce their principles *as if they were true*. Thus we literally *become human* through the operations of discourses *which tell us what it is to be human*:

> If I tell the truth about myself . . . it is in part that I am constituted as a subject across a number of power relations which are exerted over me and which I exert over others.
>
> (Foucault 1988: 39)

Methodology and Methods

The 16 women interviewed for this chapter worked in different occupations in higher education and local government institutions, the NHS, the Probation Service and Social Services. They were, variously, married, single or divorced (both the latter categories including those who were involved or cohabiting), and their ages ranged from late twenties to early fifties. Seven of the 16 had children. The data were analysed inductively, with the intention of identifying what the respondents see as important in their bodily and working lives, and the interaction between the two. Full transcripts of each interview were produced which, as Atkinson and Heritage (cited in Silverman 1993: 117) point out, is a research activity in itself, given the required level of familiarity with what has been said. Subsequently, the researcher read the transcripts several times in order to 'tease out themes, patterns and categories' (Easterby-Smith et al. 1991: 108). These emergent 'themes, patterns and categories' were then explored by reference to a selection of the relevant literature, and connections and disjunctures noted as appropriate. This was done to identify ways in which the complex issues raised by the respondents could be fruitfully understood, especially given that the body is a relatively under-researched area in organizational analysis. However, given the use of non-representative sampling techniques, the size of the respondent group and the semi-structured nature of the interviews, these experiences of female bodies are not in any significant way seen to be representative of the ways in which other working women understand their bodies. Rather, what each woman said is treated here as perceptual, as: 'an informed statement by the person whose experiences are under investigation' (Brown and Sime, cited in Silverman, 1993: 107). Of course, respondents may have also dissembled in their accounts – thus the aim in the interviews was to capture a series of *impressions and interpretations* of the experience of having a female body.

Furthermore, it is recognized that claims to pure inductivism here are misguided because the question and answer format of even the least structured interview always constrains the respondent to some degree, allowing the researcher to dictate the flow of what is discussed (Hughes, cited in Silverman 1993: 117). Moreover, the data have also been produced at least in part as a result of the researcher's own identity – she is both female and fascinated by the (somewhat unpredictable!) workings of her own body. Therefore, the data here are not in any way independent of the researcher (Easterby-Smith et al. 1991: 104). Their collection, analysis and reportage are in fact an artificial construction of what respondents thought, said and meant, as mediated by the researcher's self-image. This has inevitably done damage to the respondents' own sense of their words, quite apart from the fact that the researcher has arguably secured her own identity in imposing an arbitrary order on the data (Silverman 1993: 26–7; Knights 1995: 234–5).

Experiencing the Female Body at Work

In this section, the main themes drawn from the data will be considered, starting with the respondents' shared sense that their knowledge about their bodies is, in the main, socially produced – by others' reactions, by cultural images of bodily beauty and by comparisons to others' bodies – and changes over time. There were also conflicts within the body images described by the respondents; for example, Marie (late forties, married, lecturer) feels better about herself than she did when she was younger, but still wants to present a 'perfect front' to the outside world. From this basis, the comments offered by the respondents regarding the ways in which they prepare their bodies for work present themselves for discussion. Here it becomes apparent that their experience of their female bodies in the organizational setting actually begins in the home. Moreover, none of these women, despite a range of bodily inse-curities, suggested that they spend much time on their morning regimes. Time taken varied between 30 minutes and an hour, and rou-tine activities usually included washing, hair-styling, making up and dressing. In describing her routine, Hannah (late twenties, single, lec-turer) said:

> I don't do a *lot* of like mass[ive], massively pampering, it's more of a, again it's a functional thing . . . I don't really put any effort into it and I don't feel like I want to either . . .

Similarly, Lorraine (late forties, married, clerical assistant) finished her description of her preparations by saying: 'And, um, that's sort of me really . . . it doesn't take me long . . .', and both Marnie (late thirties, married, part-time secretary) and Marie used the term 'fine art' in this regard. The emphasis in these comments seems to be on spending as little time as possible on the feminine-coded activity of bodily 'titiva-tion'.

In contradistinction, upon arrival at work, these women suggest that they are usually defined by their gender, as a result of their biologically sexed bodies. Olivia (late twenties, single, local government housing manager) stated that her clients may abuse an overweight member of staff, especially if that individual is female. Rachel (late forties, divorced, Social Services manager) agreed that working women who are over-weight may suffer as a consequence, echoing another point of Olivia's in saying that her own size perhaps signifies that she is unable to control herself and therefore raises questions for others about whether she is fit to do her managerial job. Importantly, both Rachel and Olivia suggested that overweight men would not be judged in this way. However, in what appears to be the reverse of these accounts, Tania (late twenties, single, lecturer) told of how colleagues (who obviously felt she was too thin) had accused her of having an eating disorder.

Rachel also suggested that the age of one's body can act as a powerful signifier to others at work, describing how she was resented during her time as a day sister because her staff group were 'twice her age'. Belinda (mid-thirties, single, substance misuse team manager) offered a similar account. At 21, whilst running a ward, she was asked by an elderly patient if she was on a YTS scheme and offered a pound to buy ice cream! Likewise, Melissa (late twenties, divorced, local government housing manager) commented that, when she first began to secure promotions at work, her mainly older colleagues tended to see her as a 'jumped-up little secretary'. She also linked gender and age in saying that clients may now refuse to believe she is a manager because they see her as 'a whippersnapper' or 'a girl'. This terminology seems to imply an assumption that Melissa's 'femaleness' is understood as immaturity, and concomitant inability to hold a managerial position.

Marian (late forties, married, technical support assistant), on the other hand, said she was scared to make any kind of career move because her age would militate against her finding another job. Meg (late thirties, married, NHS service manager), moreover, linked older age and gender in remarking that she will feel 'even more pressured' to look good at work as she gets older *because* she is female.

The ways in which these women see their bodies as signifying to others at work suggest that they understand these bodies as markers of difference or Otherness. Their management of their bodies in the working context, moreover, shows that many strive to reduce this difference. Hannah certainly feels more comfortable 'blending in'. She tends to wear a suit when she is 'on show', such as at university Open Days, to detract from the fact that she is a woman, and a young woman to boot. Brenda (early thirties, married, lecturer), similarly, says that wearing a jacket to work gives her a feeling of 'being businesslike, professional, um, yes, a working woman . . .'. On the other hand, Belinda acknowledged the need to come across as 'almost asexual really' in some of her workplace encounters, but also said that she doesn't 'like to *conform* too much . . . I like to be smart, um, but I like still sort of always [to] have an element of me in it . . .'. She describes, for example, wearing 'wacky earrings' to work; thereby, we might suggest, drawing attention to her gender. Marie is also comfortable with 'standing out', saying that her professionalism (acceptance of the need to 'act masculine'?) sometimes clashes with her desire to rebel. Moreover, she quoted a male colleague as follows:

> If you're a male out there you spend most of your day, day meeting and talking to other boring middle-aged males . . . So how would you react if you get a, you know, a female coming in of whatever age really?

In sum, then, not all respondents react to their bodies signifying a lack of organizational 'fit' in the same way. Many work to play down their Otherness but others prefer to emphasize it and/or acknowledge that having a female body can be beneficial at work *precisely because* of its being different – as Marie does. Belinda, Rachel and Melissa all said that women's bodies can be useful at work because they tend to have a more calming effect than men's bodies, being smaller and slighter. In a similar vein, Marian commented that: 'if a woman stamps her foot and screams and throws a wobbly men are now so embarrassed at work he'd give into her [laughs] . . .'. She also says that this is legitimate because it might be 'the only way women can get their foot under the [organizational] door'. Melissa likewise says she will be a 'little bit girly' sometimes, using a wheedling tone of voice with male colleagues.

However, these respondents also have a definite sense of where to draw the line. Melissa disapproves of a colleague who wears tight, low-cut tops and leans across desks to use her body as a 'control type mechanism'. Holly (early thirties, single, Probation Service manager) suggested that women can overplay their sexuality, saying a colleague of hers wears short skirts and a Wonderbra to work and that this apparel, rightly or wrongly, 'undermines the job that she's doing' in others' eyes. None the less, she also stated that acting in a *masculine* way at work may mean that a woman is labelled as 'hard-faced', whereas men behaving the same way would be seen as exercising 'some sort of natural authority that people assume it's OK to have . . .'.

Staying with the theme that women's bodies are markers of their 'difference' at work, the respondents also tended to contrast men and women's bodily experiences in organizations. To begin with, the respondents rejected any idea that their biological bodies render them less suited to the work environment than men, preferring to understand female biology as relatively manageable, even malleable. For example, Belinda mentioned rearranging workload around one woman's menstrual cycle, and Hilary (mid-thirties, single, nurse) said that she uses 'mind over matter' at work when she has period pain. None the less, most agreed with Marian's claim that:

> if women have really horrendous periods then of course it's going to affect how they, they're working. I mean some have to take a day off a month for instance, don't they? Um, if you go on to pregnancy, some people, they're continuously sick for the first 3 months, um, they're not giving their all to work . . . which men haven't got . . . [they've] got it made, haven't they?

Harriet (early fifties, single, lecturer) likewise, doesn't feel that men '*swing* in, in quite the same way [as women]'. This leads us to the claim by many of the respondents that men do not understand women's bodies, at work especially. Hannah, discussing an incident where another respondent (Belinda) had experienced a leakage of breast milk whilst about to speak at a conference, thought that the reaction from the men present may have been: 'Oh God, this is what to expect when you have women doing these situations . . . bloody hell, if we'd got a man we wouldn't have been in a situation like this.'

Marian said that, in the same situation, she would have wanted to be 'swallowed up' because the men present would not have been sympathetic. Moreover, Harriet remarked that organizations in general are simply not 'equipped' to take account of variations in women's performance according to their biological cycles.

However, Belinda and Lorraine both suggested that men now make more of an effort to understand female biology than they have in the past, and Tania agreed that most of her male colleagues are 'quite good' about such issues, because their relationships with their own partners mean that they understand women better.

As we have seen, then, the respondents here largely agree that their bodies precede and define them at work, and that female biology may pose problems in the organizational context. None the less, they also suggest that their bodies are relatively insignificant in the work that they do (professional, managerial or administrative in the main). Lorraine said: 'I mean if you were a model or somebody then you know your body is, is your job, OK, whereas here . . . I don't think so.' Lorraine uses her mind as opposed to her body at work, and Rachel agrees, also pointing to modelling and 'sort of receptionist-type situations' as examples of more 'embodied' work. Brenda, likewise, mentioned modelling and added:

I think the body is quite important, err, in, for example, clothes shops. You often look at the person in the clothes shop and she or he is wearing some of the clothes that are for sale in the shop and their body image and their body shape is quite, um, quite important there as well.

Here Rachel and Brenda suggest bodies are part of certain service jobs in the sense that they represent what the organization has to offer. Hannah made a similar point about the occupation of flight attendant; that customers here are often business*men* who are 'looking for certain things' in the bodies of those who minister to them. She also remarked that professional sportspeople use their bodies at work and noted how sportswomen's bodies are commodified in that they are starting to wear more revealing clothing. Hannah asks: 'why aren't blokes wearing midriff [skimming tops]?... that piece of fabric there is not restricting you 'cos the blokes don't do that...'. Her point seems to be that sportswomen are now expected not only to excel at their chosen sport, but also to look sexy whilst doing it.

However, the most frequently mentioned occupations that 'used' the body were those in the sex industry. Marnie, for instance, suggested that the only line of work she could think of which genuinely used the body was prostitution, given that, even in stripping, 'I mean no one touches you, I mean they're not supposed to, are they? They're not allowed to. It's just a "looky looky"...'.

Of the few respondents who did acknowledge that their jobs required their bodies, Helen (late forties, married, lecturer) and Brenda alluded to the ways in which body language helps in teaching. Hannah also suggested that she might use her body more when she is running an Open Day, to 'sell' the university through her gestures. Marnie agreed that she needs her body at work – but her view was more functional, emphasizing the use of hands, feet, eyes and ears at work.

Overall, it would seem these women are not especially aware of using their bodies to carry out their work, despite acknowledging the significance of the body in other organizational respects. Although some talked of the way that the body might communicate, and Marnie implied its functionality, the general theme seemed to be one of the body as only used at work in aesthetic, energetic or sexualized ways.

Discussion

The above data initially suggest a sense on the part of the respondents that their body knowledge is largely constituted by their exposure to prevailing discourses, as represented by others' reactions, others' bodies and cultural images of bodily beauty. This implies a Foucauldian, 'outside-in' process of identity formation, in that these women have learnt about their bodies as a result of being-in-the-world, making sense of their materiality through the ideas, images, structures, behaviours, institutions and regulations available to them both historically and presently. The multiplicity of such discourses is also illustrated by the respondents' descriptions of how their body image has changed, and the conflicts which several identified in their relationships with their bodies – which speaks of Knights and Vurdubakis's (1994) claim that identity is an ongoing, dynamic project of making unified sense of oneself.

Moreover, these women all expressed a sense of not measuring up to discursive imperatives around the female body (Bartky 1988; Fine and Macpherson 1994; Gamman and Makinen 1994; Moore 1994), often despite their efforts to the contrary. None the less, they also said that these efforts are not directed at preparing their bodies for work. Why, then, do these women choose to streamline their morning regimes in the ways described? We could argue that, for the mothers, the emphasis on minimizing time for self stems from what they understand as 'good' mothering. Certainly, Marie referred to her hour of preparation, at the higher end of the scale described by the respondent group, as: 'pretty self-absorbed for a mother', although she tends to get up earlier to compensate. Marnie, likewise, said she spent much longer on her morning regime before becoming a mother. Here again we might note the multiple and contrasting power effects of discourses. On the one hand, Western discourse on body shape emphasizes the importance of the outward presentation of the body (Featherstone 1991: 171; Shilling 1993: 92; Butler 1993: especially 16). On the other, Martin (1989), in discussing the discourse surrounding motherhood, points out that children are often seen as women's 'products', to be raised in particular ways – one of these arguably being to spend as much time with children as possible. The contrasting cases of investment manager and mother of five, Nicola Horlick, and former president/chief executive of Pepsi-Cola North America, Brenda Barnes, who left her job to spend more time with her three children (Vine 1997; Gordon 1997), are also examples of the ways in which prevailing discourses construct motherhood. Horlick's notability centred on her seeming ability to mother *and* hold down a demanding job, whereas the motif in the Barnes reportage was her quitting her job to focus instead on 'what really matters': her family. Accordingly, we might suggest that those respondents with children are subject to an understood pressure to look as good as possible at all times, but also to care for their children in ways that mean a certain self-sacrifice – hence the minimal attention paid to morning routines.

In addition, perhaps, these circumscribed routines imply a particular kind of identity performance. Kerfoot and Knights' (1993) argument that gender identity derives from discourse around gender difference is relevant here because it allows women to identify with and work to embody masculine values. Moreover, we have already established that the organizational environment may require working women to construct a sufficiently masculine identity to assure their survival (Sheppard 1989; Collinson and Collinson 1997). Consequently, given that the process of 'titivating' is discursively labelled as feminine, striving to accomplish masculinity for working women may involve paying less attention to dress, make-up and hairstyle.

None the less, as we have seen, the respondents here sense that they are very much defined by their gender at work as a result of having female bodies, echoing the earlier point that gender, *discursively at least*, derives from biological sex. Rachel and Olivia referred to being categorized as overweight and therefore lacking self-control/the ability to control others, which they both felt was much more likely to happen to women. This connection between body size and an individual woman's ability to do her job raises questions about the different bases on which the sexes are judged at work. Rachel and Olivia's sense that working men are less likely to be stigmatized if they are overweight implies that, amongst their colleagues at least, there is an assumption that men naturally possess (masculine) discipline, whereas women are expected to prove that they possess it, and to demonstrate this in an embodied fashion. However, it is also worth recalling Holly's comments that women risk going 'too far' in embodying masculinity, as well as research findings that women who adopt a highly masculine persona at work may be subject to punishment from their colleagues (Bartky, cited in Martin 1989: 21; Sheppard 1989: 146, 148; Yount 1991; Gherardi 1995: 135; Brewis 1998; Cassin 1998). Indeed, Tania's confrontation with colleagues about her having an eating disorder strongly suggests that she was being labelled as *un*feminine (as opposed to Rachel and Olivia's being seen as *too* feminine), whilst also speaking of the emphasis on 'getting the body right' in the modern West (Foucault 1980: 57).

Similarly, the respondents' discussion of the signifying power of the body at work as regards age reflects Gherardi's (1995: 133) claim that age is a basis for categorizing others in the organization. Comments centred partly on being defined as too young for one's position – and, although none of these respondents made the explicit connection between age, judgements of organizational ability and the female body that Olivia and Rachel did between weight, judgements of organizational ability and the female body, we might surmise that there is something of this in their accounts. Indeed, Melissa's 'whippersnapper'/'girl' comments, where the use of these pejoratives apparently denotes immaturity/lack of managerial ability, suggest that this immaturity is connected in the minds of her clients with her gender, as signified by her body. However, Marian's fear that she will be discriminated against in the job market because she is older suggests another way in which the discourse around age operates – and echoes research findings regarding age discrimination (Bendick, Jackson and Romero 1996; Walker and Maltby 1997). Again, it is possible to speculate that older age is more problematic for women because, just as youth denotes immaturity, so the physical appearance of older age is discursively connected with a decline in reasoning ability, which, like discipline, is coded as masculine. The ageing female body, then, like Olivia and Rachel's overweight female bodies, might be seen as signifying the *particular* lack of a capacity valued at work. Meg's comments on gender and age suggest she has some sense that this is the case.

However, although the respondent group agreed that their bodies are understood as Other in the working environment, the ways in which they choose to react to this coding vary. Hannah, Tania and Brenda prefer to play down their difference by aiming for a more masculine appearance at work – representing apparent instances of power dressing in an effort to conform, organizationally speaking (Williamson 1980; McDowell and Court 1994: 745; Brewis, Hampton and Linstead 1997: 1287–8). Pringle's (1989: 177) analysis of power dressing is also reflected in Brenda's remarks about her jacket making her feel like a *working woman*. None the less, there are also instances where respondents suggest that they prefer to 'stand out', and several comments as to the potential value of the female body at work – for example, remarks on its size being less threatening. Indeed, Brewis, Hampton and Linstead (1997: 1284–5) suggest that a deliberate emphasis on femininity can disrupt gender codings in an organization, and perhaps force others to realize that, even if a woman behaves in a 'hyper-feminine' fashion, she is no less capable of performing her job – although they also argue that such subversion may actually be understood as compliance with more traditional understandings of femininity, and could therefore be problematic. Holly's comments regarding her colleague's chosen work dress point to the difficulties associated with the strategy of hyper-femininity.

Another dimension of organizational Otherness which respondents discussed was female biology at work. Their comments on Belinda's experience echo Hite's finding that 69 per cent of women believed men lack knowledge about women's bodies (cited in Synnott 1993: 67), possibly because, as the respondents also point out, men and women have very different bodily lives. Moreover, seeing organizations as environments which are designed by men, for men, explains Harriet's sense that organizations are not 'equipped' to take account of the possible effect of women's biology on their performance, as well as echoing Martin's (1989: 123) point about the structuring of time and space in organizations.

However, although these women see their bodies as significant in certain ways at work, they tended not to suggest that they use their bodies in actually carrying out their jobs, associating this with, for example, service jobs such as that of flight attendant, and reflecting Tyler and Abbott's (1998: 441) argument that the female flight attendant's body:

> acts as the material expression of the airline by which she is employed, as the medium through which the airline itself is personified and through which it comes into contact with its public.

Tyler and Abbott's empirical data suggest that, consequently, particular emphasis is placed on these women being thin, well groomed and 'poised'. Hannah also identified sport as a highly embodied profession – as does Pateman, in her comment that sport is an occupation in which 'bodies are up for sale and in which employers have an intrinsic interest in their workers' bodies' (1988: 205–6). However, for Pateman, the occupation in which bodies, *and therefore selves*, are genuinely sold is prostitution. Because she sees us as confirming our gendered selves through sexual activity, she suggests that 'when a prostitute contracts out use of her body, she is thus selling *herself* in a very real sense' (1988: 207). Although Pateman arguably overestimates the selling of body/self in prostitution, because some prostitutes actively enjoy their work, there is still considerable evidence of the use of distancing techniques to avoid subjective damage in this profession (Brewis and Linstead 1998: 241–2, 235–6). Prostitution, moreover, was also mentioned several times by the respondent group as falling into the category of embodied professions.

The above understandings of occupations which actually use the body might be seen to be constituted through the classic Cartesian mind/ body dualism, so that respondents see their bodies as the receptacle of energy, instincts and sexuality, essentially separate from and controlled by their minds. It would therefore be interesting to conduct similar research with female manual workers, to assess how far they divide mind from body and to what extent they see their mental capacities as influencing their work activities.

Conclusion

This chapter explores the ways in which 16 female respondents experience their bodies, their working lives and the relationship between the two. Although no claims about the significance of the data are intended beyond its relevance in understanding these specific experiences, it is worth emphasizing that there are similarities, differences and dynamics in the ways that these women relate to their bodies. For example, they agree that the body is a powerful signifier of gender in the organizational context but, while the majority choose to underplay their gender at work, others prefer to assert their difference from the organizational 'norm'.

These similarities, differences and dynamics in the respondents' accounts, as well as the ways in which they distinguish their bodily lives from men's, imply the dual status of the body as a source of human commonality *and* a source of difference (Shilling 1993: 22–3; Synnott 1993: 242–4). Moreover, what that difference *means* in particular contexts (for example, work), and what the consequences are of addressing or ignoring difference in such contexts, may be what is significant here, as opposed to difference *per se* (Rhode 1992: 153). This is especially evident in the respondents' accounts of female biological processes at work, where they seem to feel that their material difference is dismissed in such a way as to create organizational inequality.

Overall, the data strongly suggest these women see their bodies as materially real (possessing sex, weight, age and so on), but that this materiality is accessible only through the operations of discourse. These women's bodies, then, are sites which discourses (re)inscribe in various complicated ways. As Butler (1993: 10) says:

> To claim that discourse is formative is not to claim that it originates, causes or exhaustively composes that which it concedes; rather, it is

to claim that there is no reference to a pure body which is not at the same time a further formation of that body.

Acknowledgement

Arguments drawing on the same broad data-set appeared as:

Brewis, J. 1999. 'How Does it Feel? Women Managers, Embodiment and Changing Public-Sector Cultures', in S. Whitehead and R. Moodley (eds), *Transforming Managers: Gendering Change in the Public Sector.* London: Taylor and Francis, pp. 84–106.
Brewis, J. and Sinclair, J. 2000. 'Exploring Embodiment: Women, Biology and Work', in J. Hassard, R. Holliday and H. Willmott (eds) *Organizing the Body.* London: Sage, pp. 192–214.

References

Bartky, S.L. 1988. 'Foucault, Femininity and the Modernisation of Patriarchal Power' in I. Diamond and L. Quinby, L. (eds.), *Feminism and Foucault: Reflections on Resistance*. Boston: Northeastern University Press, 61–86.
Bendick, M., Jr., Jackson, C.W. and Romero, J.H. 1996. 'Employment Discrimination against Older Workers: An Experimental Study of Hiring Practices', *Journal of Aging and Social Policy* 8 (4): 25–46.
Brewis, J. 1998. 'What is Wrong with This Picture? Sex and Gender Relations in *Disclosure*', in J. Hassard and R. Holliday (eds.), *Organisation-Representation: Work and Organisations in Popular Culture*. London: Sage, 83–99.
Brewis, J., Hampton, M.P. and Linstead, S. 1997. 'Unpacking Priscilla: Subjectivity and Identity in the Organisation of Gendered Appearance', *Human Relations* 50 (10): 1275–304.
Brewis, J. and Linstead, S. 1998. 'Time after Time: The Temporal Organisation of Red-Collar Work', *Time and Society* 7 (2): 223–48.
Butler, J. 1993. *Bodies that Matter: On the Discursive Limits of 'Sex'*. New York, London: Routledge.
Cassin, M. 1998. 'Making it Work: Organisational Change and Being a Woman Manager'. Paper presented to the *Women in the Community: Working at Being Women Conference*, University College Scarborough, Scarborough, July.
Collinson, D.L. and Collinson, M. 1997. '"Delayering Managers": Time-Space Surveillance and its Gendered Effects', *Organization* 4 (3): 375–407.
Easterby-Smith, M., Thorpe, R. and Lowe, A. 1991. *Management Research: An Introduction*. London: Sage.
Featherstone, M. 1991. 'The Body in Consumer Culture' in M. Featherstone, M. Hepworth and B.S. Turner (eds.), *The Body: Social Process and Cultural Theory*. London: Sage, 171–96.
Fine, A. and Macpherson, P. 1994. 'Over Dinner: Feminism and Adolescent Female Bodies', in H.L. Radtke and H.J. Stam (eds.), *Power/Gender: Social Relations in Theory and Practice*. London: Sage, 219–46.

Foucault, M. 1977. *Discipline and Punish: The Birth of the Prison*. London: Allen Lane.
Foucault, M. 1979. *The History of Sexuality, Volume One: An Introduction*. London: Allen Lane.
Foucault, M. 1980. *Power/Knowledge: Selected Interviews and Other Writings 1972–1977*, ed. C. Gordon. Brighton: Harvester Press.
Foucault, M. 1982. 'The Subject and Power', in H. Dreyfus and P. Rabinow (eds.), *Michel Foucault: Beyond Structuralism and Hermeneutics*. Chicago: Chicago University Press, 202–26.
Foucault, M. 1988. *Politics, Philosophy, Culture: Interviews and Other Writings 1977–1984*, ed. L.D. Kritzman. New York: Routledge.
Gamman, L. and Makinen, M. 1994. *Female Fetishism: A New Look*. London: Lawrence and Wishart.
Gherardi, S. 1995. *Gender, Symbolism and Organizational Cultures*. London: Sage.
Gordon, G. 1997. 'I Gave Up £1m A Year For My Three Babies', *Daily Express*, London, 25 September, 7.
Kerfoot, D. and Knights, D. 1993. 'Management, Masculinity and Manipulation: From Paternalism to Corporate Strategy in Financial Services', *Journal of Management Studies* 30 (4): 659–77.
Knights, D. 1995. 'Refocusing the Case Study: The Politics of IT Research and Researching Politics in IT Management', *Technology Studies* 2 (2): 230–54.
Knights, D. and Vurdubakis, T. 1994. 'Foucault, Power, Resistance and All That', in J.M. Jermier, D. Knights and W.R. Nord (eds.), *Resistance and Power in Organizations*, London: Routledge, 167–98.
Martin, E. 1989. *The Woman in the Body: A Cultural Analysis of Reproduction*. Milton Keynes: Open University Press.
McDowell, L. and Court, G. 1994. 'Performing Work: Bodily Representations in Merchant Banks', *Environment and Planning D: Society and Space* 12: 727–50.
Moore, S. 1994. 'Make Way for the Third Sex'. *Guardian*, 13 October, 5.
Pateman, C. 1988. *The Sexual Contract*. Cambridge: Polity.
Pringle, R. 1989. 'Bureaucracy, Rationality and Sexuality: The Case of Secretaries', in J. Hearn, D.L. Sheppard, P. Tancred-Sheriff and G. Burrell (eds.), *The Sexuality of Organization*. London: Sage, 158–77.
Rhode, D.L. 1992. 'The Politics of Paradigms: Gender Difference and Gender Disadvantage', in G. Bock and S. James (eds.), *Beyond Equality and Difference: Citizenship, Feminist Politics and Female Subjectivity*. London, New York: Routledge, 149–63.
Sheppard, D.L. 1989. 'Organizations, Power and Sexuality: The Image and Self-Image of Women Managers', in J. Hearn, D.L. Sheppard, P. Tancred-Sheriff and G. Burrell (eds.), *The Sexuality of Organization*. London: Sage, 139–57.
Shilling, C. 1993. *The Body and Social Theory*. London: Sage.
Silverman, D. 1993. *Interpreting Qualitative Data: Methods for Analysing Talk, Text and Interaction*. London: Sage.
Synnott, A. 1993. *The Body Social: Symbolism, Self and Society*. London and New York: Routledge.
Tyler, M. and Abbott, P. 1998. 'Chocs Away: Weight Watching in the Contemporary Airline Industry', *Sociology* 32 (3): 433–50.
Vine, P. 1997. 'Battling the Myth of the Superwoman', *British Journal of Administrative Management*, November–December: 12–13.

Walker, A. and Maltby, T. 1997. *Ageing Europe*. Buckingham: Open University Press.

Williamson, J. 1980. *Consuming Passions: The Dynamics of Popular Culture*. London, New York: Marion Boyars.

Yount, K. 1991. 'Ladies, Flirts and Tomboys: Strategies For Managing Sexual Harassment in an Underground Coal Mine', *Journal of Contemporary Ethnography* 19 (4), 396–422.

11

Equal Opportunities Strategies: Ways of Developing Feminist Embodiment as a Physical Reality in Bureaucracies?

Cinnamon Bennett

Introduction

This chapter starts from the premise that the design and processes of bureaucracies express systematic sets of relations which are both gendered and sexed. It accepts the contention of a distinct body of academic thought which now rejects the Weberian rational legal model of bureaucracies and explicitly searches for the personal (Savage and Witz 1992). Joan Acker's (1992) conceptualization of embodiment combining gender and sexuality paradigms is central to its analysis. Embodiment focuses on the 'lived body' – an actor's embodied experience. It takes account of the societal, economic and social structures that shape organizational gender relations as well as localized expressions of people's sexuality, influenced by the norm of masculine heterosexuality. Acker contends that the conception of the neutral Weberian bureaucrat is nothing of the sort. This ideal-type bureaucrat is assumed to have a male body and to behave and experience organizational relationships from a man's perspective. Female or non-hegemonic male bureaucrats will struggle to match their different 'lived body' experience to the expectations of what they are supposed to feel and the dominant form of structural interactions which are supposed to come naturally to them.

One group of bureaucrats for whom this 'neutral' embodiment has been a particular problem are women's equal opportunities officers. Not only do this group have different bodies from the hegemonic male, they are also charged with changing the structural and cultural contexts which suits 'him' best. Arguably the history of their experience at work contains many valuable insights about the shaping of the 'lived body' in organizations.

This chapter explores different strategies pursued by feminist bureaucrats in state bureaucracies in Australia and Britain. It argues that these women in their posts as women's officers represent antithetical/counter-embodiments to the dominant type of embodiment (associated with the male body) in the organization. Likewise the equal opportunities strategies they pursue to change the structure of services and organizational cultures can be seen to be posing the same challenge.

Developing a Theory of Feminist Embodiment

There have been many critiques of Weber's rational, functional model of the bureaucracy. The two key areas of contention that concern this chapter are the absence of gender, and sexuality, from his understanding of organizational structure and interactions. The first of these has been formulated as the 'gender paradigm' (Savage and Witz 1992). It is based on a feminist structuralist viewpoint that seeks to explain women's unequal position in public organizations in terms of the existence of a corporate patriarchy. Corporate patriarchy systematically advances men's interest by upholding certain sets of gender relationships in an organization in which men dominate and women are subordinated. These relationships reflect the imbalance in external power systems, such as the labour market, welfare structures and domestic sphere. They are reinforced internally in the design of organizational hierarchies and the processes for operating and progressing within them. This paradigm challenges the neutrality and rationality of the Weberian bureaucrat and also the bureaucracy's objectives of productivity and efficiency.

The absence of analysis on sexuality in organizations was raised in response to the development of the gender paradigm. Hearn et al. (1989) demanded that the emphasis for women's relative disadvantage should be shifted from the general to the specific, following a poststructuralist critique. They argued that thinking in terms of economic and social structures missed the subtleties of the localized interaction, which were the nuts and bolts of dominant male power. In their view the strategic deployment of male power on a day-to-day basis is exercised through sexuality. The 'sexuality paradigm' recognizes the diffuse and dynamic nature of men's authority and its rapid adaptation to changed circumstances. It has brought to academic attention issues such as workplace harassment, sexual relationships, sexualized verbal exchanges, dress codes and hence the importance of considering individual agents – and their bodies.

Joan Acker (1992) has been among several scholars who have attempted to break down the dichotomy that has developed between these two paradigms; with gender on one side becoming associated with the systematic properties of structures and sexuality on the other describing the cultural sphere. Her conception of exploring organizational relationships through the medium of the 'lived body' attempts to combine a person's experience of their own gender and their own sexuality into one material whole. By looking at the problem from this angle, culture, organizational structures and societal structures are not different levels of analysis, starting from the individual and moving to the contextual, but instead are mutually reinforcing, indivisible parts of an overall experience:

> The recursive nature of the structural context and the interactional content of organizations work through participants' knowledge and understanding of organizational rules, procedures and injunctions. Because these participants do not 'leave their bodies behind' when they 'go' to work, part of this understanding is an embodied one.
>
> (Witz et al. 1996: 176)

Starting from the 'lived body', Acker asks what lived body is underneath the grey-suited Weberian bureaucrat? The body she identifies is male, heterosexual, with minimal involvement in procreation and very controlled emotional expression. This embodiment has been normalized (seen as neutral). It is subsumed in organization design and demanded of participants. Other commentators have expanded on Acker's characteristics: Witz et al. (1996) argue that it is not the male body *per se*, but rather a specific male type that has been institutionalized – the male disciplined body – which lacks sexual desire, is isolated in concerns about its performance and accepts regimentation through disassociation of its work from knowledge of itself. While many people would probably recognize the workplace expectation for 'professionalism' (the 'face they wear at work') the importance is that this seemingly asexual body is male. Societal structures, such as domestic care of dependants by women, make the disciplined body's level of absorption and self-unawareness very difficult for women to achieve.

How have women reacted to the domination of the male 'lived body' in organizations? Colgan and Ledwith (1996) have explored the path women follow as they become aware of the gendered relationships around them. They describe this path as a trajectory of increasing awareness. The conclusion of this journey for individuals is 'a clear sense of themselves as a woman', or in other words, a clear sense of their own embodiment in contrast to that of the organization's dominant form. A woman's level of gender awareness determines her ability to control gendered relationships for her own advantage and for the advantage of other women in the organization.

Colgan and Ledwith describe four stages of awareness of female embodiment. 'Traditional women' tolerate the gender role and sexual treatment they receive, although they may not agree with it in every instance. Many women at this stage are 'muting their own awareness' of being an embodied woman, and therefore their difference from men. Becoming 'one of the lads' is a typical response. Women gain a different perspective when the male ideal they are striving for becomes too different from their personal knowledge of themselves. These women are then 'in transition'. Colgan and Ledwith describe them as being in 'painful turmoil' as they have not resolved on a new set of values and therefore on how to behave. Women in this state are often fearful of the implications of their new awareness and reject the label feminist. By moving through this uncertainty to acknowledge their female embodiment, women arrive at being feminist. Among this group of women are those who are 'women-aware', but mediate their expression of this awareness in the strategies they enact. Short-term specificity is at the heart of any action they take to advance themselves or other women. These are the 'safe' feminists who push the differences of their embodiment no further than outcomes they are able to anticipate. They will work both individually and collectively with, and separately from, men. In contrast 'fuller feminists' allow their knowledge and gender awareness to explicitly inform all their actions. They pursue long-term strategies for change. They may prefer to work only with other women as many share 'an altruistic sense of reciprocity and sisterhood' which implicitly enables them to sustain an oppositional stance.

Embodied View of Feminist Agency in Equal Opportunities Programmes

Using Acker's conceptualization of organizational relationships grounded in the male 'lived body' and Colgan and Ledwith's description of women's experience of these relationships, is it possible to reinterpret the nature of the obstacles to feminist practice in organizations and what that practice represents?

The policies and procedural changes which feminists have initiated in state organizations, have primarily been located within the gender paradigm. The practitioners' accounts (including Button 1984; Perrigo 1986; Goss 1986; Harriss 1989) explain women's disadvantage in terms of their position in social and economic structures, such as the sexual division of labour at home and in the workplace, gendered hierarchies of male power, and women's lack of confidence and expectations. Equal opportunities programmes have therefore aimed to address these areas. Programmes have typically included family-friendly polices, fair recruitment procedures and the promotion of non-traditional occupations for women. Despite these programmes being supported by liberal arguments for equal treatment and economic benefits, they have not been well received in organizations. The majority of men have not embraced opportunities for paternal leave or flexible working. Informal procedures continue to affect recruitment decisions and positive action strategies have provoked conspiratorial backlashes. It is apparent that hidden barriers remain.

Responding to the lack of tangible progress, feminist practitioners have gone on to analyse resistance in terms of organizational cultures. These cultures are blamed for holding women and men back from taking up new working arrangements. Parkin and Maddock's (1994) description of organizational cultures recognizes distinct male role types. For example, a 'locker room' culture expects its members to behave like 'one of the lads', accepting a certain amount of sexist banter as a way of common identification among members of the team. Members are expected to put the team first and work hard and play hard. They conclude that women are disadvantaged from participating in this culture because of their greater domestic responsibilities and the homosociability it is rooted in. An analysis based on cultural barriers corresponds closely with the sexuality paradigm. It draws attention to language, sex role expectation and behaviour. Practitioners' attempts to change culture include initiatives such as corporate codes of conduct around sexual harassment, women's assertiveness training and schemes of women's mentoring.

This chapter contends that neither sets of actions alone is enough to bring about significant change. Singly or in parallel these equal opportunity approaches (reflecting the gender and sexuality paradigms) fail to address the nub of the problem – the shadow of the disciplined male bureaucrat that lurks in everyone's consciousness. A theory of male embodiment underpinning all organizational relationships could form the basis of a more comprehensive understanding of the objectives of equal opportunity programmes and therefore could enable practice to be more strategically and effectively applied. The symptoms of the problem have been identified, but the problem itself remains under-theorized.

Significantly, management literature has already set a precedent for considering organizational change in terms of embodiment. There has been an enormous amount written by organizational theorists on the subject of change agents in organizations. Their credentials and skill sets have been extensively catalogued (Kirton 1989). Responding to the barriers which organizational cultures erect to the introduction of new procedures, the skills of interpersonal management have become a focus of considerable attention. Interpersonal management skills rely on an individual's self-conscious comportment in any interpersonal exchange as well as clear knowledge of how to mitigate what one imports from the personal internal world into the work situation (Colgan and Ledwith 1996: 33). This analysis can be applied to a feminist theory of women's embodied strategies for change. As Colgan and Ledwith (1996: 22–3) have established women's current lived experience in male-dominated organizations predisposes them to discover for themselves their feminist embodiment – they are all potential change agents within the specificity of their organizational context.

Men's Embodiment in Organizations: Equal Opportunities Intervenes

The appointment of specialist workers to deliver equal opportunities programmes came about in the early 1980s following a decade of fem inist politicization. This new approach recognized that the legisla tive framework[1] and paper-based equality instructions had not been invoked in practice. Women's structural disadvantage in the home and labour market remained largely unchanged. Cynthia Cockburn (1990) suggests that the thinking behind the development of specialist equality officers was based on a series of assumptions which feminist actors made about the nature of organizational relationships: first, there was an implicit belief that individuals are both able to influence and are influenced by the structures around them (after Giddens). Women as individuals could therefore change the way power was used in organiza- tions. Second, it was assumed that women's methods and values would be different from those of men, based on their past experience of oppression. This last premise draws on a key concept of the women's movement that the personal is – and should be made – political. The movement to specialist equality initiatives, unlike the legislative approach before, enshrined the idea of agency into general thinking about equal opportunities.

Cockburn has argued that both the legal and specialist approaches are necessary and lie on the same continuum. At one end is the short agenda which is limited to top-down actions to extend existing rights, often on technical paper points of law or policy. The long agenda is an ambitious 'utopian' strategy, based on positive action. It demands broad-based support and requires a long time-scale. Cockburn (1990: 74) describes it as:

> The transformational project [long agenda], while it necessarily includes access of more individuals of disadvantaged groups to positions of relative advantage, is not only about quantity. It is also qualitative, proposing the *restructuring and resocialising* of the organization, its purpose and its behaviour.
>
> (author's emphasis)

Although agency and the 'resocialization' of organizational relations has been part of the equal opportunities concept since the early 1980s, no coherent theory has emerged to explain how the two go together. By mapping Cockburn's continuum of equal opportunities implementation to the stages of embodied practice identified by Colgan and Ledwith (1996), it is possible to argue that equal opportunities can be seen in terms of a strategy of embodiment (See Figure 11.1). Its aim is to change the organizational understanding of the lived experience of its members.

The short agenda for reform does not require feminist agents to act as its heralds. It can be grounded in liberal arguments for fairness which are based on women being given the same opportunities as the normalized male bureaucrat. Women-aware agents may follow the short agenda however, as a first step, to win acceptance for a more radical change at a later stage. In contrast, the long agenda cannot be achieved without deconstruction of existing male-dominated forms of interaction. The fuller feminist perspective, based on an antithetical position, is a crucial element of this process, since it keeps the goals of the long-term agenda concurrent. Overt feminist behaviour, however, may not accompany this perspective since it can produce a severe backlash to an equality programme and persecution for the individual attempting it. A woman-aware strategy may therefore be preferred.

In the remaining section, this chapter explores the practice of specialist equality workers. It contrasts two equal opportunities programmes, exploring how they can be reinterpreted in terms of a challenge to male embodiment of organizational relationships. The first describes the 'femocracy' at the national state level in Australia, and the second

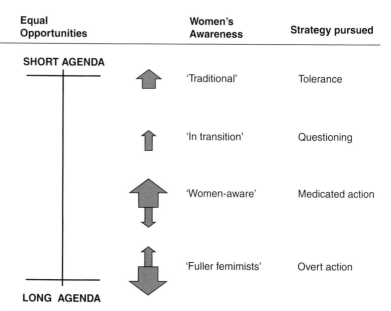

Equal Opportunities	Women's Awareness	Strategy pursued
SHORT AGENDA	'Traditional'	Tolerance
	'In transition'	Questioning
	'Women-aware'	Medicated action
	'Fuller femimists'	Overt action
LONG AGENDA		

Figure 11.1 Mapping Cockburn's (1990) continuum to Colgan and Ledwith's typology of embodied feminists' practice (1996).

examines the experience of women's committees and units in local government in Britain. The size and political context of these two bureaucracies has determined the form of the counter-embodiment being pursued.

Exploring the 'Lived Body' Experience of Women's Officers

How have women's officers through equal opportunities work challenged the interactional relationships of state organizations? Although the circumstances in which women's officers in Australia and Britain have worked are very different, the accounts they give of their experience in the position are markedly similar.[2] This section gives brief examples from both experiences to support the arguments first, that feminists in organizations have come to represent an alternative – and in many cases unwelcome – female form of embodiment, and second, that their practice consequently focuses on different ways to legitimate their embodied position in their organization. This analysis is the subject of further work in my doctoral thesis.

British and Australian literature emphasizes the innovation and novelty of feminists' presence in the state bureaucracy. The job description of women's officer had no precedent. Women's officers were doubly different from traditional bureaucrats. First, they joined a minority of managerial women in hierarchies predominantly run by men: 'Each male bureaucrat, whatever his style or his location in the hierarchy, had a tradition of ten thousand years of bureaucratic power behind him, stretching back to Babylon' (Eisenstein 1990). Second, and most significantly, these women were organizational symbols of female embodiment in opposition to the status quo. The job of women's officer to generate partisan 'political' policies for women was a direct challenge to the role of the 'impartial' male bureaucrat. They challenged all aspects of 'his' work relationship; scrutinizing the procedural and work-place experience of women as employees, as well as the bureaucracies treatment of women as customers, patients, clients, tenants and constituents of state services.

In the case of Britain, the partisan stance of women's officers was seized upon and used to undermine the legitimacy and value of their work. The label of 'lipstick lesbian' invoked by the right-wing tabloid press embodied these officers as irrational women in a way that was both socially classed and sexualized. No other type of local government officer in Britain has assumed such a strong and negative image in the public's imagination. In Australia, the most vociferous criticism of women's officers came from the women's movement itself, expressing disappointment that their deportment was not overtly feminist. The term 'femocrat' to describe the number, power and status of women's advisers had a double edge. It also implied their co-option and collusion with the male bureaucrat (Eisenstein 1990: 90).

There are many empirical examples that demonstrate the antithetical position women's officers assumed. The degree of symbolic difference they represent has rested on individual women's officers' decision of what behaviour to enact along the trajectory of gender awareness (Colgan and Ledwith 1996). This enactment is a constant process of mediation back and forth, making adjustments according to the specificity of the organizational context. For example, in some circumstances a 'woman-aware' position, despite being compromising, will achieve more real change on the ground than the 'fuller feminist' position that necessarily incites resistance from women and men.

British women's officers have found it important to position their embodiment carefully within the bureaucracy, as spatially they are very isolated. The majority of women's initiatives had a total administrative staff of only two or three members, to implement policies in a bureaucracy of hundreds, in some cases thousands, of members of staff.

An important site of feminist embodiment has therefore been the location of these officers in the hierarchy.[3] Questions of whether to site the administrative support staff in the Chief Executive or Personnel Department may appear to be bureaucratic trivia, however to women's officers their spatial proximity to key actors has been of crucial importance to shield, publicize and legitimize their different embodiment.

In Australia, spatial relations have been less significant due to the greater number of high-level appointments. Their primary dilemma (also shared by British officers) has been about behavioural collusion. Femocrats are pragmatic. They have chosen to work in close alliance with traditional bureaucrats as an effective change strategy. Partnerships with other specialist areas means that 'one's authority as a feminist expert was recognised and even sought: one's gender was legitimate' (Eisenstein 1990: 102).

In both cases, women's officers have problematized their relationship and use of established power structures. Spatially, verbally and physically aping the status quo gives access to key actors and information and therefore the potential to wield more influence over the design of policies. However, it also holds the risk that women will be co-opted in the bureaucracy's own image. Women's officers' embodied positions are a constant matter of judgement. No interaction is free of calculation and concern. Their prevarication is unsatisfactory to both the bureaucracy and the women's grassroots movement, both of which have accused women's officers of disloyalty and viewed their motives with suspicion. Accusations by grassroots feminists have been especially painful. Women's officers have always defended the importance of their relationship with grassroots groups. To sustain an embodied female identity within the bureaucracy, a constant reminder from this source appears to be essential.

Australian Experience: Female Embodiment as a Mirror Image to Men's

During the 1970s the Labor Party campaigned in opposition on the issues of social change and equality of opportunity. It tacitly recognized that the exclusion of women along with other social groups was a challenge to the legitimacy of the state in liberal terms (Franzway et al. 1989: 135). The coincidence of a strong women's movement provided the impetus for the institutionalization of Labor's equality commitment when it was elected to government in December 1972. The women's movement was dominated by the Women's Electoral Lobby (WEL), an organization akin to the liberal feminist National Organization for Women (NOW) in America. Its strategy was to ally with the left to effect the reform of existing procedures and legislation.

In partnership with the new government, WEL supported the initiative to create positions and structures in government to represent women's affairs. The first post-holders were drawn from women in its ranks. They were appointed as high-level women's advisers to the Labor executive. The importance which the wider women's movement attached to the first of these appointees, Elizabeth Reid, Women's Adviser to the Prime Minister in 1973, demonstrates that the feminist agenda of these posts was explicit. Federal governments followed the Whitlam government's lead and by 1987 there were 24 prominent well-staffed women's units nation-wide. WEL attempted to raise national awareness of the issue of women's representation through skilful use of the media. It surveyed and then graded political candidates on their knowledge and attitude towards feminist concerns such as abortion, family planning and childcare. In these ways from the beginning of Australian government's equality initiative, the importance of personal awareness and agency was established.

In Australian politics the bureaucratic process is recognized to be partisan (Franzway et al. 1989). Therefore the presence of women bureaucrats acting as feminist advocates conformed to the unwritten expectation of bureaucratic behaviour. This contrasts to the experience in Britain where the civil service has a strong tradition of objectivity. The large numbers of women appointed as women's advisers in the Australian government produced the standard bureaucratic response to a new area of work: it became professionalized. As many British visitors to Australian politics have commented, they were 'dazzled' by the contrast with Britain; 'these feminists were intensely practically minded and they were immersed, too, in a kind of [procedural] detail that I found overwhelming and mystifying' (Eisenstein 1990: 89). The definition of femocrat job descriptions and career progression made feminist embodiment in the bureaucracy a physical reality. This process was self-perpetuating since the existence of clear structures and legitimized posts attracted more women to take up the challenges of embodied feminism.

In recent years the growing institutionalism of women's issues has prompted the women's movement to accuse individual femocrats of 'selling out' to power and personal success. Femocrats have been contrasted with the 'true believers in boilersuits who inhabit the lesbian separatist communities of Glebe and Balmain' upholding the heart of feminist revolution (Eisenstein 1990: 89). Disagreement within the women's movement and the rejection of their bureaucratic counterparts appears to be based on the physical manifestation of embodiment which femocrats portray. They appear to the feminist community to be too similar in spatial location and personal presentation to the hegemonic bureaucrat.

There is a tension in the Australian strategy of embodiment, which sets up a women's form as a mirror-image to that of the traditional bureaucracy. The conception of the 'femocracy' is inherently contradictory. Its similarity to the bureaucracy makes it seem equally exclusive to grassroots women. They argue that femocrats should take up a more overt form of women's embodiment, represented on Colgan and Ledwith's typology as a 'fuller feminist' position. However as femocrats strengthen their antithetical embodiment they also increase their dichotomy from the bureaucracy which they are attempting to influence. What needs to be to be resolved is not which embodied positions, 'woman-aware' or 'fuller feminist', femocrats should adopt, but more fundamentally, what form of organizational embodiment should femocrats aim for? What does an ideal-type (female, feminine-male, masculine) embodied bureaucrat look like? And which structural forms and equality strategies can best effect it?

British Experience: Islands of Feminist Embodiment

The limited legal advocacy structures for equality, combined with a tradition of bureaucratic neutrality, have made the British state particularly opaque to outside influence (Gelb 1989: 95). The radical separatist and Marxist traditions of the British Women's Liberation Movement (WLM) reinforced feminists' scepticism about the ability of equal rights campaigns to have any significant impact on gender relationships of state bureaucracies. Consequently, women's engagement with the state was ad hoc as individual women seized local opportunities offered by the progressive wing of the Labour Party in the late 1970s (Harriss 1989). The Greater London Council (GLC) undertook the first institutional provision addressing women's issues. A political committee, the Women's Committee, and an administrative unit in the bureaucracy were set up in 1982. These structures and posts came about following discussions between a handful of feminist Labour councillors and women's groups already funded by the administration. The committee was initially not a representative group, just 'people who knew people' (Lovenduski and Randall 1993: 194). In the four years of its existence its high level of funding supported the growth of a vibrant women's voluntary sector throughout the metropolitan boroughs (Lovenduski and Randall 1993). These grassroots groups became more and more involved in determining its agenda and priorities. Other Labour Councils around the country followed the example of the GLC. Committees and units were established following manifesto promises exacted by feminists from their local parties. The mushrooming of initiatives a peaked at 43 in 1987 (Coyle 1989). Although they were loosely allied in a voluntary national structure, the National Association of Local Government Women's Committees (later renamed the Women's Local Authority Network), initiatives experienced disparate political contexts and different levels of funding and staff. The only thing they had in common was their uniqueness.

Feminist embodiment, contained in women's units in local government bureaucracies, was never as coherent as it is in Australia. It was not sponsored by the Conservative central government, but instead was very much defined as the vanguard movement of the 'loony left'. Individual officers were isolated and unsupported; the NALGWC had a staff of two who, within the scope of their resources, arranged meetings on a quarterly basis. In some local authorities feminist structures had been sprung upon an unwilling male-dominated constituency party through the actions of a handful of committed women members. Therefore neither the party, the chamber nor the authority at large was aware of the objectives of the initiative and its rational. Some key politicians and managers deliberately found ways of marginalizing equality work and questioning women's officers and councillors' credibility.

The lack of male political involvement, and the close connection of women's initiatives with the grassroots women, meant that women's officers often took up 'fuller feminist' strategies. They not only intended to reform existing services but to transform the way in which those services were delivered. Many women's committees and units pioneered mechanisms of public consultation which were unprecedented in the local government arena in 1980s. They opened up town halls to women's meetings, crèches and campaigns and co-opted local women into the formulation of policies and programmes. These strategies introduced different forms of embodiment into the decision-making process. They explicitly challenged the command culture of bureaucracies whose rational was grounded in the all-knowing objective professional.

The bureaucracy retaliated by marginalizing the embodied practice which women's initiatives were attempting to instil. For example, women's units were commonly created as appendages to the existing central management team, women's officers reporting in a vacuum to the top tier of management. Their effectiveness therefore depended on the political will of key gatekeepers to transmit their message, since they had no structural authority of their own. Where they did have structural authority they suffered resistance in the form of jokes and deliberate obstruction from departmental staff, which again undermined their ability to act. Without adequate resourcing and authority, many initiatives were merely token symbols of the bureaucracy's commitment to equality (Halford 1992). By placing the responsibility for change with an isolated number of women's officers, members were able to continue in their traditional relationships and ways of operation.

In the 1990s there was a change to the approach of using specialist women's officers. In some authorities, women's officers were removed in favour of corporate mission statements that elevated equality to one of the organization's primary business objectives. It was hoped that this would overcome the marginality of equality work, by engendering broad ownership from every organizational participant. European thinking, driven by economic imperatives to accommodate and encourage women's participation in the labour market, inspired this shift (Rees 1998). 'Mainstreaming equality' is gender-inclusive. It attempts to win people's hearts and minds, to convince them to take a gender perspective in all aspects of their work. This demands that they systematically and habitually consider the different impacts on men and women of all policies they are involved in, from their initial inception through to their implementation (EC 1996: EOC 1996). 'Mainstreaming equality' is aimed at the long agenda of equality. Implicitly it is asking all organization members to take up an embodied perspective and to use this to inform their work.

The last section of this chapter considers in more detail the equal opportunities strategy of mainstreaming by looking at the activities of one case-study local authority. The case-study research was conducted in February 1996 in a district authority close to London. It comprised of a series of semi-structured interviews with key actors and textual analysis of primary and secondary documentary sources. Although embodiment is not overtly referred to as an objective, the strategy being pursued is fundamentally about personal and interpersonal behaviour.

British Case Study Authority: 'Mainstreaming Equality'

In the late 1980s the Chief Executive Officer of the authority, with the support of the Leader of the Council, implemented a top-down equalities programme that was administered via specialist equality officers.

This enforcement produced a culture of fearful adherence to political correctness, while real prejudices were buried beneath the surface of its relations. A new incoming Chief Executive Officer, appointed with a remit to transform the equal opportunities programme, has instituted a mainstreaming strategy. This aims to retire the role of equality specialists from the central management team and share their responsibility with every member of the organization.

New corporate objectives have been formulated through negotiation with all first- and second-tier managers, who meet regularly for open and frank discussion of what the role of the authority should be. These meetings are facilitated though training, to introduce contemporary debates around the objective under discussion. The equality objective has been described as 'respect for the dignity of people at work' by 'valuing everyone's contribution equally'. These terms aim to escape the ubiquity of the concept of equality by using common language, and to avoid the association of equality work with specialist – and therefore exclusive – knowledge. The gathering of so many managers (120 in all) actively demands that they live out the principle of respect in the meetings, which it is hoped they will pass on to their relationships with their staff. Mass participation aims to remove the need for champions and share responsibility for the equality objective.

In combination the authority has undergone significant structural change. Decentralization of the authority's functional departments has disrupted male-dominated networks, which often resembled small fiefdoms. Those heads of service that cannot, or will not, accept changes in the status quo have been eased out of their posts. The 'dead wood' individuals, expressing inappropriate embodied forms, have therefore been removed from organizational relationships. In their place new individuals, reflecting a more balanced constituency, have been recruited, including many women. This gives visibility – embodiment– to the new relationships being developed. Finally, community liaison and the importance of front-line service counter staff is paramount in management discourse. This emphasizes that the old embodiment of the bureaucrat who stands apart and above 'them' – the community – is no longer acceptable.

The mainstreaming approach of this authority is saying that multiple forms of embodiment (women's and men's) are acceptable and have value, rather than asserting the absence of a woman's form of embodiment. The factors for successful outcomes are the small size of the organization (approximately 600 members of staff) and the

commitment of the management team to give the process of negotiating a new bureaucratic conception the time and resources it requires.

'Mainstreaming equality' has only recently come to be implemented
in isolated bureaucracies across the country. This looks set to increase, as
pressure for this approach grows from the national government and the
European Commission. Equality practitioners have expressed concern
that without a gender vantage-point provided by women's officers the
approach could simply be a way of mainstreaming a watered-down
version of the status quo, underneath the discourse of a radical agenda.
Interpreting mainstreaming in terms of an attack on embodied forms
takes a more optimistic view. There are problems, however, that need to
be resolved. The time-scale and size of initiatives are certainly crucial
to their likely success. There are difficulties in measuring and
checking that progress from traditional to gender-aware positions have
been undertaken and are being expressed by individuals in daily
organizational contact. Lastly, the importance of changing structures
(gender paradigm) as well as cultures (sexuality paradigm) must be
asserted if the approach is to have a lasting rather than a circumstantial
effect.

Conclusion

This chapter has used Joan Acker's (1992) conception of the 'lived body'
to explore the gendered and sexual nature of organizational relationships. Her contention that organizations have been designed to suit an
embodied form, which is based on the male body, throws up a challenge
to equal opportunity strategies that aim to change organizational relationships. An equal opportunities approach that takes either a gender
perspective or a sexuality perspective on the power relationships at work
will fail to address the insidious strength of this male bureaucrat in
participants' heads.

Women potentially are more able to recognize this embodied form
than most men since, as Colgan and Ledwith (1996) describe, their own
sense of themselves as a woman stands in contrast to the expectations
made of them by the dominant masculinized role. Women who attain
this gender awareness are potential change agents, as they can use this
knowledge to manipulate and surprise organizational relationships to
their own and other women's advantage. Feminist women's officers are
examples of gender-aware women.

Using Acker's, and Colgan and Ledwith's, conceptualizations, the
chapter has attempted to reinterpret equal opportunities programmes

and the work of feminist women's officers as strategies of embodiment. They are both aiming to change an organization's consensus of how a bureaucrat should function. Individual feminist officers in state bureaucracies represent an alternative, and often unwelcome, female form of embodiment. Their practice, which is explicitly partisan, challenges normalized types of impartial operation. Their programmes of work have prompted resistance from bureaucrats trying to protect the status quo. Women's officers have consequently been compelled to find ways of legitimating their different embodied position in the organization, through spatial, behavioural and verbal strategies. The embodied positions which women's officers assume are a constant matter of judgement – never free from calculation. They chose between overtly feminist and gender-muted positions aiming at shorter or longer agendas of change, according to the specific circumstances they find themselves in.

The two examples of equal opportunities strategies in the British and Australian states which have been explored, present very different strategies of embodiment. Each strategy is shaped by the peculiar nature of its bureaucratic context. The Australian example of a mirror-image 'femocracy' faces the problem of distance from both the wider feminist community and from the bureaucratic relationships it is trying to affect. British authorities, by mainstreaming gender equality, appear to be attempting a long agenda of change by asking all the organization's members to adopt an embodied awareness. This raises issues around the difficulties of ensuring this process is progressing towards a pluralistic acceptance of many different forms of embodiment, rather than reverting to a more moderate form of the existing conception. More analysis of organizational relationships, from the perspective of the 'lived body', is needed, to establish if a theory of embodiment offers a more comprehensive understanding of the objectives of feminist equal opportunity programmes, which will enable practice to be more strategically and effectively applied.

Notes

1 The legislative framework for state-run equality initiatives had been promoted in a piecemeal process since the late 1950s by the European Union and formalized in Britain by the Sexual Discrimination Act 1976. Australian feminism was heavily influenced by the example of American women's rights movement of 1960s.
2 'Women's officers' is used as a generic term for posts within the British and Australian state bureaucracies which have a dedicated brief to advance women's issues.

3   In none of the research undertaken to date have women officers been asked to reflect on their embodied relationship to their colleagues and organizational values and strategy. However, from research done on the barriers they perceive to their practice, it is possible to infer the lived (physical and mental) difference they have felt and also the differences the organization has projected onto their physical and ideological presence.

References

Acker, J. 1992. 'Gendering Organizational Theory', in A. Mills and P. Tancred (eds.), *Gendering Organizational Analysis*. London: Sage.

Britton, D. M. 1997. 'Gendered Organizational Logic: Policy and Practice in Men's and Women's Prisons', *Gender and Society*, Vol. 11 No. 6, December.

Button, S. 1984. *Women's Committees: A Study of Gender and Local Government Policy Formulation*. Working chapter 45. SAUS Bristol: University of Bristol.

Cockburn, C. 1990. 'Men's Power in Organizations: "Equal Opportunities" Intervenes', in J. Hearn and D. Morgan (eds.), *Men, Masculinity and Social Theory*. London: Unwin Hyman.

Colgan, F. and Ledwith, S. 1996. (eds.), *Women in Organizations: Challenging Gender Politics*, Chapter 1. London: Macmillan Business.

Coyle, A. 1989. 'The Limits of Change: Local Government and Equal Opportunities', *Public Administration*, Vol. 67, Spring, 39–50.

Eisenstein, H. 1990. 'Femocrats, Official Feminism and the Uses of Power', in S. Watson (ed.), *Playing the State: Australian Feminist Interventions*. London: Verso.

EOC [Equal Opportunities Commission] 1996. *Interim Report: Mainstreaming Gender Equality in Local Government, Part of the Fourth Medium-term Action Programme on Equal Opportunities for Women and Men (1996–2000)*.

EC [European Commission] 1996. *Communication on Incorporating Equal Opportunities for Women and Men into All Community Policies and Activities – 'Mainstreaming'*. COM(96)0067.

Franzway S., Court D. and Connell R. W. 1989. *Staking a Claim: Feminism, Bureaucracy and the State*. Cambridge: Polity.

Gelb, J. 1989. *Feminism and Politics: A Comparative Perspective*. Chapter 4. London: University of California Press.

Goss, S. 1986. 'Women's Initiatives in Local Government', in M. Boddy and C. Fudge (eds.), Local Socialism? *Labour Councils and New Left Alternatives*. London: Macmillan.

Grant, J. and Tancred, P. 1992. 'A Feminist Perspective on State Bureaucracy', in A. Mills and P. Tancred (eds.) *Gendering Organizational Analysis*. London: Sage.

Halford, S. 1992. 'Feminist Change in Patriarchal Organizations: The Experience of Women's Initiatives in Local Government and Implications for Feminist Perspectives in State Institutions', in M. Savage and A. Witz (eds.), *Gender and Bureaucracy*, Oxford: Blackwell.

Harriss, K. 1989. 'New Alliances: Socialist-Feminism and the Eighties', *Feminist Review*. No. 31, Spring.

Hearn, J., Sheppard, D. L., Tancred-Sheriff, P. and Burrell, G. 1989. (eds.), *The Sexuality of Organization*. London: Sage.

Kirton, M. J. 1989. (ed.) *Adaptors and Innovators: Styles of Creativity and Problem-solving.* London: Routledge.

Korvajarvi, P. 1997. 'Working within and between Hierarchies', in L. Rantalaiho and T. Heiskanen (eds.), *Gendered Practice in Working Life.* Basingstoke: Macmillan.

Lovenduski, J. and Randall, V. 1993. *Contemporary Feminist Politics: Women and Power in Britain.* New York: Oxford University Press.

Martin, P. Y. 1993. 'Feminist Practice in Organizations: Implications for Management', in E. A. Fagenson (ed.), *Women in Management: Trends, Issues and Challenges in Managerial Diversity. Vol. 4 Women and Work.* London: Sage.

Parkin, D. and Maddock, S. 1994. 'Gender Cultures Determine Women's Choices and Strategies at Work', in M. J. Davidson and R. T. Burke (eds.), *Women in Management: Current Research Issues.* London: Paul Chapman.

Perrigo, S. 1986. 'Socialist-Feminism and the Labour Party: Some Experiences from Leeds', *Feminist Review.* No. 23, June.

Savage, M. and Witz, A. 1992. (eds.) *Gender and Bureaucracy.* Oxford: Blackwell.

Rees, T. (1998) *Mainstreaming Equality in the European Union: Education, Training and Labour Market Policies.* London: Routledge.

Witz, A., Halford, S. and Savage, M. 1996. 'Organised Bodies: Gender, Sexuality and Embodiment in Contemporary Organizations', in L. Adkins and V. Merchant (eds.), *Sexualizing the Social: Power and the Organization of Sexuality,* Explorations in Sociology 47, British Sociological Association.

12
Working with Energy: Accessing Activist Bodies

Debra King

Introduction

Historically, bodies have been a powerful political tool in activist work. They have been used as an instrument or object in campaigns where bodies might be chained to trees, placed in front of bulldozers, camped outside of nuclear bases or marched down to Parliament House. Bodies have also been put at risk in actions: zapped by radioactive waves, beaten by opposing forces, or deprived of adequate food, water and medical supplies. Particular bodies have often been the premise for activism. For example, bodies with a specific disability have been a basis for doing activism in the area of disability rights, while sexed bodies have been important to gay and lesbian, and some feminist activism. Feminism has also operated on the basis of socially constructed bodies, with this conception of the body being relevant to forms of activism based on class, race and age. In various ways, then, bodies can be seen as important to activist work. The difficulty, though, is that in analysing the body as an object of activist work, there is the risk that the subjective body will disappear and that many of the dichotomies that sustain hegemonic western knowledges will simply be reinforced. The body as a 'thing' retains its opposition to the mind, to discourse and to society, and remains constructed in terms of dualisms such as nature/social and inner/outer.

Problematizing these dichotomies lies at the base of much recent theoretical and empirical interest in the body (for example, Haraway 1987; Freund 1988; Turner 1992; Garrett 1993; Grosz 1994), and this has extended to include the realm of working bodies (Ronai 1992; Sherlock 1993; Martin 1994; Witz et al. 1996). Attempts at transcending dichotomous boundaries has often meant focusing on how workers experience their lived body. For example, following Butler's theory of performativity (1990) there has been a small but significant body of research examining how working bodies are implicated in the performance of various aspects of identity (McDowell and Court 1994; McDowell 1997; Adkins and Lury 1998). Such research endeavours to incorporate both subjective and objective perspectives on the body with the aim of, at the very least, redrawing some of the boundaries around sex/gender and nature/social.

While viewing working bodies in terms of performativity provides a means of bringing these dichotomies into question, there appears to be a paradox between wanting to conceptualize (and analyse) the lived experience of workers' bodies and imposing the abstract objectifying framework of performance upon those same bodies. There is often little to suggest that the workers see themselves as embodying their work by constructing it as a performance. In accessing activists' lived experience of their bodies I wanted not only to analyse how they used their bodies, but also to take account of the ways in which they recognized themselves as embodied and how such embodiment influenced their work. For activists this process was about energy.

So while activist bodies could have been accessed through a variety of different theoretical frameworks – as a political tool, as socially constructed, as performance – it was evident that it was the notion of energy that was central to the way in which activists themselves perceived the relation between their work and their bodies. This notion of energy was discussed in three quite distinct ways such that their embodiment could be seen as simultaneously socially constructed, corporeal and communicative. Thus energy becomes another means of problematizing the social/nature dichotomy. In addition to locating this dichotomy within the body however, it also locates the body as one that is constructed in relation to both society and a 'nature' conceptualized more broadly as 'the body of the world' (Jackson 1983). This raised new questions about how to conceptualize nature and the social in the construction of embodied activists.

This chapter explores some of these questions by examining how activists used energy to embody themselves and their work. Following a brief description of the methodology and the research project within which energy emerged as a significant theme, attention then turns to the historical context of discussions of energy in relation to work. Although recognizing its limitations I argue for the notion of energy to be extended and reclaimed because of its continued relevance to workers' bodies, in this case activists. The third section moves on to an analysis of the three discourses of energy which activists used in discussing their work. Each discourse has a different emphasis regarding the body in theoretical as well as practical terms. There are, in effect, three different types of activist bodies in relation to work. Through the discourse of energy-as-drive activists can be seen to be 'embodied workers' with socially constructed bodies. Through the discourse of energy-as-boundary activists can be seen to be 'working bodies', constructed primarily in terms of their corporeality. And through the discourse of energy-as-tool activists can be seen to be 'bodies at work', where their bodies are constructed as communicative and expressive. In the final section of the chapter the relationship between nature and the social raised in these discourses of energy, work and the body is discussed in terms of the implications for the development of theories about activist or worker identities.

Researching Activist Work

Energy was a theme that emerged from two years of ethnographic research into the realm of activist work. The term 'activist work' had a dual purpose in the research. On the one hand it designated the case study as being the work performed by social activists. As a form of work which problematized the paid/unpaid, public/private paradigms within which work is usually conceptualized within sociology, activism provided an ideal focus for accessing various supra-economic aspects of work (Vallas 1990: 356) such as passion and creativity. Information was collected from in-depth work history interviews with 20 persistent (Downton and Wehr 1997) activists[1] who did paid and/or unpaid work in either the peace, labour or feminist movement. In addition, I became a member/researcher in three activist organizations throughout 1995 and 1996, enabling me to examine group processes and actions, conduct numerous informal interviews and check the relevance of emergent themes. The interviews were mapped (Jones 1985; Trochim 1989) to help develop the coding before creating a database on QSR NUD*IST (Richards 1994), which then became the main analytical tool.

On the other hand, activist work was also used a conceptual tool, one which signified a relationship between work and the worker. Activist work was not just about work; it was also about the activist who performed that work. The desire to capture this relationship is reflected in my emphasis on the subjective, lived experiences of activist work in the collation and analysis of the data. It was through analysing the ways in which the activists discussed the relationship between how they constructed themselves as *activists* and the *work* that they did as activists, that the theme of energy emerged. Energy was, therefore, the term used by the activists to embody themselves and their work. Initially, their use of energy appeared somewhat unusual. However energy has a long, albeit potted, history in relation to work and remnants of that history can still be found in definitions of motivation and burnout. What was interesting was that the activists' discourses of energy both reinforced and extended these traditional uses of the concept of energy in the sphere of work.

Reclaiming Energy

Energy is not a new concept in the work literature. Indeed until the 1960s it enjoyed quite a prominent place in positivist research. The amounts of energy expended by various workers and their metabolic processes were placed under examination, with minute movements being recorded as well as their sustainability and overall levels of physical exertion (for example, Turner 1955; Scholz 1957; Levey et al. 1959). Interest in energy stemmed back to the nineteenth century when physicists 'discovered' its universality and the applicability of natural laws to the social arena. Rabinbach, in *The Human Motor: Energy, Fatigue and the Origins of Modernity* (1990), argues that the application of these laws and the language of energy to the realm of work was an integral part of the transformation of the discourse of work from a moral to a scientific one (1990: 6). In tracing the development of this discourse from Marx's notion of labour power through to the development of Taylorism (in America) and the Science of Work (in Europe), Rabinbach highlights the ways in which the worker's body came to be seen as a motor fuelled by energy, which was thought to be derived from nature.

These theories were sustained by an assumption that the body had a given amount of energy which was used in the labour process and which could be replenished if the worker had adequate sleep and nutrition, which of course took place in the private sphere. By the middle of the twentieth century this view of the working body was being questioned. Not only did such a view fail to take into account the energy required for household and recreational activities (Durnin and Passmore 1967), but it also had difficulty in accounting for the use of mental energy (Brown 1982) and affective energy (Wallman 1982) in the labour processes. By this stage, changes in the work milieu in the developed countries also meant that there was less interest in the physical labour required for production, and more on the mental and emotional labour required in the service and communications sectors. Energy, as a concept that linked the worker's body to their work, became almost obsolete.

This was, however, a very limited view of energy and its relationship to work. The focus on the expenditure of physical or calorie based energy, the need to measure energy in quantifiable terms, and the dominance of the scientific paradigm in our understanding of energy produced a particularly western concept of energy which was about power, strength and heat. For example, there appeared to have been little, if any, engagement with eastern concepts of energy with their focus on harmony, balance and light. The Chinese *ch'i*, the Hindu *prana* and the Hawaiian *mana* are theories of vital energy which is recognized as being the underlying fabric of the material body. This vital energy is not limited to the body's physical or material state, but also accounts for the conscious and unconscious mind, as well as the relationship between human and non-human flows of energy (Waysun 1990; Samways 1992). While western conceptions of energy see nature as merely a resource for replenishing human energy, eastern views see the relationship as more complex.

Eastern notions of energy focus on its flow according to cycles, with positive energy created by living in harmony with these cycles. This is a more interconnected view of energy, which links personal energy to social energy, and that of 'universal nature'.[2] A significant minority of the activists in the research used these ideas about energy in their activist work. For these activists the lunar cycles were recognized as influencing their personal energy, where it increased with the full moon and decreased with the dark moon. Full moons and solstices were used to time certain political actions so as to optimize the positive universal energy available to them. Human energy was also recognized as being cyclical, and while most long-term activists could point to periods of high and low energy in their activism, some of them recognized this as an inherent feature of their lives and built into their activism periods of stillness in order to balance those periods of intense action.

The notion of energy, then, can be analysed at a much broader level than the original work literature suggested. In terms of this research into activist work, seven different forms of energy were identified as being used or needed in various contexts. In addition to physical energy, activists also spoke about emotional energy, social energy, mental energy, spiritual energy, sexual energy and environmental/universal energy. Although often overlapping and interconnected, these forms of energy were analytically separate.[3] It was obvious that for the activists in this research, energy was not just about power and their physical ability to do their work, but also about their passion or moral purpose: it was the way that they felt connected both to other people and the environment, as well as connecting their own emotions, thoughts, body and sense of spirituality.

In analysing the data, it was evident that as workers, activists had three different discourses of energy – as drive, as boundary and as a tool. In examining these it became apparent that they related to three different perspectives on activist bodies and activist work. As a drive, energy was embedded in the discourses of motivation and moral purpose that emphasize the social construction of activists as *embodied workers*. Where energy was discussed as a boundary, the emphasis was more on the corporeal body and the threat of burnout, thereby influencing the construction of activists as being *working bodies*. For some activists, energy was also a tool that required specific skills and knowledge if it were to be used effectively. From this perspective the discourses of ritual, communication and magic influenced the construction of activists as *bodies at work*. The focus on energy, then, provided three ways of looking at the body in relation to work.

The Three Discourses of Energy

Energy as Drive: Embodied Workers

Being moved by an issue, being inspired by a speaker or being empowered to take action were all ways in which activists discussed their drive, or energy, for their social change work. Within the activist/work literature the concepts of moral purpose and motivation encapsulate this notion of energy as drive (Muchinsky 1990; Porpora 1997). Common to each of these bodies of literature is the idea that energy is primarily a social, rather than corporeal, aspect of work. Viewed in this way, energy produces embodied workers where the body is present but relatively passive, it is subjected to the will of the mind; a mind that is emotional, rational, social and moral.

The question of why people get involved in activist activities and what keeps them there is often framed in terms of motivation, a concept that also has currency in the work literature. In theories of motivation, energy is considered to be 'a force within people that arouses behaviour', and is one of the three major components of motivation, together with direction and maintenance (Steers and Porter, in Muchinsky 1990: 323). Interestingly however, empirical research into motivation tends to emphasize these latter two components and not energy. Rather, energy appears to be seen as an effect of these choices and is not, in itself, a focus of investigation. This contrasts to recent research into moral purpose which uses the notion of passion, or emotional attachment, as a means of accessing the energy for activism.

The grounding of moral purpose in emotions is central to arguments such as Porpora's (1997) regarding the ways in which activists in the United States responded to Central American issues in the 1980s. He argued that the difference between activists and non-activists was the ability of activists to engage emotionally with these issues because of their attachment to particular world-views (1997: 14). Their energy for activism came from their emotional attachment to a moral vision which was broad, or perhaps deep, enough to transcend personal structural situations so as to incorporate a larger cosmic political and moral vision (1997: 13–14). In so doing, the grounding of moral purpose in emotions can be seen as relevant not only in terms of creating energy and passion for activism, but also in contributing to debates about political and philosophical ideas. It is therefore the experience of having emotional attachments to certain moral positions which moves the body towards taking a particular type of action.

In the following excerpt from an interview, Kerry[4] speaks about how her passion – her moral purpose – inspired her to become one of the main organizers for an anti-uranium mining campaign in the mid-1980s:

> it was a passion I had for life ... The holocaust was possible, present, and I just really felt, I mean, I had a baby, and I just felt really motivated to be part of saving the planet ... I think when people are acting out of that passion which we, so many of us were, in the 80s, the fierceness with which people believe it and hold on to it, is different to the more distance of a professional working relationship. And while people's livelihoods are tied up, it's more about self-interest, whereas the passion that I saw in the anti-nuclear movement was a passion of survival, and it was a passion about community, that wasn't about materialism, it was something almost spiritual ...
>
> (Kerry, peace activist, 36 years old)

Kerry's work involved her camping for weeks at a time in a hostile environment, putting her body at risk in terms of radioactive poisoning, and depriving her body of sleep and adequate nutrition. Yet it was her willingness to place her body in such a position (along with other protesters) that drew attention to the health and environmental risks surrounding uranium mining and nuclear energy. Her story illustrates how activists can be seen as embodied workers by viewing energy as drive. The body was important but relatively passive in terms of the ways that decisions were made about actions to take: her body did what her mind told it to. Yet Kerry also spoke of living on 'caffeine and adrenalin' for months at a time, indicating an interaction between her corporeal body and her ability to sustain her moral energy. While this allows for a somewhat stronger role for the corporeal body in any theory of energy as drive, it still remains primarily a socially constructed body.

As a drive, energy is substantially a matter of activists developing their consciousness and will to act – it is the impetus that moves them along a particular course of action. While certain physiological factors may influence the level of drive, the development of moral energy does not require a conscious consideration of the body. In terms of the embodied worker, energy can be seen as being socially constructed with there being little sense of any interaction with a corporeal body, except inasmuch as the way that energy moves the body in one direction or another. In effect, while the boundary between rationality and emotion may be redefined through the notion of moral purpose, there remained a mind body distinction wherein the mind 'controlled' the body. However, there appeared to be limits to the extent of this control, a point at which the body asserted itself and imposed a boundary on moral energy. This boundary was usually discussed in terms of burnout.

Energy as Boundary: Working Bodies

Long working hours, hard campaigns, dangerous actions and the long-term nature of their work often meant that activists were well aware of the limits of their bodies and the possibility of burnout. In the work literature, burnout is related to energy through the notion of exhaustion, whether it be physical, emotional and/or mental exhaustion (Schaufeli and Buunk 1996: 314–15) and it occurs when more energy is being used than is being replaced. However, it is rare for any focus on energy to be sustained in research into this area (but see Cruikshank 1989), and where it does the relationship to embodiment is not explicit. Instead the focus tends to be on the causes of exhaustion and the implications for the work environment (for example, Jayaratne and Chess 1983; Pines 1983; Sakharov and Farber 1983; Poulin 1993; Schaufeli and Buunk 1993). In contrast, the activists in my research clearly linked burnout to their embodied capacity to continue doing activist work.

The activists' awareness regarding the extent to which their work put their bodies at risk in terms of their life and/or health highlighted a notion of energy that is bounded. Energy was not simply produced and reproduced through activist work, but also expended. It was therefore necessary for activists to monitor their energy so that they could avoid burnout and sustain their activist work over long periods of time. However, monitoring did not necessarily mean conserving energy, as was proposed in the early 'working body' literature, but optimizing its use. The activists developed strategies to avoid becoming physically, emotionally and mentally exhausted, many of which focused on creating energy, thus rejuvenating themselves for continuing with their work. The recognition that social change was a long-term project, requiring life-long work on their behalf refocused attention on the boundaries of their energy and the limits of their bodies.

The extent to which the working body was an issue for the activists partly depended on how close they had been to burning out. However, their level of awareness was also related to the type of activism engaged in and the gender of the activist. Activists who focused on labour politics and the socialist project of social change were less likely to problematize the limits of their bodies, and men were also less likely than women to consider the needs of their working body.[5] Consequently, there was a small number of activists in my research who did not see burnout as an issue for themselves; however, they often recognized that it was likely to be an issue for other activists. Nevertheless, most of the activists either had ideas about, or engaged in strategies to avoid burnout.

At one end of the spectrum, avoiding burnout was seen to be merely a matter of prioritizing where and how energies were spent, as indicated in Robert's statement:

> I mean one of the things I think we need to consider is whether we're putting our energy, using our energies, prioritizing our energies to work differently so that we don't get tired out. (Robert, state president of a national peace organization, age 60 years)

The idea that activism can be tiring was raised consistently by the activists. For some the solution was one of management: rethinking their campaign tactics and projects so that the available amount of energy could be used in the most effective way. The main strategies for avoiding burnout for activists at this end of the spectrum were to take brief periods of 'time-out', to restructure their activist work, and/or re-energize themselves by reconnecting with universal nature:

the single most important thing is having loving relationships around me, and having opportunities to actually, you know, experience the stars and this wonderful sky that we have and, like going out camping and things like that. Those things are the rejuvenations that I feel, like I can get very tired and depressed at different times around things, and feel very vulnerable. They're the things that rejuvenate me.

(Kerry, peace activist, age 36)

At the other end of the spectrum were activists like Emma. As a feminist labour movement activist, Emma radically restructured her activist work to incorporate burnout-avoidance strategies after becoming quite ill through her activism. She described her burnout in terms that highlight the body's reaction to her work, which was, at that time, employment as a full-time union officer:

in a way the body exerts itself. Like it changed my direction. The body, in a sense, said: 'that is enough', and it broke out in shingles and it got RSI and whatever. It just said this: 'you have to work part-time'. So the body asserted itself and eventually I had to listen to it.

(Emma, feminist trade union activist, age 41)

Listening to her body meant finding ways of doing activist work that were not so 'hard' on her. Although still very much involved in the feminist side of the labour movement, Emma developed a number of self-care strategies including taking part- time paid activist work, doing re-evaluation counselling, making space for a personal life, ensuring that she had social support networks and finding ways of being energized through her work. These strategies were typical of activists at this end of the spectrum, all of whom became much more reflexive about their body's relation to energy and work.

Unlike the activists' discussion of moral energy that had a weak sense of the corporeal body, their discussion of burnout brought the corporeal body more clearly into focus. Many of the activists were much more aware of their body being a working body. This is not to say that the social relations, discourses and structures within which they worked were not significant. They certainly found ways to manipulate their energy levels as their emphasis on finding ways to create energy demonstrates. There was however, an awareness of there being a boundary to their energy beyond which their body became conscious of itself and required attention. Their bodies were not simply socially constructed, but neither were they simply corporeal entities. The tension between energy-as-drive and energy-as-boundary indicated a complex intertwining of social nature, mind body and inner outer, rather than an assertion of one over the other. There was no hierarchical relationship; rather the constant contestation of the boundaries of energy highlighted the inescapable association between the concepts. This called into question the notion that bodies can ever be completely socially constructed. Unlike the passive model of the body incorporated into much of the discussion around 'embodiment', a focus on the working body gave recognition to the body as actively participating in the way it is constructed.

Whereas energy-as-drive and energy-as-boundary both focused on a notion of energy as individually bounded, where the body was constructed 'in itself', the following discussion looks at the body 'in relation' by focusing on how activists used energy as a tool in their work. In this sense the body becomes an important medium for conveying meaning, for forming connections and for monitoring group dynamics. It was a body at work.

Energy as Tool: Bodies at Work

Many activists found that using their energy as a tool enabled them to be more effective in their work. It was seen as particularly useful for mobilizing people around issues, creating and maintaining groups and organizations, and in maximizing the success of an action. It was through sharing, shaping and harnessing energy that they felt better able to connect with other people – whether that is as individuals or groups – as well as with universal nature. In analysing the ways in which activists used energy it became evident that communication strategies went beyond the dissemination of information with its focus on textual discourse, and beyond the structures and rules which govern group and organizational processes to also include embodied ways of constructing knowledge and connecting to others. In this way activists' bodies were central to their work.

Perhaps the most common example of the ways in which activists used energy as a tool was with regard to mobilizing people for action through public speaking. As public speakers, activists aimed to challenge the hegemonic perspective on the world and empower people to take action. This meant engaging people at a level beyond the cognitive, reasoning level of the mind by simultaneously disseminating (alternative) knowledge about issues while also transmitting their passion, their energy and integrity, to other people (see also Caldicott 1996: 131). Some organizations acknowledged the importance of the skills required to project and share moral and emotional energy and held workshops for activists to develop these skills. The purpose in using their energy as a tool was to get audiences to respond to issues, not only by the reasoning and logic of argument or 'knowing by thinking', but also by getting to 'know by feeling' with regard to the urgency and moral importance of the topic.

Activists also discussed the need to monitor the energy levels of meetings to make sure that they did not ebb too low for fear of losing members, making poor decisions or having the meeting (and eventually the organization) disintegrate. Strategies were devised and used to shape group energy and some activists took it upon themselves to act in the capacity of 'energy monitor' or 'vibes watcher'. The importance of optimizing energy in meetings and organizations is also recognized in the activist literature (Ludwick 1985: 85–6; Coover et al. 1977: 88–93; MNS 1979: 39–40) where numerous strategies are suggested. Kate, a self-appointed 'energy monitor', incorporated jokes and having fun into meetings that she attends and organizes:

> I just think it's more sparky to play up and tell a few jokes. We actually use it as quite a deliberate thing. I know that in meetings when we all feel like 'ugh', and because international politics is usually urgent, you know, things have to be done quickly and there's a lot of pressure. And so it's good to have fun, it just helps you keep in touch with the people and humanity and that.
>
> (Kate, state co-ordinator of a women's peace organization, age 54)

Some activists also took the levels of social energy into account when planning and participating in events such as rallies. At the planning stage, issues such as the type of rally, its format and the chant were recognized as important for shaping the energy of a particular action. During the rally, activists spoke of the skills that they needed to draw people together with a common focus and to maintain the level and type of energy that they felt would have the most effective outcome. The activists who worked with energy in rallies often differentiated the type of rally that they thought would be effective from the traditional type of rallies where emotional energy was inflamed by laying 'blame', where social energy was usually a spontaneous outcome and not well directed.

The idea that energy is a significant factor when organizing or participating in these types of activist ritual implies that these operate at a level that is beyond words or institutionalized practices. It is also necessary to attend to their energy, in particular its forms, levels and flow.

Developing an awareness of how social energy operated, of how energy flowed through groups, meant using both the body and the mind – their own as well as that of the group members. They recognized that the body communicates in both verbal and nonverbal modes. It not only hears and speaks, for example, but also sees and feels.[6] Secondly, the activists needed to be able to tap into the social energy of a group without getting caught up in it. This required them finding a balance of connection and distance from the form and level of energy they were trying to shape. Thirdly, the activists had to have developed enough knowledge about how energy works in individuals and groups to be able to choose the right option for shaping energy as required. Part of this process seemed to be developing an understanding of their own energy, its patterns and flows, as well as the ways in which they could shape or change it.

A few of the activists in this research also engaged in what Epstein calls 'magical politics' (1991: 157–94), with these activists being possibly the most skilled in their use of energy. Magical politics emerged out of the neo-pagan and feminist spirituality movements of the early 1980s and has had quite an influence on the nonviolent direct action movement particularly around feminist, peace and environmental issues.[7] One of the differences between magical politics and more traditional forms of political practice appears to be the emphasis on harnessing and using different forms of energy. This energy appeared to be used mainly for creating and maintaining spiritual, psychic and environmental connections. For women who had been to Greenham Women's' Peace Camp in Berkshire (England), for example, magical politics was a crucial part of their programme of direct action.

Phoebe was an Australian feminist activist who had been at Greenham and she spoke of a number of actions that she was involved in which used 'magic' in some way. At 44 years of age, Phoebe had been actively involved in the women's movement for 28 years, during which time she had belonged to numerous coalitions and played a leading role in shaping the agenda around women's issues. Describing herself as a 'feminist anarchist', Phoebe acknowledged the impact that living at Greenham had on her activism. In particular, the use of 'magic' at Greenham led her to rethink the ways in which people communicate and connect with each other. There were a number of actions that she was involved in which used 'magic' in some way: psychic energy was used to connect to other women – send messages to women in prison, or to 'call' women from around the world to come and join them; spiritual energy was used to 'do protections'; environmental energy was harnessed to flood the base; visualizations were used to get information about the layout of towers within the base. In the way that Phoebe discussed energy, it was about developing a completely different concept of communication which was not premised on the spoken word or direct contact, but on channelling energy through the body in rituals and disseminating it across time and space. Developing intuitive and psychic skills, both of which are embodied ways of knowing the world, were seen as integral to this type of practice. Greenham women also learnt about tapping into environmental energy: full moons and solstices, for example, were seen as good times to engage in magical politics.[8]

Magical politics, monitoring energy and mobilizing for action all utilize energy as a tool for furthering activist programmes and campaigns. This is a notion of energy as something that flows through bodies and connects activists to the energy of other bodies/people, the energy of the environment and to a spiritual energy. Activist bodies in this section can be seen as 'bodies at work'. The body is communicative and expressive, connected via energy to the social, spiritual and environmental spheres. When the three perspectives on energy are reintegrated, as they are in the activists' lived experience of their bodies in relation to work, then focusing on energy provides a way of looking at the activist/worker subject as simultaneously socially constructed, corporeal and communicative; as both a body-in-itself and a body-in-relation.

Using Energy to Reconceptualise Social/Nature

In recent years the dichotomous separation between nature and the social in constructions of embodied subjects has been problematized and alternative models proposed. Grosz used the Möbius strip to conceptualize social/nature as being intertwined and mutually constructed to the extent that one side becomes another (1994: xii). Alternatively, Frank used the three angles of a triangle to argue that the body is constituted in the intersections between institutions, discourses and corporeality (1991: 49). What both these models illustrate is the inherent relationship between nature and the social rather than their opposition. However, while these models use a notion of the social as both interior and exterior, as existing in the psyche and in institutions and discourses, they have a more limited view of nature. In effect nature is reduced to the corporeal body, one that is interior even though it may 'leak' aspects of its corporeality into the exterior through illness, bodily difference (Frank 1991: 83–8) and flows (Grosz 1994: 187–210). When flows of energy are considered, however, this notion of nature can be seen to be problematic.

Through analysing the activists' experiences of creating, manipulating and using energy, I have argued that the body is not only social and corporeal, but also communicative. It is through this communicative dimension of activist bodies that energy could be seen as connecting the corporeal to the social through discourses, institutions and contact with other bodies, *as well as* being connected to what I called universal nature. It is this dimension of nature, the relation between the interior and exterior, that appears to be missing from theories of the body. Within these theories there are no avenues for accounting for the ways in which activists' used universal nature to re-energize themselves, for analysing the relationship between the corporeal body and universal nature. Nor could I explain the harnessing of universal energy for actions, for activists' use of natural cycles or their calling of the earth's elements to assist them in actions: in other words, for the relationship between the social body and universal nature. Focusing on energy as a means of embodying activists and activist work facilitated an analysis of these modes of connectedness.

It was apparent that if energy still had relevance to the realm of work, then it was necessary to incorporate some of the eastern aspects, including that of cycles and the interconnectedness between human energy and universal energy, and consciousness and the body. At this stage any model of the relationship between social/nature based on this reclaimed notion of energy would be tentative, as there remains much to be researched. Nevertheless as a step in this direction I propose a model that would locate the human body within the body of the world, with both bodies having material and social dimensions, perhaps illustrated in Figure 12.1.

By positing permeable boundaries, the connectedness between the individual and universal dimensions of the social/nature relationship is emphasized, thereby allowing for a more complex analysis to evolve. It does, for example, provide avenues for examining the relationship between the corporeal and social body of an individual, between an individual and universal nature, between an individual and society, and between society and universal nature. All these relationships, I argue, are integral to understanding both how individual identities are constructed and how individuals construct their world. This point is illustrated by Aboriginal people in Australia, who have consistently argued for public acceptance of the significance of space and place for their sense of identity and cultural survival. Any examination of the use

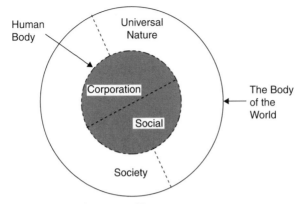

Figure 12.1 Reconceptualizing social/nature

and fluctuations in moral, physical and communicative energy among Aboriginal people and their communities would, then, need a theoretical framework which could facilitate an analysis of the relationship between universal nature and the social and corporeal bodies of individuals.

This relationship may also be significant for the development of some work identities. For example, while the social influence on universal nature is recognized in occupations such as farming, mining, seafaring and environmental management, little attention is given to how universal nature shapes the social, either in terms of the work or the work identities associated with performing these occupations. Given that energy is likely to be relevant to forms of work other than activism, it is possible that conceptualizing social/nature as being multidimensional could open up new areas for research and debate. There are, already, many occupations for which social, physical and communicative energy are required: dance, sport and theatre are obvious examples, although teaching, counselling, healing and some entrepreneurial occupations are also likely to harness, shape and share different forms of energy.

There is, then, still much to be discovered about how energy is utilized, and how it relates to occupational identities and workplace organization. In addition, the recognition that an individual's energy is influenced by external energy could lead to further research into areas such as how architecture and the design of workplaces could shape the energy of those who work in particular spaces. This use of energy is widely recognized in eastern philosophies such as feng shui, and while it has been adapted into some western workplace contexts it has yet to be incorporated into western theories about work and work organization.

Finally, the concept of energy may have particular relevance to understanding women's (and increasingly, men's) multiple locations as workers. For the activists in my research, juggling their responsibilities in paid work, unpaid domestic work and unpaid community work was as much about the ability to create, harness and use energy as it was about allocations of time between the various spheres of work (King 1999: 342–60). Taken together, the concepts of time and energy may provide for interesting research into the boundaries between work, gendered identity and social relations. It seems possible, then, that reclaiming energy as a work-related concept could open up new avenues for exploring the different dimensions of the relationship between bodies, work and constructions of identity.

Notes

1   The activists participating in the research had long-term activist careers spanning between five and 62 years. Those who had been active for less than ten years were all under 30 years of age.
2   In the West, these ideas have become incorporated into some areas of physics, and have gained popular credence through theories of 'Gaia' (Lovelock 1979; 1991). Some areas of psychology and the alternative/complementary health industry are also based on these ideas about energy (Samways 1992; Hicks 1997). The extent and effect of the importation of eastern ideas into western cultural contexts does not appear to have been widely researched with respect to activism, although it is likely that some transmutation would occur. With regards to activists, these ideas are most likely to be expressed by eco-activists and spiritual feminists engaged in Dianic/Wiccan forms of spiritualism.
3   While of interest the ways in which these forms of energy overlap and relate to one another in activist or any other form of work would require dense data regarding energy that was not available for this project.
4   The names given to the activists participating in my research are pseudonyms.
5   This is backed up by other research. Sudano, for example, argues that within labour politics women take greater care of themselves than men and she sees this as part of a shift in leadership models from one which is 'self- sacrificing, omnipotent' and male, to a more female one based on principles of 'self-care' and 'positive role- modelling' (1997: 167).
6   The extent to which the other senses – smell and taste – are involved in shaping energy were not discussed by the participants in the research.
7   See Epstein (1991) for an account of its influence in the United States during the 1980s. Finley's research on a group of Dianic Wiccans (a group in the

feminist spirituality movement) argues that magic and ritual are important aspects of their political programme inspiring change-oriented activism, group consciousness and empowering women through challenging their own self-evaluations as well as traditional models of womanhood (1991: 357–8). In Australia this form of political spirituality and use of energy is being researched by Rosemary Beaumont (1997).

8 Similar uses of energy were also discussed in relation to various actions held in Australia, particularly in the anti-nuclear and environmental movement, although spiritual activism was also discussed as integral to Aboriginal activism.

References

Adkins, L and Lury, C. 1998. 'Making People, Making Bodies, Making Work'. Paper presented at the *Making Sense of the Body* British Sociological Association Annual Conference, University of Edinburgh, 6–9 April.

Beaumont, R. 1997. 'Ceremony as a Creative Strategy for Change: Re-wiring the Collective Paradigm'. Unpublished paper presented at *The 6th Women and Labour Conference*, Deakin University, Geelong, Australia.

Brown, I. D. 1982. 'Measurement of Mental Effort: Some Theoretical and Practical Issues', in G. A. Harrison (ed.), *Energy and Effort*, London: Taylor & Francis.

Butler, J. 1990. *Gender Trouble: Feminism and the Subversion of Identity*. New York: Routledge.

Caldicott, H. 1996. *A Passionate Life*. Sydney: Random House.

Coover, V., Deacon, E., Esser, C. and Moore, C. 1977. *Resource Manual for a Living Revolution*. Philadelphia: New Society Press.

Cruikshank, J. 1989. 'Burnout – An Issue among Canadian Community Development Workers', *Community Development Journal: An International Forum* 24, 1: 40–54.

Downton, J. V. and Wehr, P. 1997. *The Persistent Activist: How Peace Commitment Develops and Survives*. Boulder, Co.: Westview Press.

Durnin, J. V. G. A. and Passmore, R. 1967. *Energy, Work and Leisure*. London: Heinemann Educational Books.

Epstein, B. 1991. *Political Protest and Cultural Revolution: Nonviolent Direct Action in the 1970s and 1980s*. Berkeley: University of California Press.

Finley, N J. 1991. 'Political Activism and Feminist Spirituality', *Sociological Analysis* 52, 4: 349–62.

Frank, A. W. 1991. 'For a Sociology of the Body: An Analytical Review', in M. Featherstone, M. Hepworth and B. S. Turner (eds.), *The Body, Social Process and Cultural Theory*. London: Sage.

Freund, P. E. S. 1988. 'Bringing Society Back into the Body: Understanding Socialized Human Nature', *Theory and Society* 17: 839–64.

Garrett, C. 1993. 'Myth and Ritual in Recovery from Anorexia Nervosa'. Unpublished doctoral thesis, University of NSW, Australia.

Grosz, E. 1994. *Volatile Bodies: Toward a Corporeal Feminism*. Sydney: Allen & Unwin.

Haraway, D. 1987. 'A Manifesto for Cyborgs: Science, Technology, and Socialist Feminism in the 1980s', *Australian Feminist Studies* 4: 1–42.

Hicks, A. 1997. *Thorsen's Principles of Acupuncture*. London: Thorsens.

Jackson, M. 1983. 'Thinking through the Body: An Essay on Understanding Metaphor', *Social Analysis* 14: 127–48.

Jayaratne, S. and Chess, W. A. 1983. 'Job Satisfaction and Burnout in Social Work', in B. A. Farber (ed.), *Stress and Burnout in the Human Service Professions*. New York: Pergamon Press.

Jones, S. 1985. 'The Analysis of Depth Interviews', in R. Walker (ed.), *Applied Qualitative Research*. Aldershot: Gower.

King, D. S (1999) *Knowledge, Knowing, Passion and Power: Exploring the Realm of Activist Work*. Unpublished PHD thesis. Adelaide: Department of Sociology, Flinders University of South Australia.

Levey, S., Drucker, W. R., and Czarnecki, N. 1959. 'Energy Expenditure of Surgeons, Nurses and Anesthesiologists during Operative Procedures', *Surgery*, 46: 529–33.

Lovelock, J. E. 1979. *Gaia: A New Look at Life on Earth*. Oxford: Oxford University Press.

Lovelock, J. E. 1991. *Gaia: The Practical Science of Planetary Medicine*. Sydney: Allen & Unwin.

Ludwick, M. 1985. 'Organizing Your Group and Setting Goals', in N. Wollman (ed.), *Working for Peace: A Handbook of Practical Psychology and Other Tools*. San Luis, California: Impact Publishers, pp. 80–90.

Martin, E. 1994. *Flexible Bodies: Tracking Immunity in American Culture from the Days of Polo to the Age of AIDS*. Boston: Beacon Press.

McDowell, L. 1997. *Capital Culture: Gender at Work in the City*. Oxford: Blackwell.

McDowell, L and Court, G. 1994. 'Performing Work: Bodily Representations in Merchant Banks', *Environment and Planning D: Society and Space* 12: 727–50.

MNS (Movement for a New Society Training Action Affinity Group) 1979. *Building Social Change Communities*. Philadelphia: Philadelphia Movement for a New Society.

Muchinsky, P. M. 1990. *Psychology Applied to Work*. Pacific Grove: Cole Publishing.

Pines, A. 1983. 'On Burnout and the Buffering Effects of Social Support', in B. A. Farber (ed.), *Stress and Burnout in the Human Service Professions*. New York: Pergamon Press.

Porpora, D. V. 1997. 'Moral Emotions'. Unpublished paper presented at *Emotions in Social Life and Social Theory Conference*, HRC, Australian National University, Canberra, July.

Poulin, J. W. C. 1993. 'Social Worker Burnout: A Longitudinal Study', *Social Work Research and Abstracts* 29: 5–11.

Rabinbach, A. 1990. *The Human Motor: Energy, Fatigue and the Origins of Modernity*. New York: Basic Books.

Richards, L. 1994. *QSR NUD*IST* [Software] version 3.0, Qualitative Solutions and Research Pty. Ltd., Australia.

Ronai, C. R. 1992. 'The Reflexive Self Through Narrative: A Night in the Life of an Erotic Dancer/Researcher', in C. Ellis and M. G. Flaherty (eds.), *Investigating Subjectivity: Research on Lived Experience*. London: Sage.

Sakharov, M. and Farber, B. A. 1983. 'A Critical Study of Burnout in Teachers', in B. A. Farber (ed.), *Stress and Burnout in the Human Service Professions*. New York: Pergamon Press.

Samways, L. 1992. *Your Mindbody Energy*. Melbourne: Viking.

Schaufeli, W. B. and Buunk, B. P. 1996. 'Professional Burnout', in M. J. Schabracq, J. A. M. Winnubst and C. L. Cooper (eds.), *Handbook of Work and Health Psychology*. Chichester: John Wiley & Son.

Scholz, H. 1957. 'Changing Physical Demands of Foundry Workers in the Production of Medium Weight Castings', *Ergonomics,* 1: 30–8.

Sherlock, J. 1993. 'Dance and the Culture of the Body', in S. Scott and D. Morgan (eds), *Body Matters: Essays on the Sociology of the Body*. London: Falmer Press.

Sudano, L. 1997. 'Women Union Leaders: Mongrels, Martyrs, Misfits or Models for the Future?', in B. Pocock (ed.), *Sex and Strife: Sex and Politics in Labour Unions*. Sydney: Allen and Unwin.

Trochim, W M. K. 1989. 'An Introduction to Concept Mapping for Planning and Evaluation', *Evaluation and Program Planning* 12: 1–16.

Turner, B. 1992. *Regulating Bodies: Essays in Medical Sociology*. London: Routledge.

Turner, D. 1955. 'Energy Cost of Some Industrial Operations', *British Journal of Industrial Medicine* 12: 237–9.

Vallas, S. P. 1990. 'Comments and Observations on the Nature of Work', in K. Erikson and S. P. Vallas (eds.), *The Nature of Work: Sociological Perspectives*. New Haven, Conn.: Yale University Press.

Wallman, S. 1982. 'Time and Affect: Facets of the Social Anthropology of Work', in G. A. Harrison (ed.), *Energy and Effort*. London: Taylor & Francis.

Waysun, L. 1990. *T'ai Chi Classics*. Boston: Shambhala.

Witz, A., Halford, S. and Savage, M. 1996. 'Organized Bodies: Gender, Sexuality and Embodiment in Contemporary Organizations', in L. Adkins and V. Merchant (eds.), *Sexualizing the Social: Power and the Organization of Sexuality*. London: Macmillan.

Index

Absent presence, body as, 3, 7–10
Abstract pupil, 95, 97
Accumulation, reflexive, 152–7, 160–2
Achievement culture, 155
Acker, J., 187
Activism, activist work, xxii, chapter 12 passim
Adolescents, xvii, 14; *see also* children; school
Adoption and fostering, 9–10
Age as workplace signifier, 173
Ageing, elderly, 9
  and discrimination, 179
  and exclusion, 30–1
  and resuscitation protocols, 133, 136
  see also Grey Power, residential homes for the elderly
Agency
  feminist, 188–90
  women-aware, 191
Ainsworth, M., 42, 46
Airline industry, *see* service sector economy; working women
Althusser, L., 10
Anthropology of the body, xv, 65
Appearance, 168
Aristotle, *Politics*, 27
Articulation, 4
Attachment theory, xviii, 45–6

Bathrooms, *see* corporeal dirt; taboos
Baudrillard, P., 120, 121–2
Bauman, Z., 133
Behaviours and welfare, 7
Black dangerousness, 106–10
Bodies, regulation of, 6
Bodily inscription, 11
Bodily order, 6
Body and Society, xv
Body
  accommodated, 57
  body/mind split, *see* mind/body split
  as cultural artefact, 11

discipline in the workplace, 159
gendered, xix, 89, 92, 106–10,
  chapter 6 passim; reproduced in schools, 81
image, 172
knowledge, 167, 177
language, 176
management, chapter 4 passim
odour, 68; *and see* corporeal dirt; elimination taboos
paradoxes of, 6
as pre-social entity, 8
presentation at workplace, 177–8
private, 61
racialized, xix, 106–10; *and see* Christopher Clunis; Jayne Zito
/society nexus, 5, 6, 7, 21
-work, 167
Bowlby, J., xviii, 45–6
Brooks, Tony, 124
Built environment, and accessibility, 43–4
Bureaucracies; Bureaucrats, ideal-type, xxii, 185
Burnout, 212–13

Calves, M., 120–3
Capitalism and individualism, 28
Care in the community, xviii, xix, 45, 103; *see also* Christopher Clunis; mentally ill; cf. residential institutions; secure units
Cartesian theory, *see* mind/body split
'Cartesian Ghost', 16
Child sex abusers, 16, 17
Children Act 1989, 14, 17
Children, xvii, 12–15
  and cleanliness, 64
  as embodied subjects, 15
  and sexuality, 12, 15
  see also school
Citizen; citizenship, xvii, chapter 2 passim

225